THE PUNISHER

WAR IN BAGALIA

COLLECTION EDITOR:
JENNIFER GRÜNWALD

ASSISTANT EDITOR:
CAITLIN O'CONNELL

ASSOCIATE MANAGING EDITOR:
KATERI WOODY

EDITOR, SPECIAL PROJECTS:
MARK D. BEAZLEY

VP PRODUCTION & SPECIAL PROJECTS:
JEFF YOUNGQUIST

BOOK DESIGNERS:
RODOLFO MURAGUCHI
WITH STACIE ZUCKER

SVP PRINT, SALES & MARKETING:
DAVID GABRIEL

DIRECTOR, LICENSED PUBLISHING:
SVEN LARSEN

EDITOR IN CHIEF:
C.B. CEBULSKI

CHIEF CREATIVE OFFICER:
JOE QUESADA

PRESIDENT:
DAN BUCKLEY

EXECUTIVE PRODUCER:
ALAN FINE

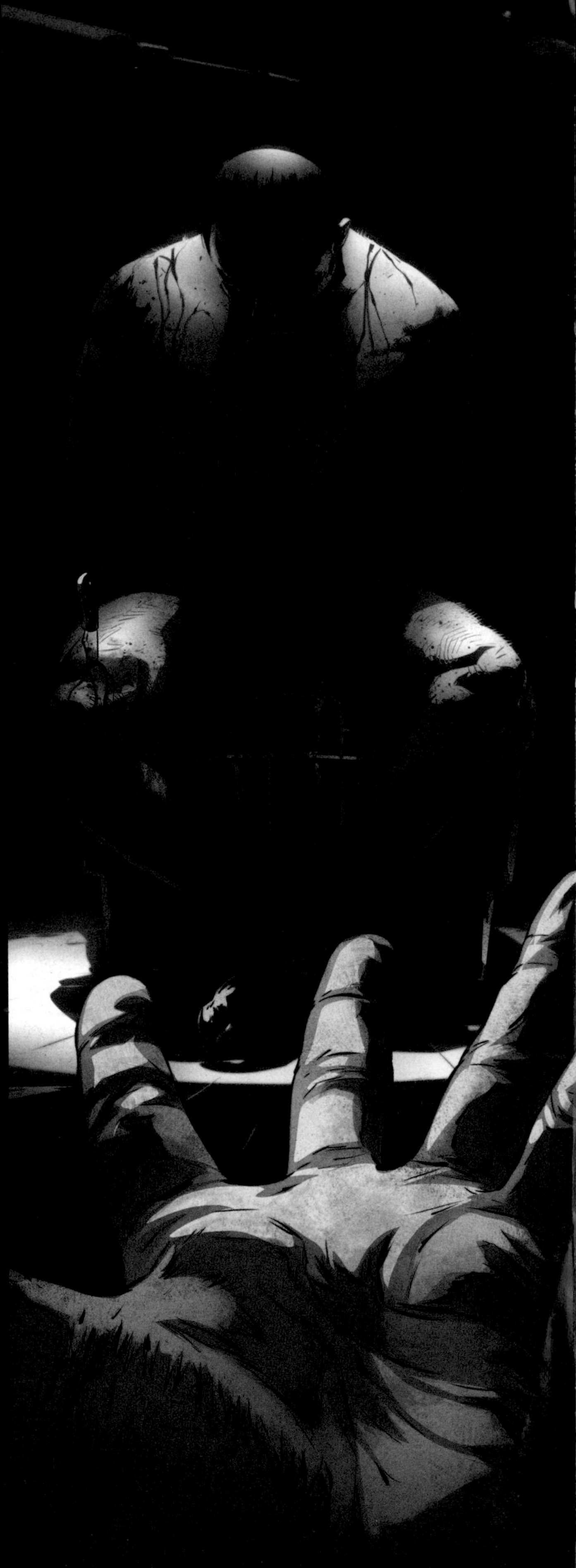

THE PUNISHER VOL. 2: WAR IN BAGALIA. Contains material originally published in magazine form as THE PUNISHER #6-11. First printing 2019. ISBN 978-1-302-91348-9. Published by MARVEL WORLDWIDE, INC., a subsidiary of MARVEL ENTERTAINMENT, LLC. OFFICE OF PUBLICATION: 135 West 50th Street, New York, NY 10020. **Printed in Canada.** DAN BUCKLEY, President, Marvel Entertainment; JOHN NEE, Publisher; JOE QUESADA, Chief Creative Officer; TOM BREVOORT, SVP of Publishing; DAVID BOGART, Associate Publisher & SVP of Talent Affairs; DAVID GABRIEL, SVP of Sales & Marketing, Publishing; JEFF YOUNGQUIST, VP of Production & Special Projects; DAN CARR, Executive Director of Publishing Technology; ALEX MORALES, Director of Publishing Operations; DAN EDINGTON, Managing Editor; SUSAN CRESPI, Production Manager; STAN LEE, Chairman Emeritus. For information regarding advertising in Marvel Comics or on Marvel.com, please contact Vit DeBellis, Custom Solutions & Integrated Advertising Manager, at vdebellis@marvel.com. For Marvel subscription inquiries, please call 888-511-5480. **Manufactured between 3/22/2019 and 4/23/2019 by SOLISCO PRINTERS, SCOTT, QC, CANADA.**

10 9 8 7 6 5 4 3 2 1

Frank Castle was a decorated Marine, an upstanding citizen and a family man. Then his family was taken from him when they were accidentally killed in a brutal mob hit. From that day, he became a force of cold, calculated retribution and vigilantism. Frank Castle died with his family. Now, there is only...

THE PUNISHER

The Punisher is out to destroy Hydra, beginning by killing the Mandarin, a representative of the Hydra nation of Bagalia, on the floor of the United Nations. Baron Zemo, Hydra's leader, fought back. He turned the world's mercenary forces against the Punisher, and while Frank foiled them all, Chameleon and Jigsaw managed to frame the Punisher for the murder of several NYPD officers.

Just as the Punisher neared the top of Hydra's forces in America, a group of heroes assembled by Nick Fury fought him to a standstill and captured him. Fury claimed he was taking Frank into custody, but instead he made a devil's bargain and had Frank extradited to Bagalia...and directly into the hands of Baron Zemo.

WAR IN BAGALIA

WRITER:
MATTHEW ROSENBERG

ARTIST:
SZYMON KUDRANSKI

COLORIST:
ANTONIO FABELA

LETTERER:
VC's CORY PETIT

COVER ARTIST:
GREG SMALLWOOD

ASSISTANT EDITOR:
LINDSEY COHICK

EDITORS:
JAKE THOMAS & MARK BASSO

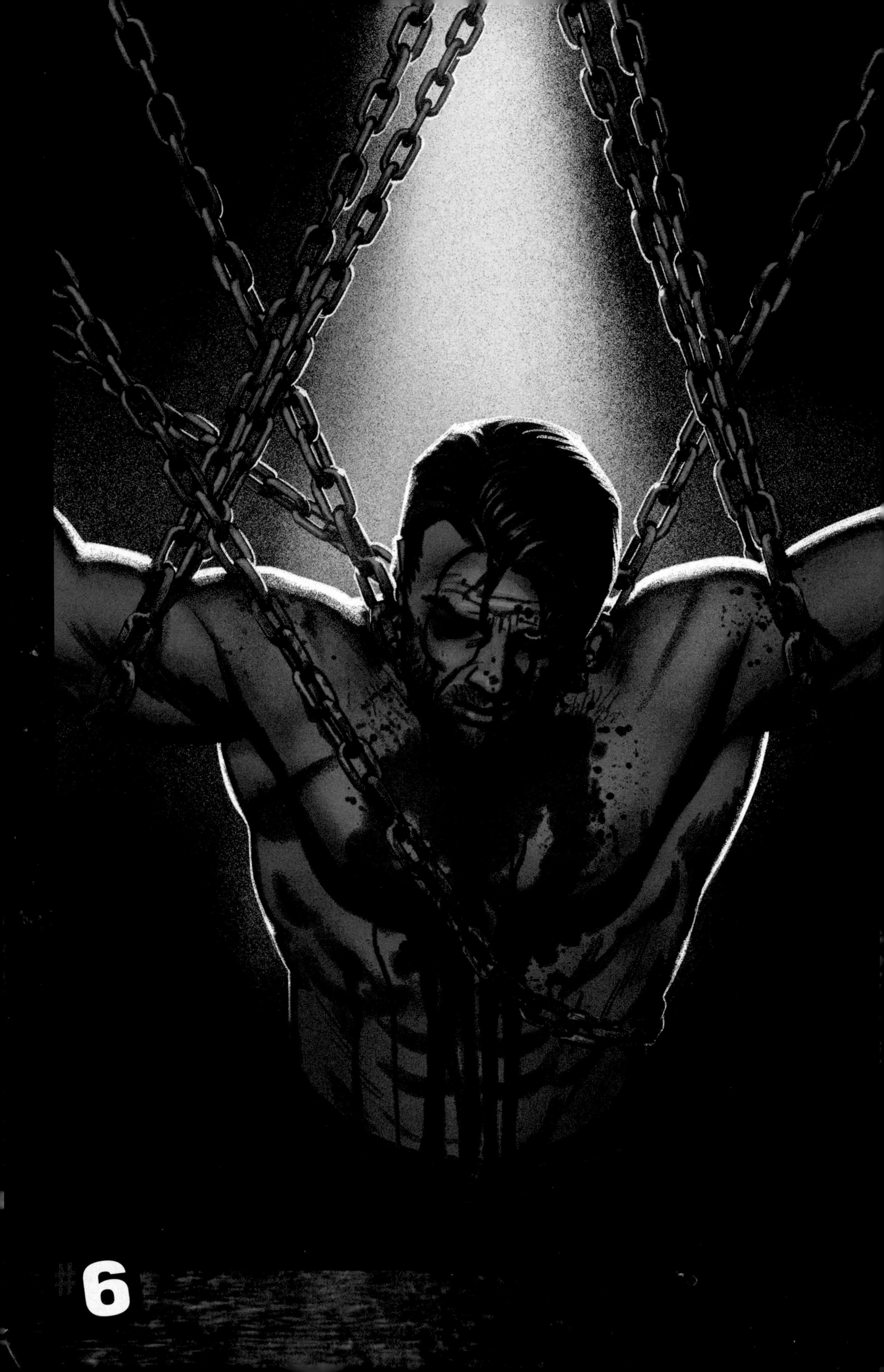
#6

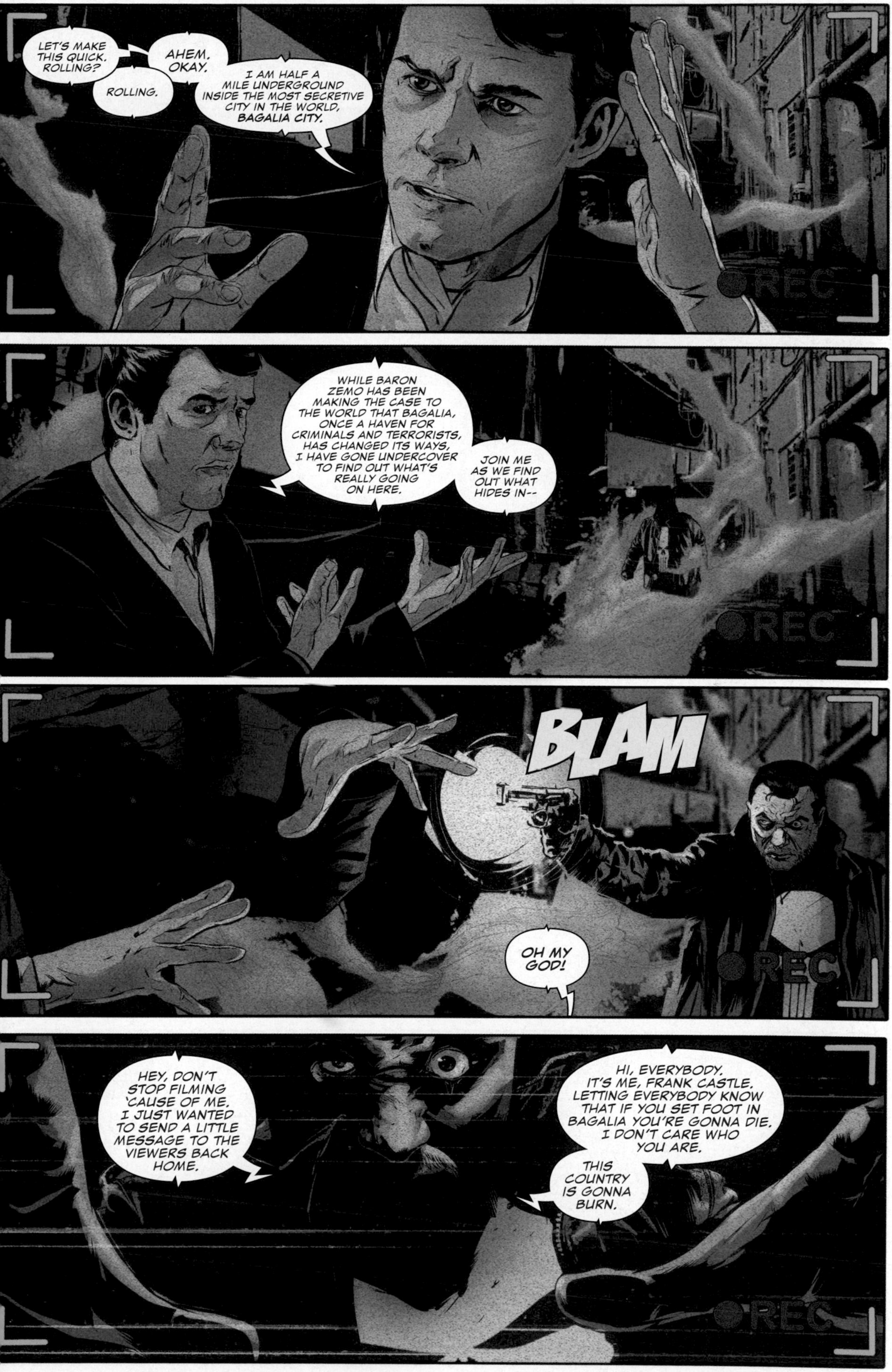
LET'S MAKE THIS QUICK. ROLLING?
ROLLING.
AHEM. OKAY.
I AM HALF A MILE UNDERGROUND INSIDE THE MOST SECRETIVE CITY IN THE WORLD, BAGALIA CITY.
REC
WHILE BARON ZEMO HAS BEEN MAKING THE CASE TO THE WORLD THAT BAGALIA, ONCE A HAVEN FOR CRIMINALS AND TERRORISTS, HAS CHANGED ITS WAYS, I HAVE GONE UNDERCOVER TO FIND OUT WHAT'S REALLY GOING ON HERE.
JOIN ME AS WE FIND OUT WHAT HIDES IN--
REC
BLAM
OH MY GOD!
REC
HEY, DON'T STOP FILMING 'CAUSE OF ME. I JUST WANTED TO SEND A LITTLE MESSAGE TO THE VIEWERS BACK HOME.
HI, EVERYBODY. IT'S ME, FRANK CASTLE. LETTING EVERYBODY KNOW THAT IF YOU SET FOOT IN BAGALIA YOU'RE GONNA DIE. I DON'T CARE WHO YOU ARE.
THIS COUNTRY IS GONNA BURN.
REC

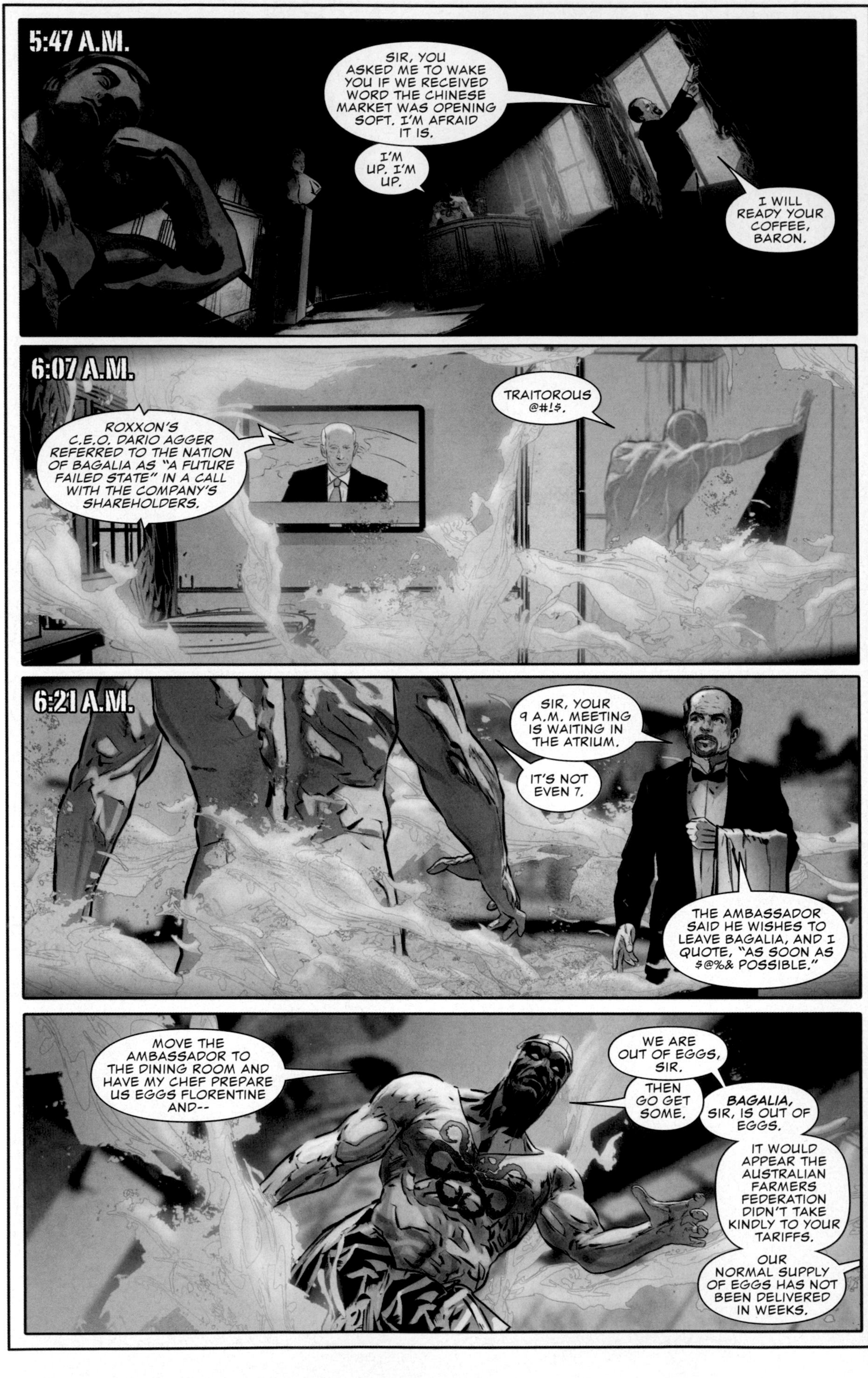
5:47 A.M.
SIR, YOU ASKED ME TO WAKE YOU IF WE RECEIVED WORD THE CHINESE MARKET WAS OPENING SOFT. I'M AFRAID IT IS.
I'M UP. I'M UP.
I WILL READY YOUR COFFEE, BARON.
6:07 A.M.
ROXXON'S C.E.O. DARIO AGGER REFERRED TO THE NATION OF BAGALIA AS "A FUTURE FAILED STATE" IN A CALL WITH THE COMPANY'S SHAREHOLDERS.
TRAITOROUS @#!$.
6:21 A.M.
SIR, YOUR 9 A.M. MEETING IS WAITING IN THE ATRIUM.
IT'S NOT EVEN 7.
THE AMBASSADOR SAID HE WISHES TO LEAVE BAGALIA, AND I QUOTE, "AS SOON AS $@%& POSSIBLE."
MOVE THE AMBASSADOR TO THE DINING ROOM AND HAVE MY CHEF PREPARE US EGGS FLORENTINE AND--
WE ARE OUT OF EGGS, SIR.
THEN GO GET SOME.
BAGALIA, SIR, IS OUT OF EGGS.
IT WOULD APPEAR THE AUSTRALIAN FARMERS FEDERATION DIDN'T TAKE KINDLY TO YOUR TARIFFS.
OUR NORMAL SUPPLY OF EGGS HAS NOT BEEN DELIVERED IN WEEKS.

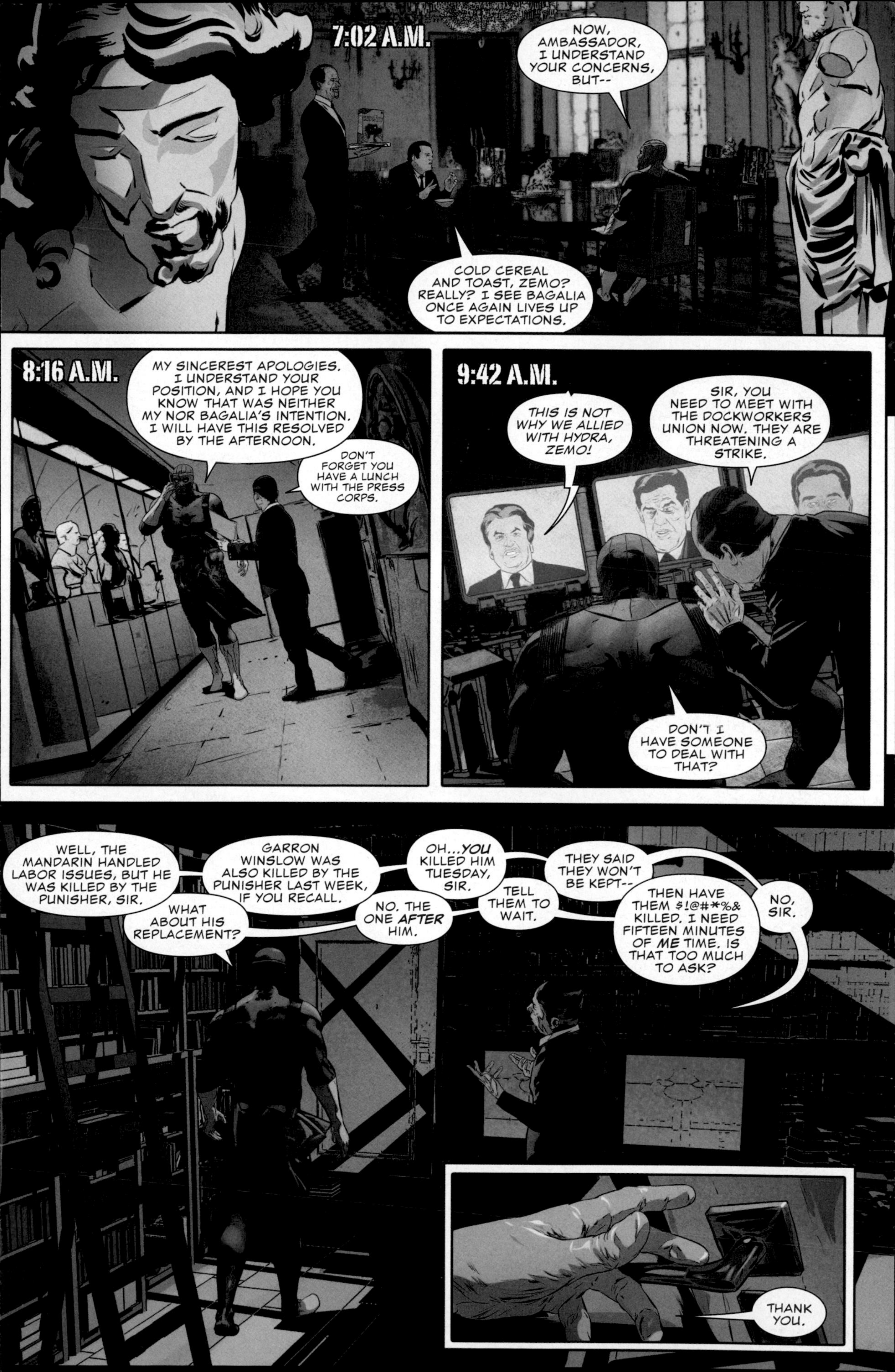
7:02 A.M.
NOW, AMBASSADOR, I UNDERSTAND YOUR CONCERNS, BUT--
COLD CEREAL AND TOAST, ZEMO? REALLY? I SEE BAGALIA ONCE AGAIN LIVES UP TO EXPECTATIONS.
8:16 A.M.
MY SINCEREST APOLOGIES. I UNDERSTAND YOUR POSITION, AND I HOPE YOU KNOW THAT WAS NEITHER MY NOR BAGALIA'S INTENTION. I WILL HAVE THIS RESOLVED BY THE AFTERNOON.
DON'T FORGET YOU HAVE A LUNCH WITH THE PRESS CORPS.
9:42 A.M.
THIS IS NOT WHY WE ALLIED WITH HYDRA, ZEMO!
SIR, YOU NEED TO MEET WITH THE DOCKWORKERS UNION NOW. THEY ARE THREATENING A STRIKE.
DON'T I HAVE SOMEONE TO DEAL WITH THAT?
WELL, THE MANDARIN HANDLED LABOR ISSUES, BUT HE WAS KILLED BY THE PUNISHER, SIR.
WHAT ABOUT HIS REPLACEMENT?
GARRON WINSLOW WAS ALSO KILLED BY THE PUNISHER LAST WEEK, IF YOU RECALL.
NO. THE ONE *AFTER* HIM.
OH...*YOU* KILLED HIM TUESDAY, SIR.
TELL THEM TO WAIT.
THEY SAID THEY WON'T BE KEPT--
THEN HAVE THEM $!@#*%& KILLED. I NEED FIFTEEN MINUTES OF *ME* TIME. IS THAT TOO MUCH TO ASK?
NO, SIR.
THANK YOU.

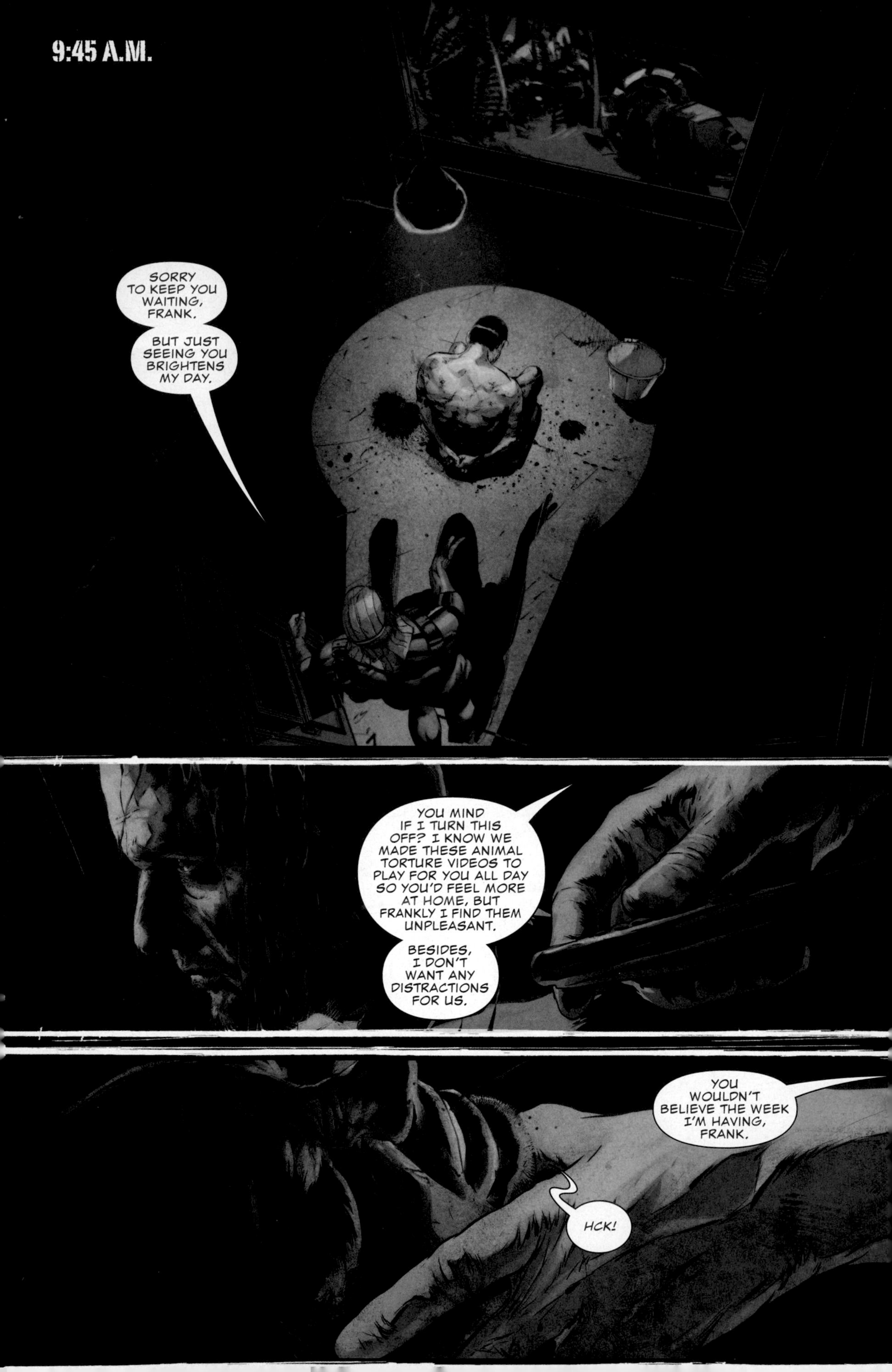
9:45 A.M.
SORRY TO KEEP YOU WAITING, FRANK.
BUT JUST SEEING YOU BRIGHTENS MY DAY.
YOU MIND IF I TURN THIS OFF? I KNOW WE MADE THESE ANIMAL TORTURE VIDEOS TO PLAY FOR YOU ALL DAY SO YOU'D FEEL MORE AT HOME, BUT FRANKLY I FIND THEM UNPLEASANT.
BESIDES, I DON'T WANT ANY DISTRACTIONS FOR US.
YOU WOULDN'T BELIEVE THE WEEK I'M HAVING, FRANK.
HCK!

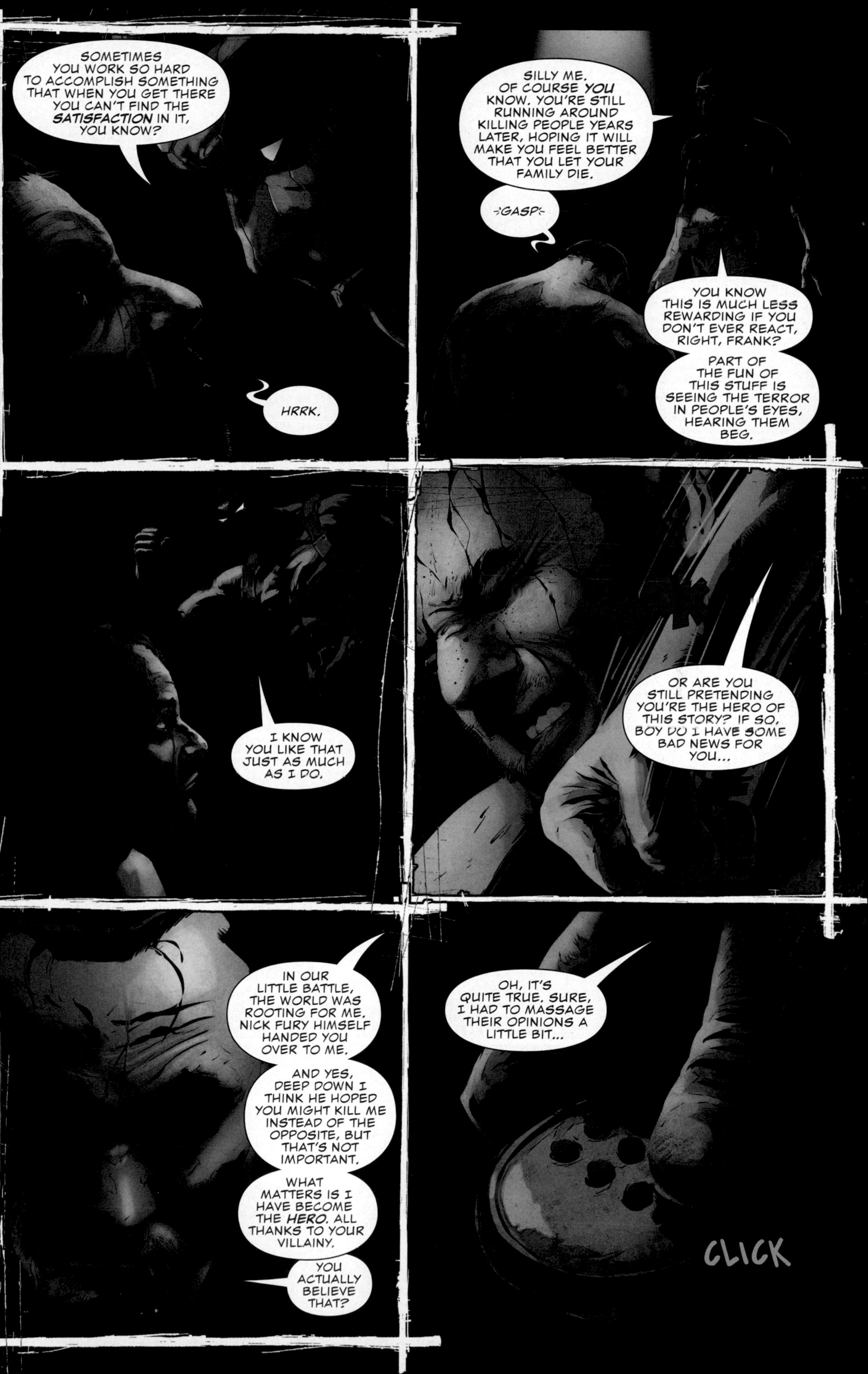
SOMETIMES YOU WORK SO HARD TO ACCOMPLISH SOMETHING THAT WHEN YOU GET THERE YOU CAN'T FIND THE SATISFACTION IN IT, YOU KNOW?
HRRK.
SILLY ME. OF COURSE YOU KNOW. YOU'RE STILL RUNNING AROUND KILLING PEOPLE YEARS LATER, HOPING IT WILL MAKE YOU FEEL BETTER THAT YOU LET YOUR FAMILY DIE.
-GASP-
YOU KNOW THIS IS MUCH LESS REWARDING IF YOU DON'T EVER REACT, RIGHT, FRANK?
PART OF THE FUN OF THIS STUFF IS SEEING THE TERROR IN PEOPLE'S EYES, HEARING THEM BEG.
I KNOW YOU LIKE THAT JUST AS MUCH AS I DO.
OR ARE YOU STILL PRETENDING YOU'RE THE HERO OF THIS STORY? IF SO, BOY DO I HAVE SOME BAD NEWS FOR YOU...
IN OUR LITTLE BATTLE, THE WORLD WAS ROOTING FOR ME. NICK FURY HIMSELF HANDED YOU OVER TO ME.
AND YES, DEEP DOWN I THINK HE HOPED YOU MIGHT KILL ME INSTEAD OF THE OPPOSITE, BUT THAT'S NOT IMPORTANT.
WHAT MATTERS IS I HAVE BECOME THE HERO. ALL THANKS TO YOUR VILLAINY.
YOU ACTUALLY BELIEVE THAT?
OH, IT'S QUITE TRUE. SURE, I HAD TO MASSAGE THEIR OPINIONS A LITTLE BIT...
CLICK

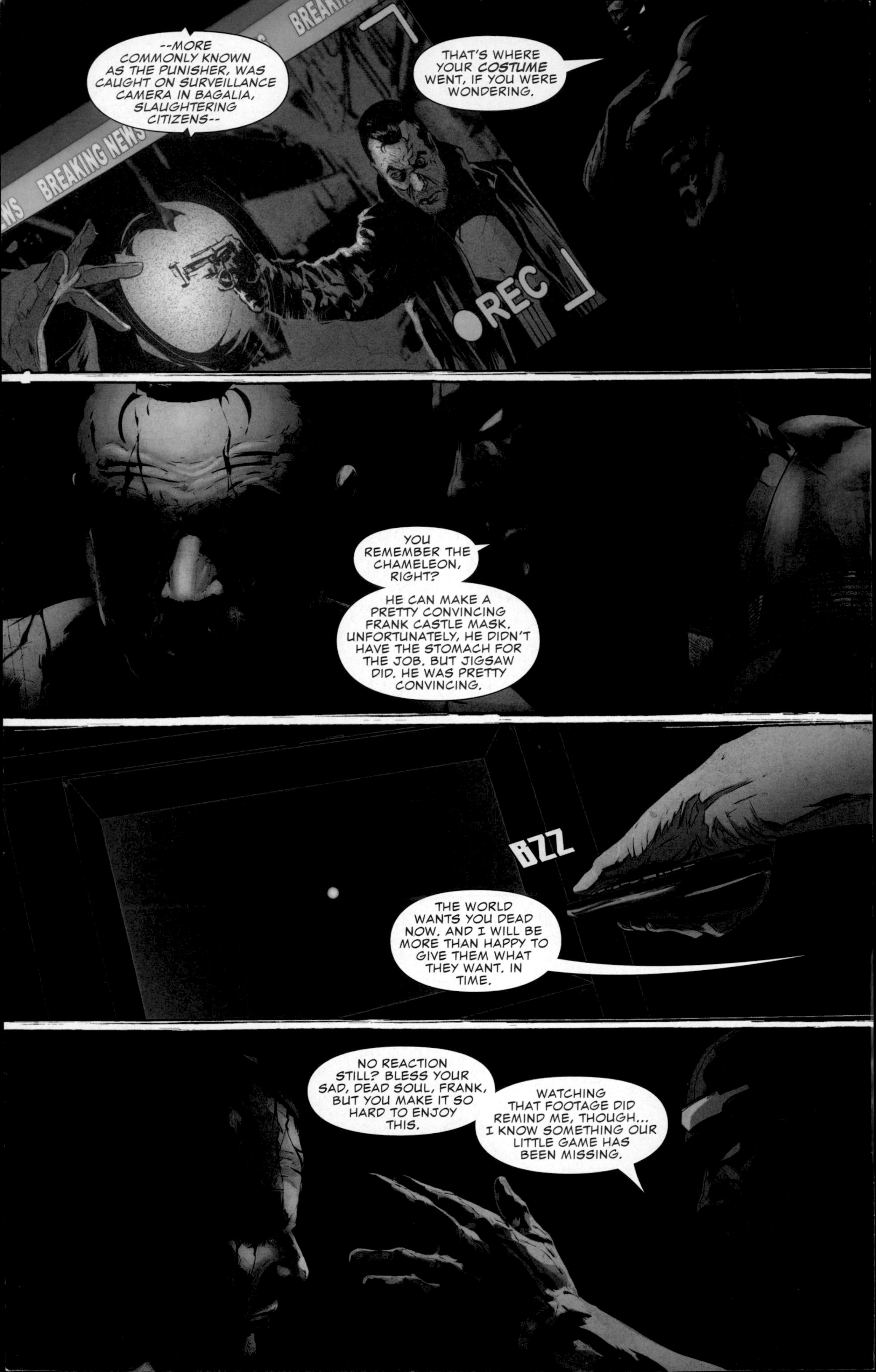
--MORE COMMONLY KNOWN AS THE PUNISHER, WAS CAUGHT ON SURVEILLANCE CAMERA IN BAGALIA, SLAUGHTERING CITIZENS--
BREAKING NEWS
THAT'S WHERE YOUR COSTUME WENT, IF YOU WERE WONDERING.
REC
YOU REMEMBER THE CHAMELEON, RIGHT?
HE CAN MAKE A PRETTY CONVINCING FRANK CASTLE MASK. UNFORTUNATELY, HE DIDN'T HAVE THE STOMACH FOR THE JOB. BUT JIGSAW DID. HE WAS PRETTY CONVINCING.
BZZ
THE WORLD WANTS YOU DEAD NOW. AND I WILL BE MORE THAN HAPPY TO GIVE THEM WHAT THEY WANT. IN TIME.
NO REACTION STILL? BLESS YOUR SAD, DEAD SOUL, FRANK, BUT YOU MAKE IT SO HARD TO ENJOY THIS.
WATCHING THAT FOOTAGE DID REMIND ME, THOUGH... I KNOW SOMETHING OUR LITTLE GAME HAS BEEN MISSING.

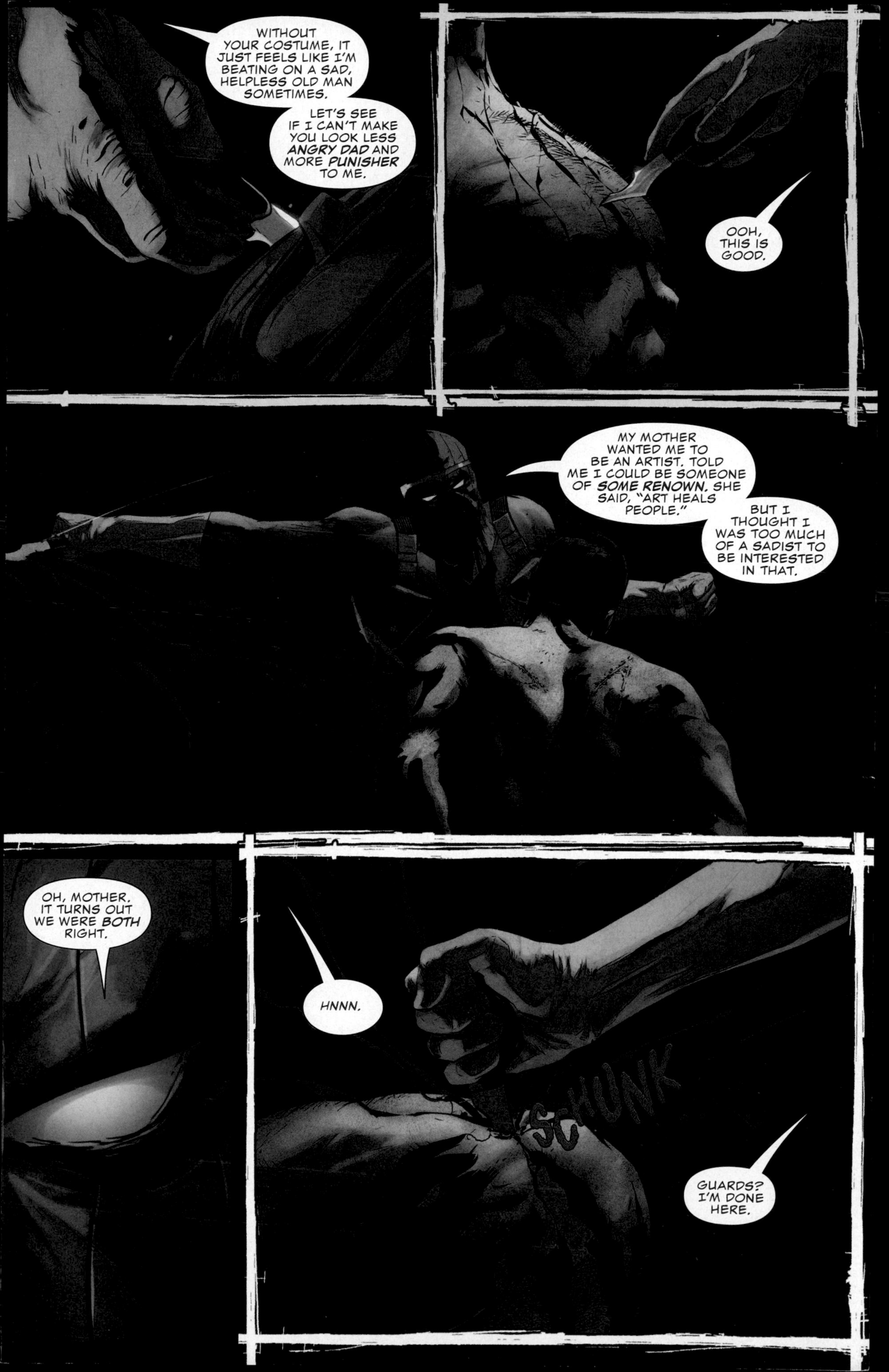
WITHOUT YOUR COSTUME, IT JUST FEELS LIKE I'M BEATING ON A SAD, HELPLESS OLD MAN SOMETIMES.
LET'S SEE IF I CAN'T MAKE YOU LOOK LESS ANGRY DAD AND MORE PUNISHER TO ME.
OOH, THIS IS GOOD.
MY MOTHER WANTED ME TO BE AN ARTIST. TOLD ME I COULD BE SOMEONE OF SOME RENOWN. SHE SAID, "ART HEALS PEOPLE."
BUT I THOUGHT I WAS TOO MUCH OF A SADIST TO BE INTERESTED IN THAT.
OH, MOTHER, IT TURNS OUT WE WERE BOTH RIGHT.
HNNN.
SCHUNK
GUARDS? I'M DONE HERE.

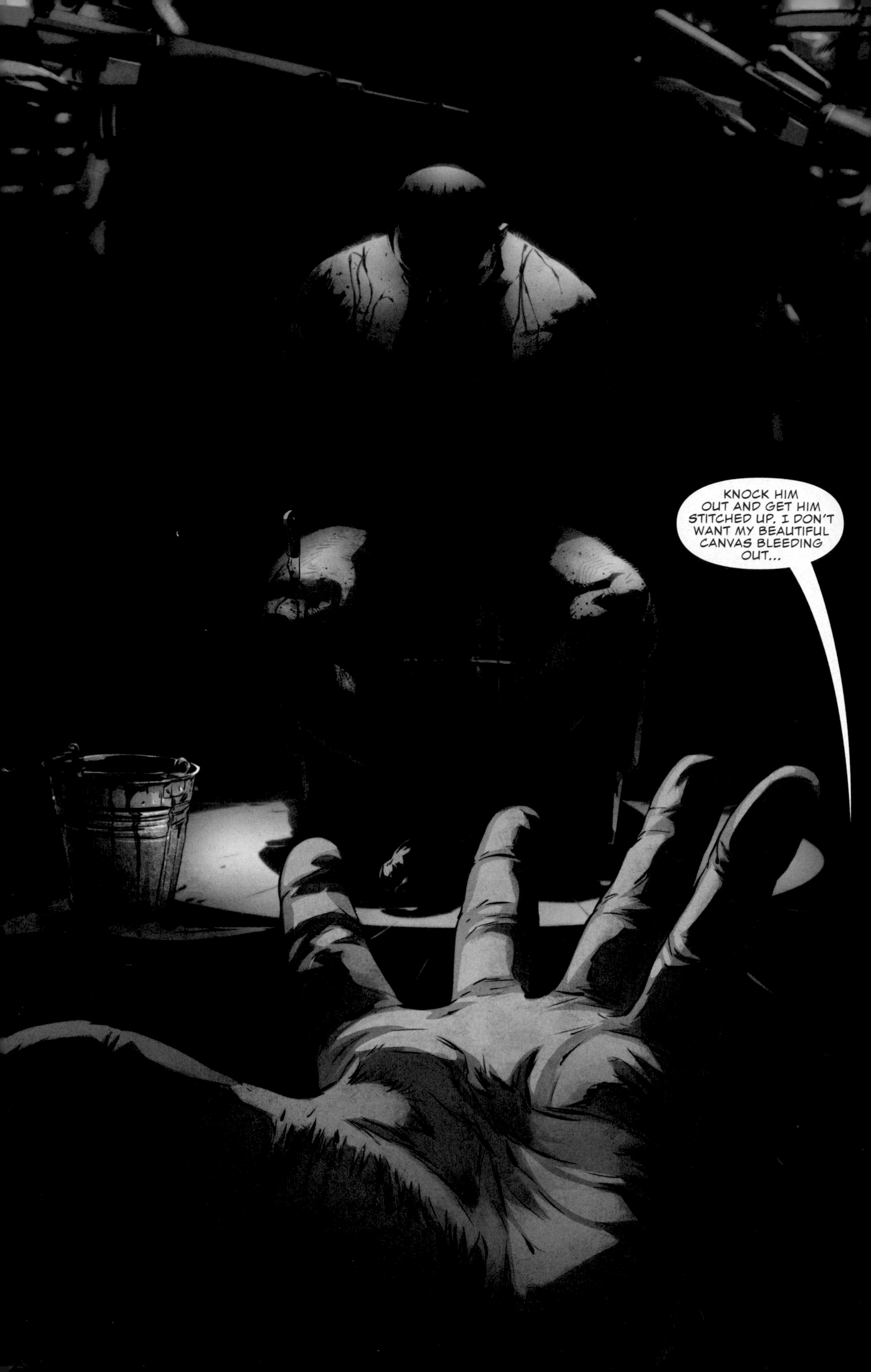
KNOCK HIM OUT AND GET HIM STITCHED UP. I DON'T WANT MY BEAUTIFUL CANVAS BLEEDING OUT...

"...NOT BEFORE OUR BIG DAY."

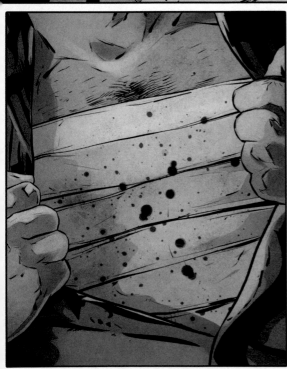

RISE AND SHINE, CASTLE, IT'S TIME TO MEET THE NEIGHBORHOOD.

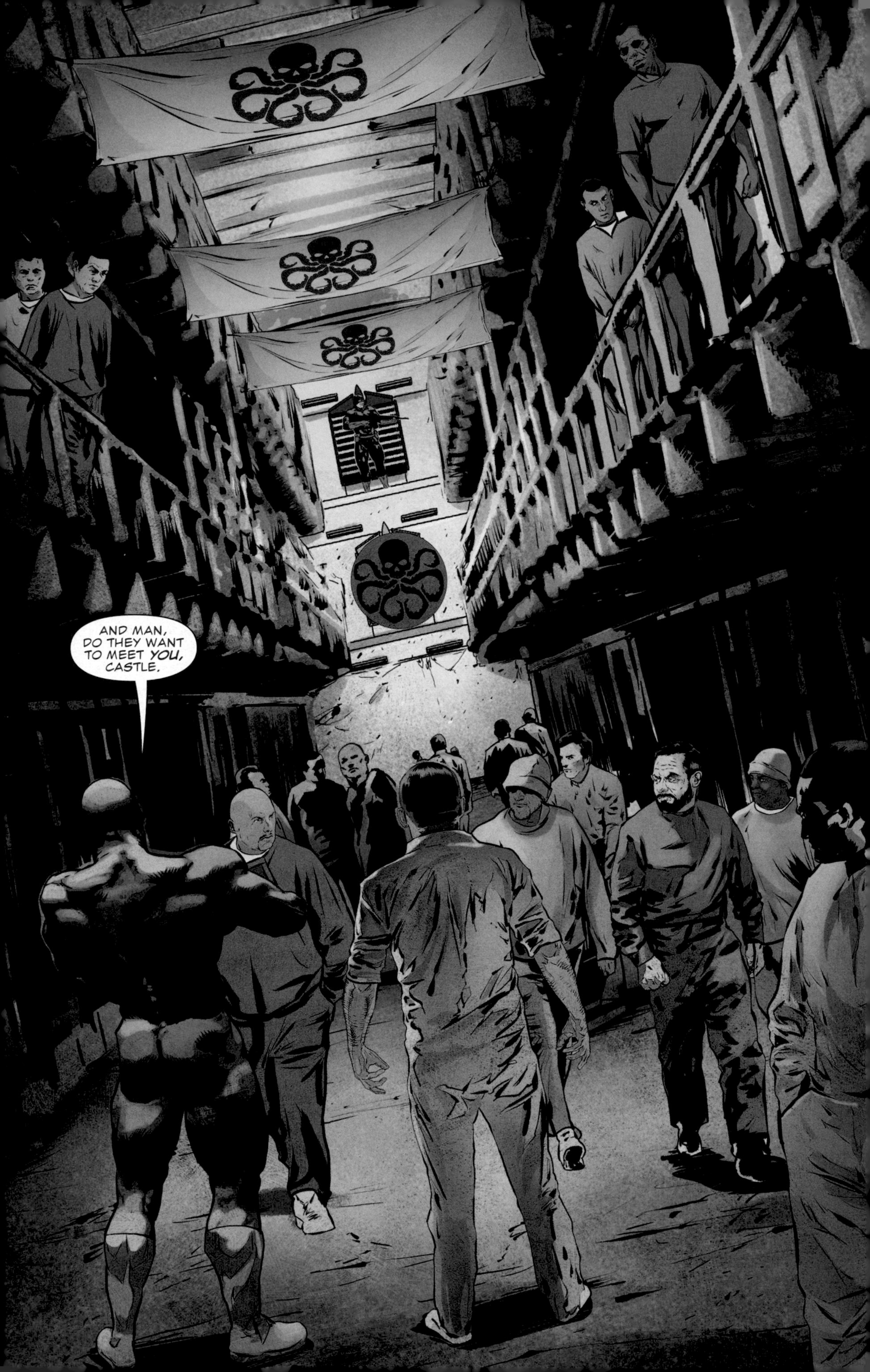
AND MAN, DO THEY WANT TO MEET YOU, CASTLE.

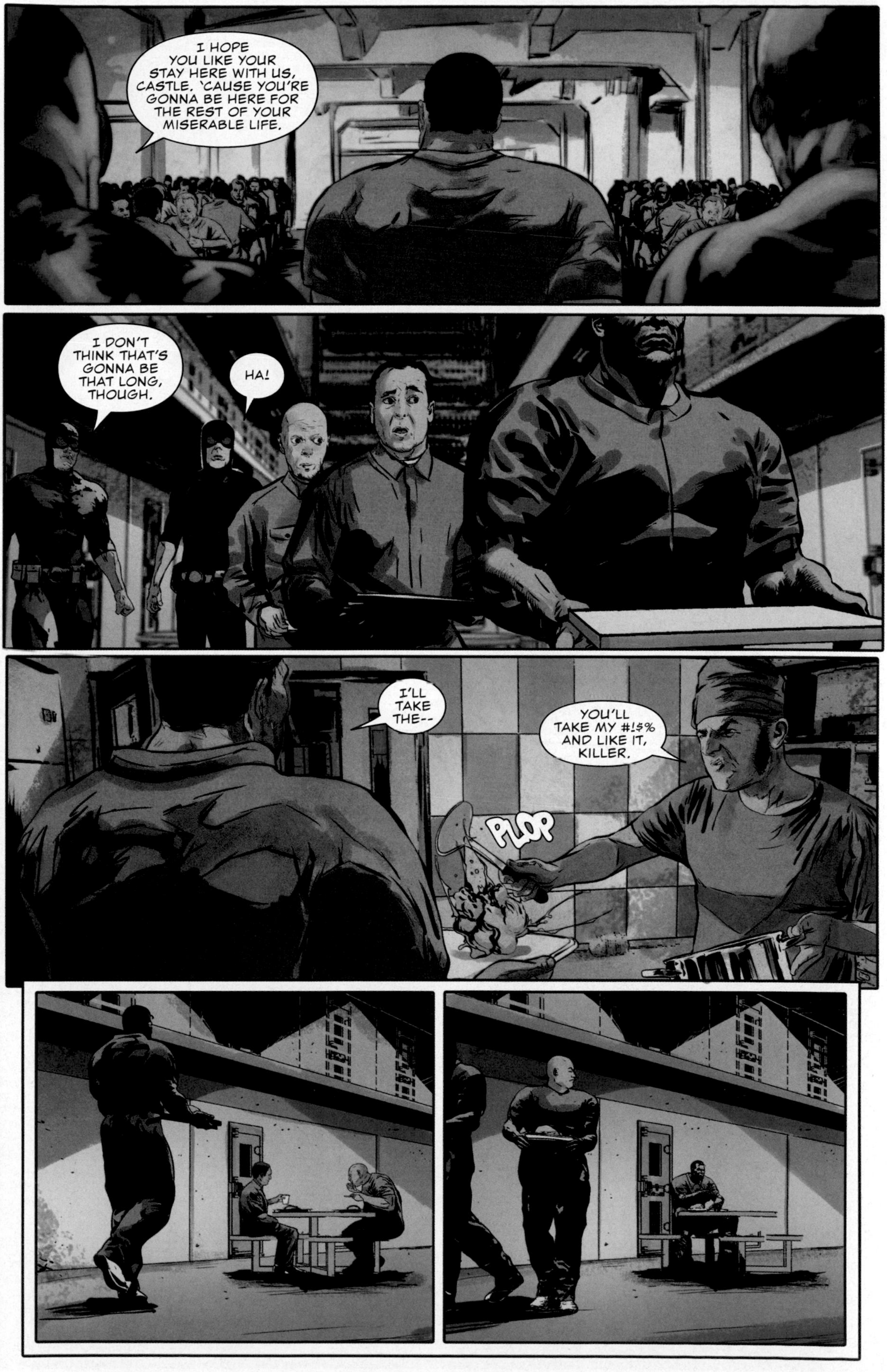
I HOPE YOU LIKE YOUR STAY HERE WITH US, CASTLE. 'CAUSE YOU'RE GONNA BE HERE FOR THE REST OF YOUR MISERABLE LIFE.
I DON'T THINK THAT'S GONNA BE THAT LONG, THOUGH.
HA!
I'LL TAKE THE--
YOU'LL TAKE MY #!$% AND LIKE IT, KILLER.
PLOP

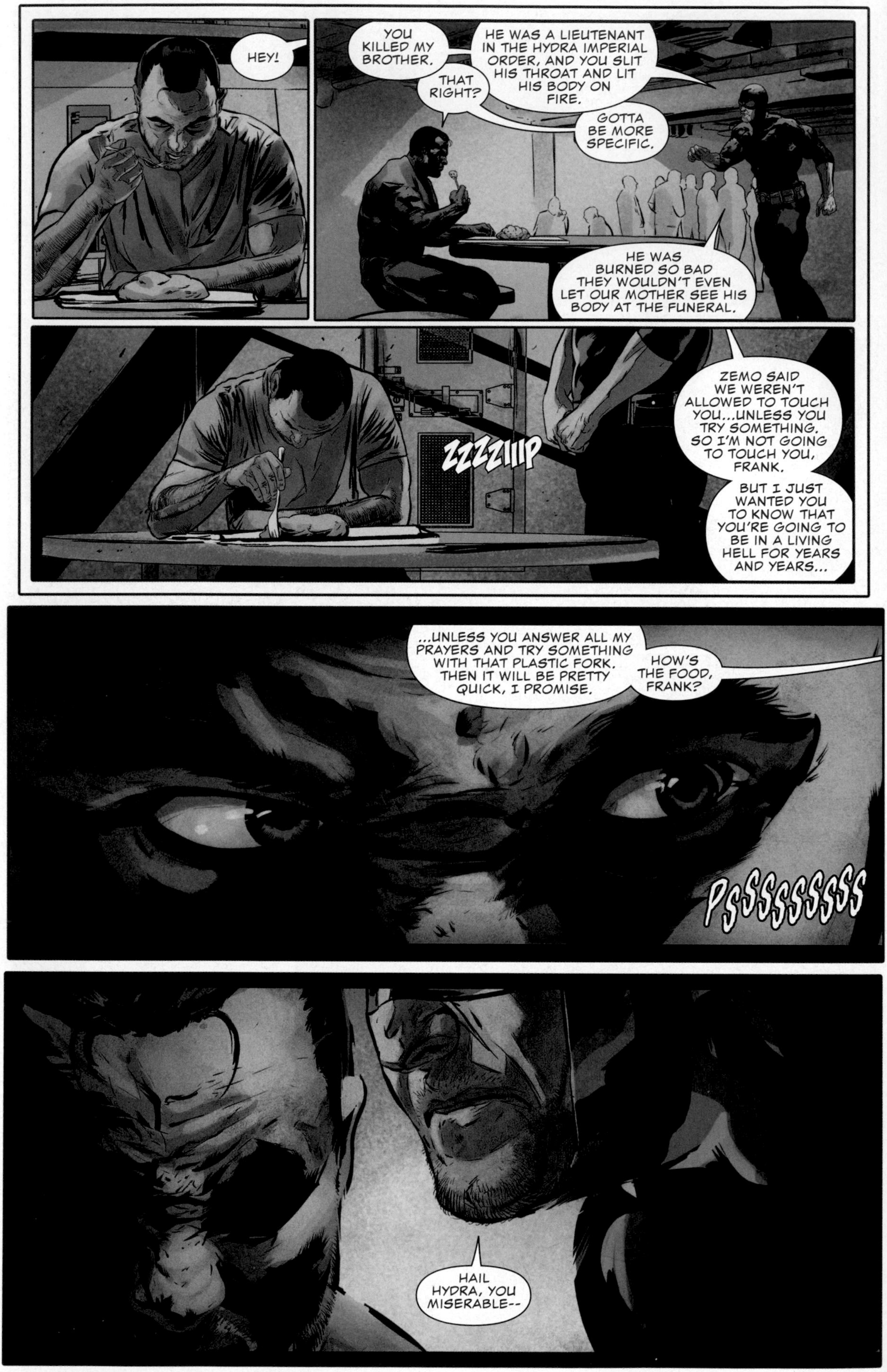
HEY!
YOU KILLED MY BROTHER.
HE WAS A LIEUTENANT IN THE HYDRA IMPERIAL ORDER, AND YOU SLIT HIS THROAT AND LIT HIS BODY ON FIRE.
THAT RIGHT?
GOTTA BE MORE SPECIFIC.
HE WAS BURNED SO BAD THEY WOULDN'T EVEN LET OUR MOTHER SEE HIS BODY AT THE FUNERAL.
ZEMO SAID WE WEREN'T ALLOWED TO TOUCH YOU...UNLESS YOU TRY SOMETHING. SO I'M NOT GOING TO TOUCH YOU, FRANK.
ZZZZIIIP
BUT I JUST WANTED YOU TO KNOW THAT YOU'RE GOING TO BE IN A LIVING HELL FOR YEARS AND YEARS...
...UNLESS YOU ANSWER ALL MY PRAYERS AND TRY SOMETHING WITH THAT PLASTIC FORK. THEN IT WILL BE PRETTY QUICK, I PROMISE.
HOW'S THE FOOD, FRANK?
PSSSSSSSSS
HAIL HYDRA, YOU MISERABLE--

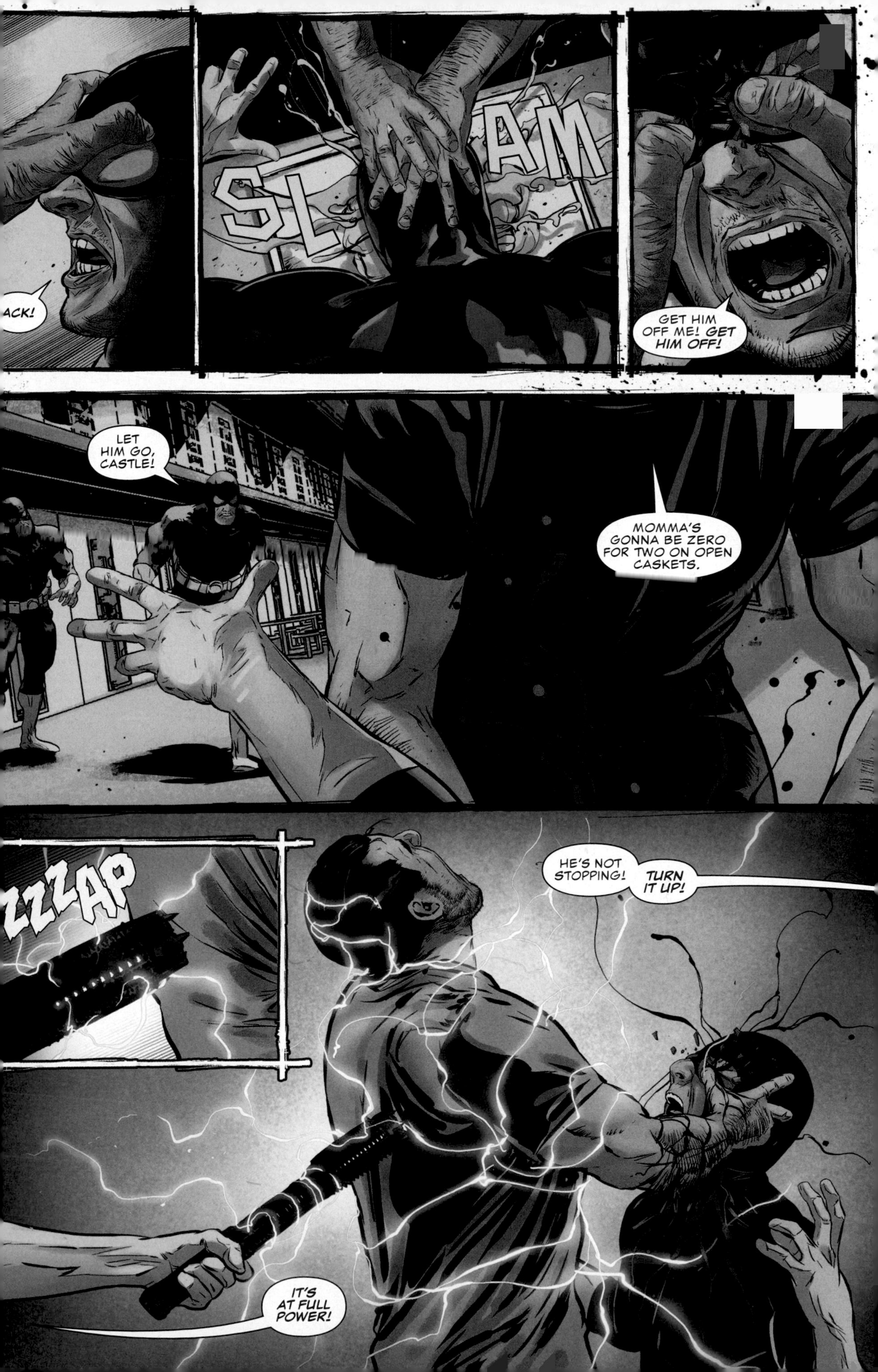
ACK!
SL AM
GET HIM OFF ME! GET HIM OFF!
LET HIM GO, CASTLE!
MOMMA'S GONNA BE ZERO FOR TWO ON OPEN CASKETS.
ZZZAP
HE'S NOT STOPPING!
TURN IT UP!
IT'S AT FULL POWER!

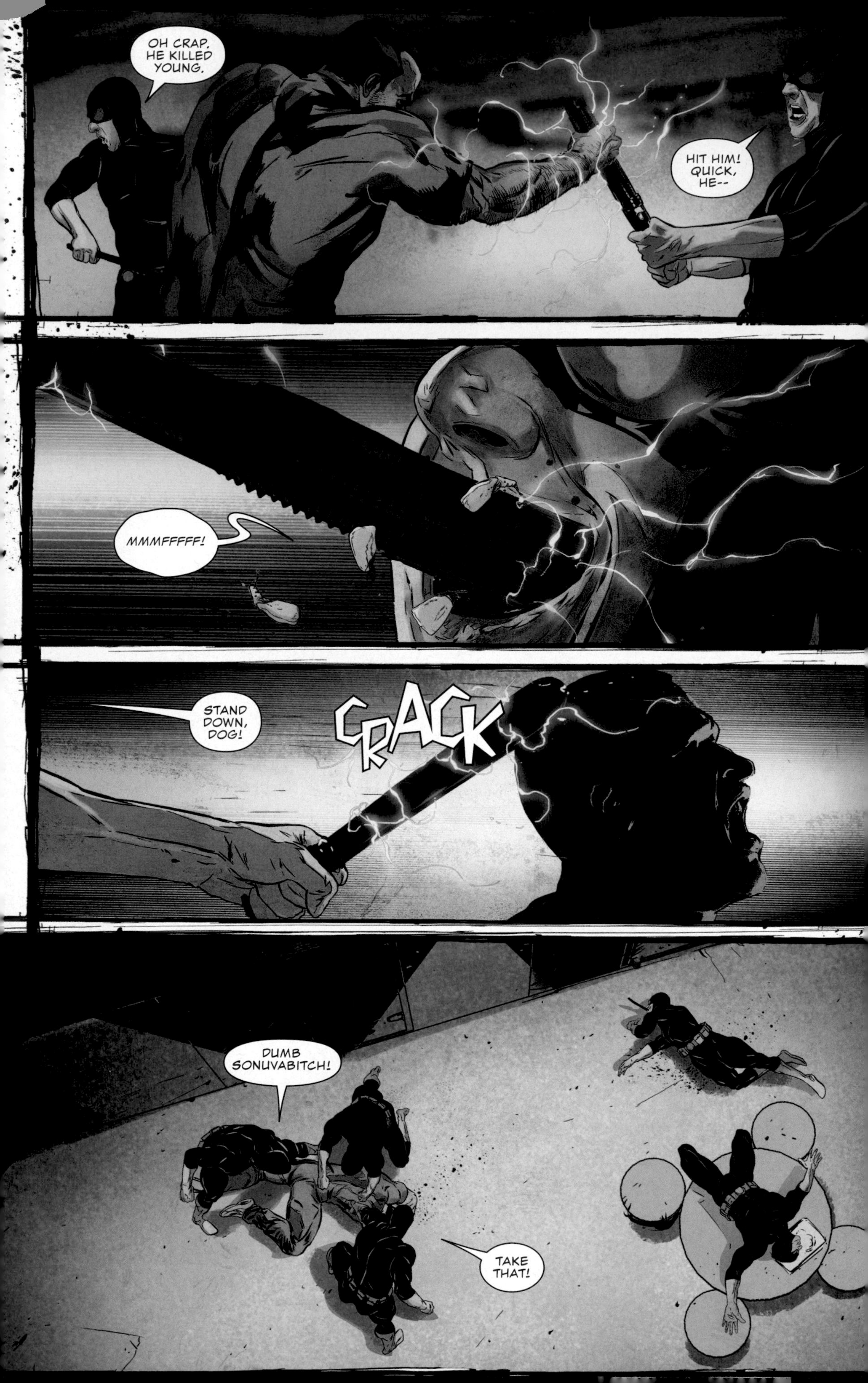
OH CRAP. HE KILLED YOUNG.
HIT HIM! QUICK, HE--
MMMFFFFF!
STAND DOWN, DOG!
CRACK
DUMB SONUVABITCH!
TAKE THAT!

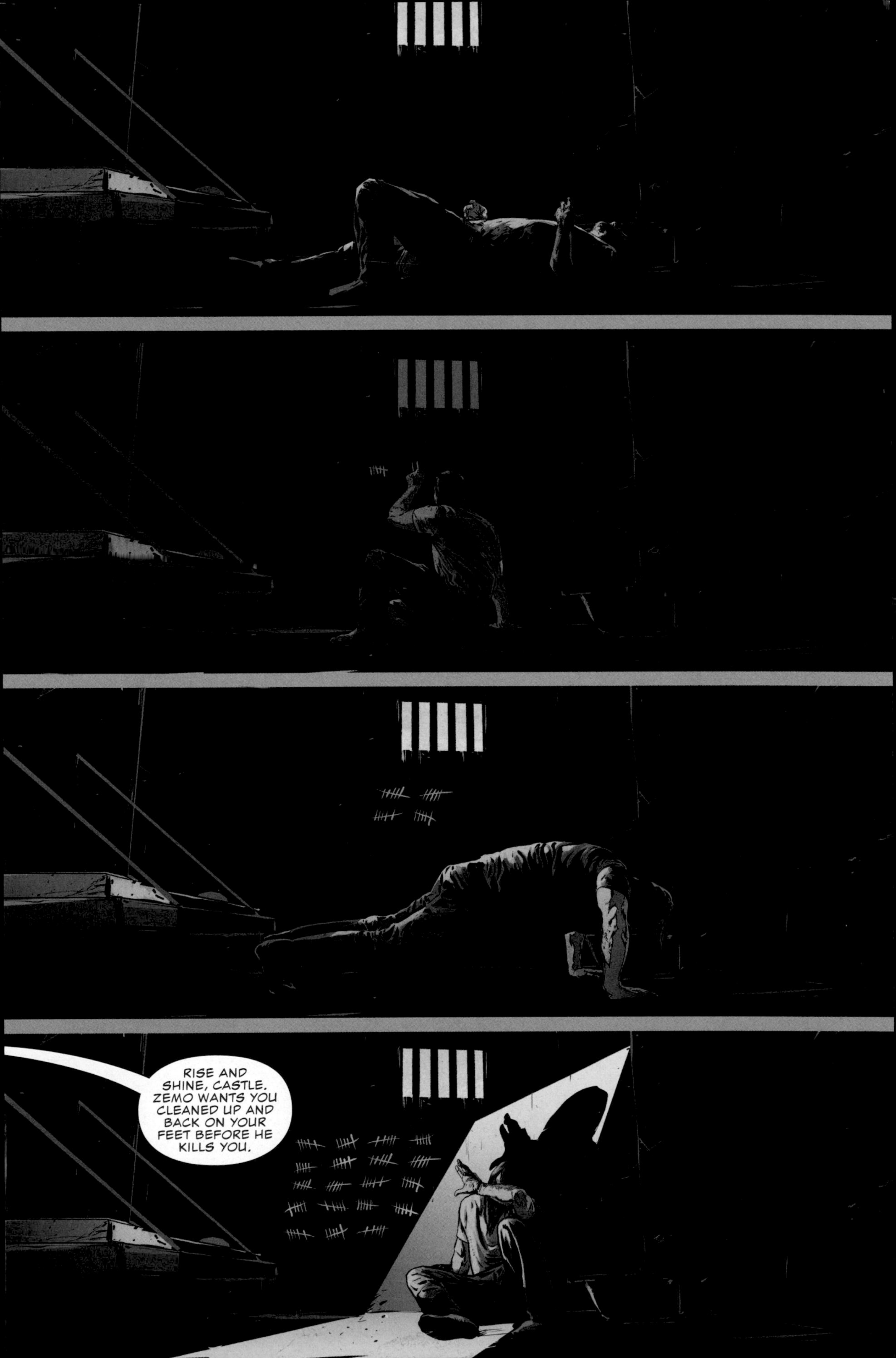
RISE AND SHINE, CASTLE. ZEMO WANTS YOU CLEANED UP AND BACK ON YOUR FEET BEFORE HE KILLS YOU.

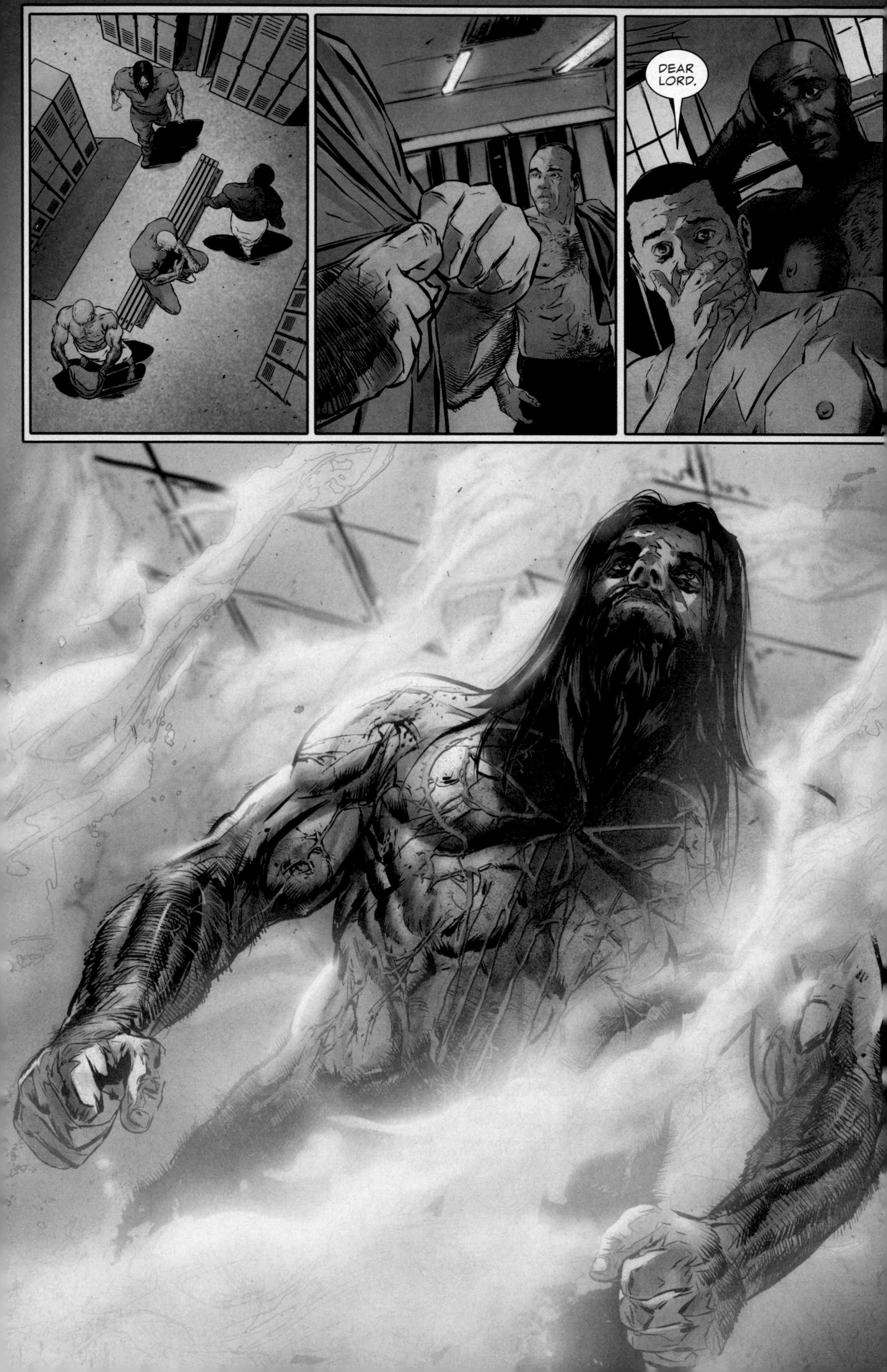
DEAR LORD.

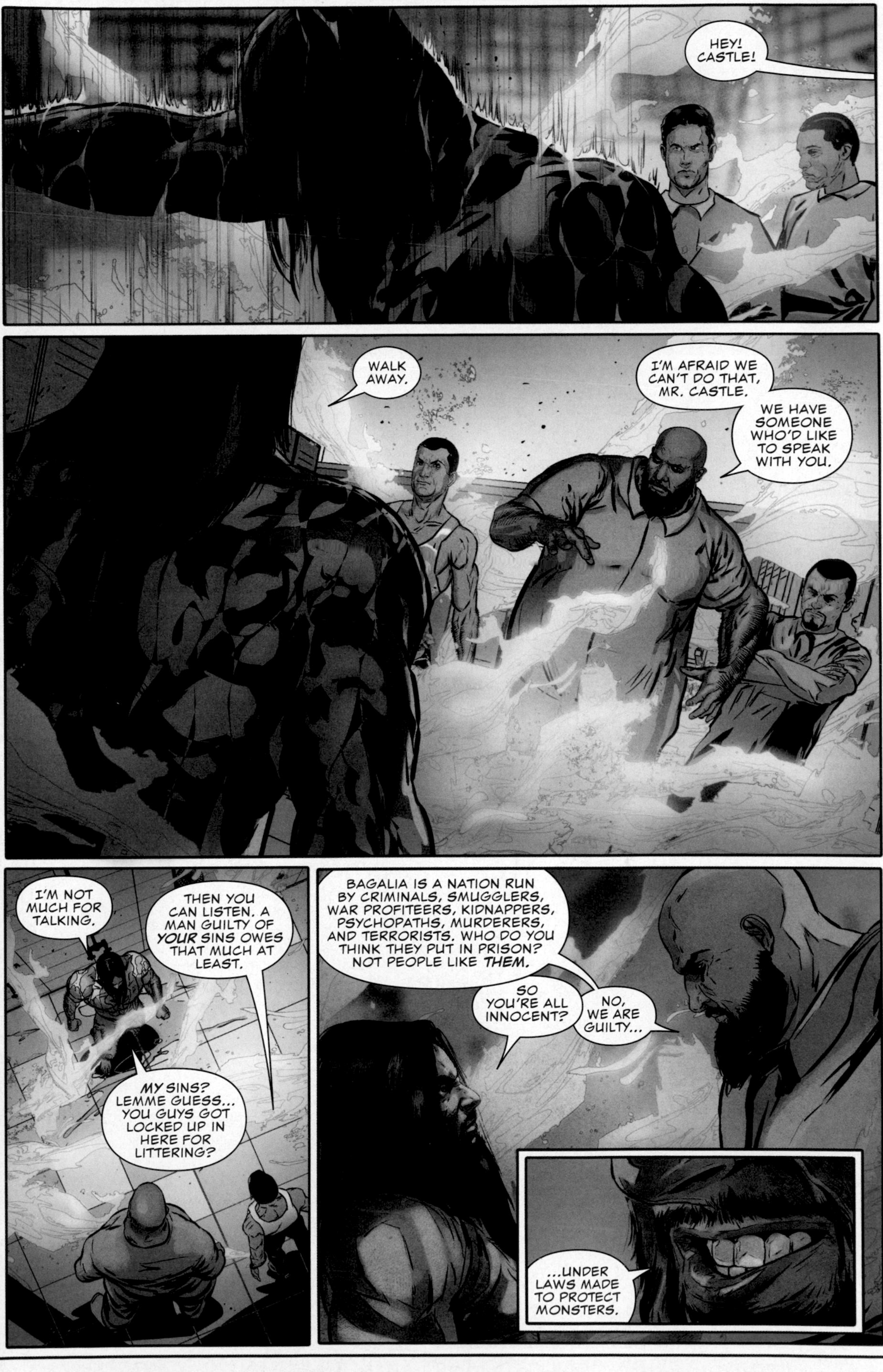
HEY! CASTLE!
WALK AWAY.
I'M AFRAID WE CAN'T DO THAT, MR. CASTLE.
WE HAVE SOMEONE WHO'D LIKE TO SPEAK WITH YOU.
I'M NOT MUCH FOR TALKING.
THEN YOU CAN LISTEN. A MAN GUILTY OF *YOUR* SINS OWES THAT MUCH AT LEAST.
MY SINS? LEMME GUESS... YOU GUYS GOT LOCKED UP IN HERE FOR LITTERING?
BAGALIA IS A NATION RUN BY CRIMINALS, SMUGGLERS, WAR PROFITEERS, KIDNAPPERS, PSYCHOPATHS, MURDERERS, AND TERRORISTS. WHO DO YOU THINK THEY PUT IN PRISON? NOT PEOPLE LIKE *THEM*.
SO YOU'RE ALL INNOCENT?
NO, WE ARE GUILTY...
...UNDER LAWS MADE TO PROTECT MONSTERS.

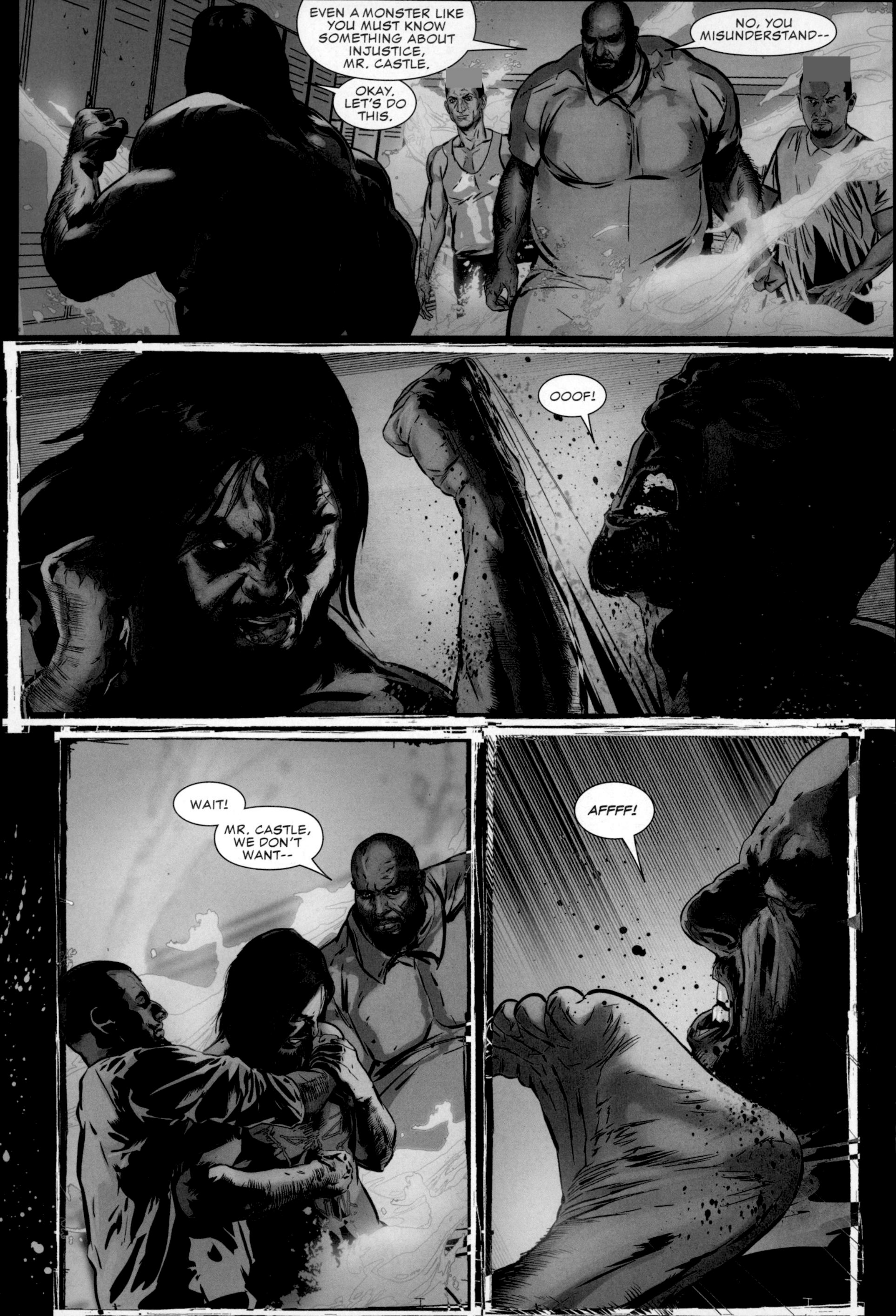
EVEN A MONSTER LIKE YOU MUST KNOW SOMETHING ABOUT INJUSTICE, MR. CASTLE.
OKAY. LET'S DO THIS.
NO, YOU MISUNDERSTAND--
OOOF!
WAIT!
MR. CASTLE, WE DON'T WANT--
AFFFF!

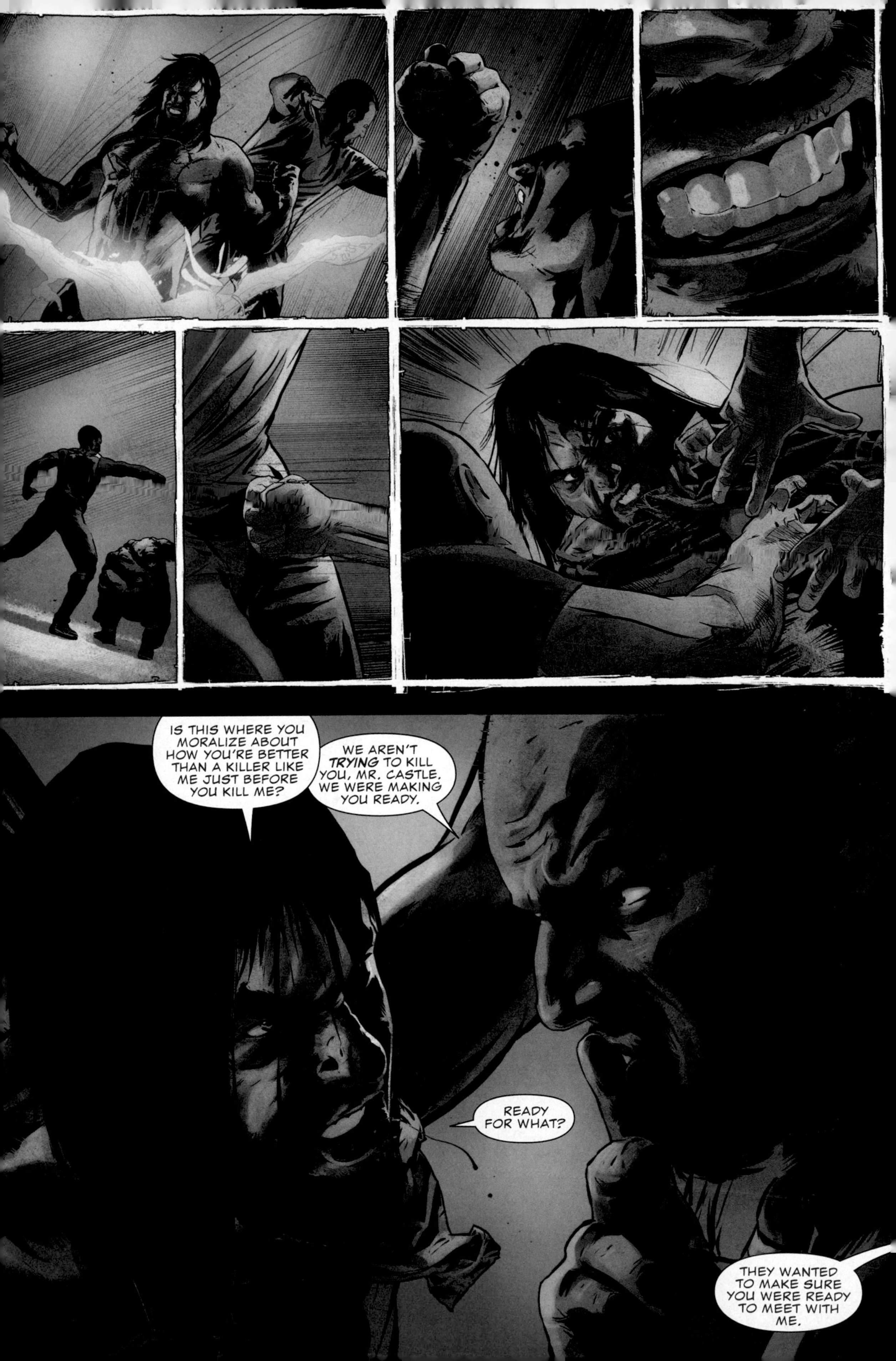
IS THIS WHERE YOU MORALIZE ABOUT HOW YOU'RE BETTER THAN A KILLER LIKE ME JUST BEFORE YOU KILL ME?
WE AREN'T *TRYING* TO KILL YOU, MR. CASTLE. WE WERE MAKING YOU READY.
READY FOR WHAT?
THEY WANTED TO MAKE SURE YOU WERE READY TO MEET WITH ME.

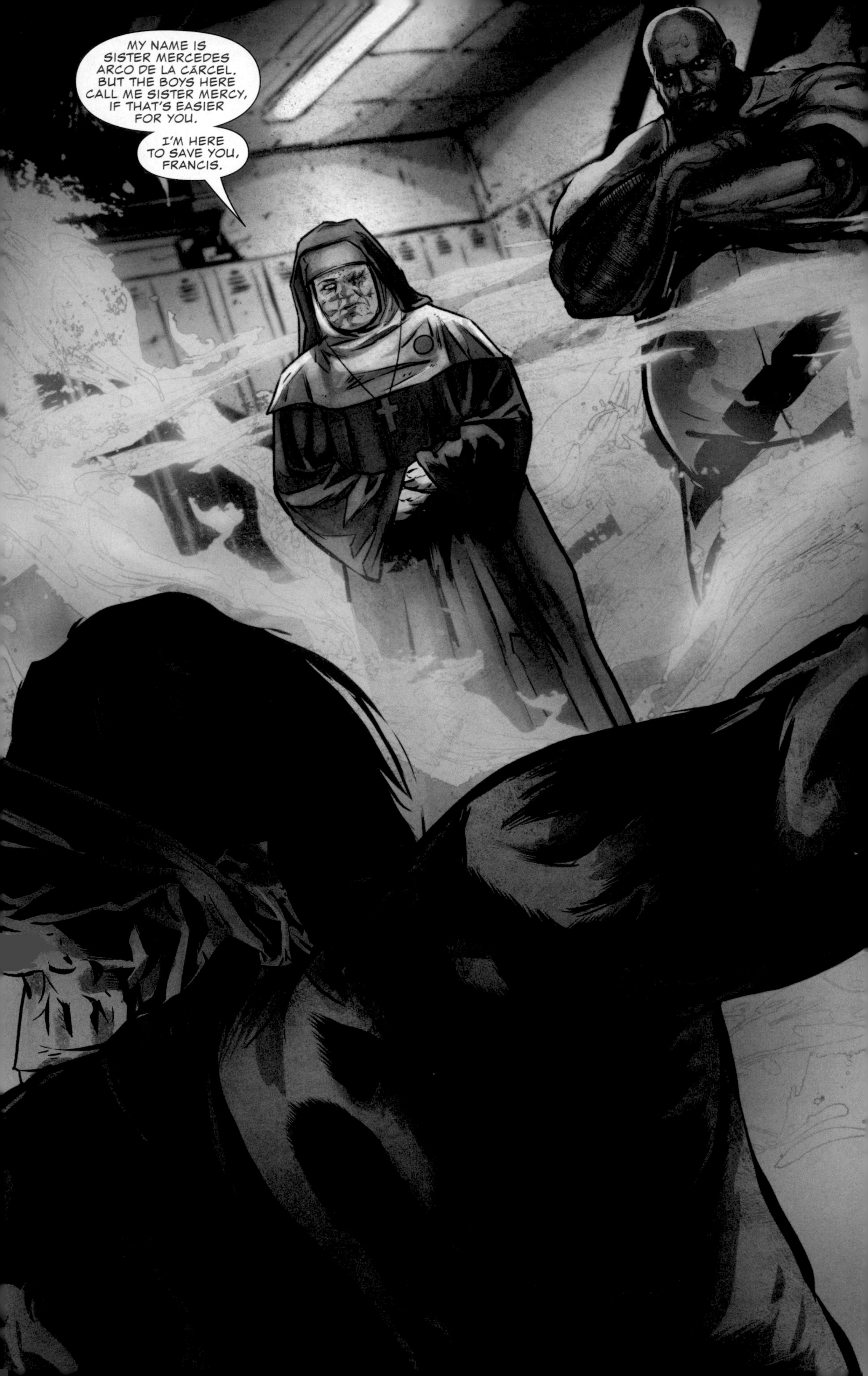
MY NAME IS SISTER MERCEDES ARCO DE LA CÁRCEL. BUT THE BOYS HERE CALL ME SISTER MERCY, IF THAT'S EASIER FOR YOU.
I'M HERE TO SAVE YOU, FRANCIS.

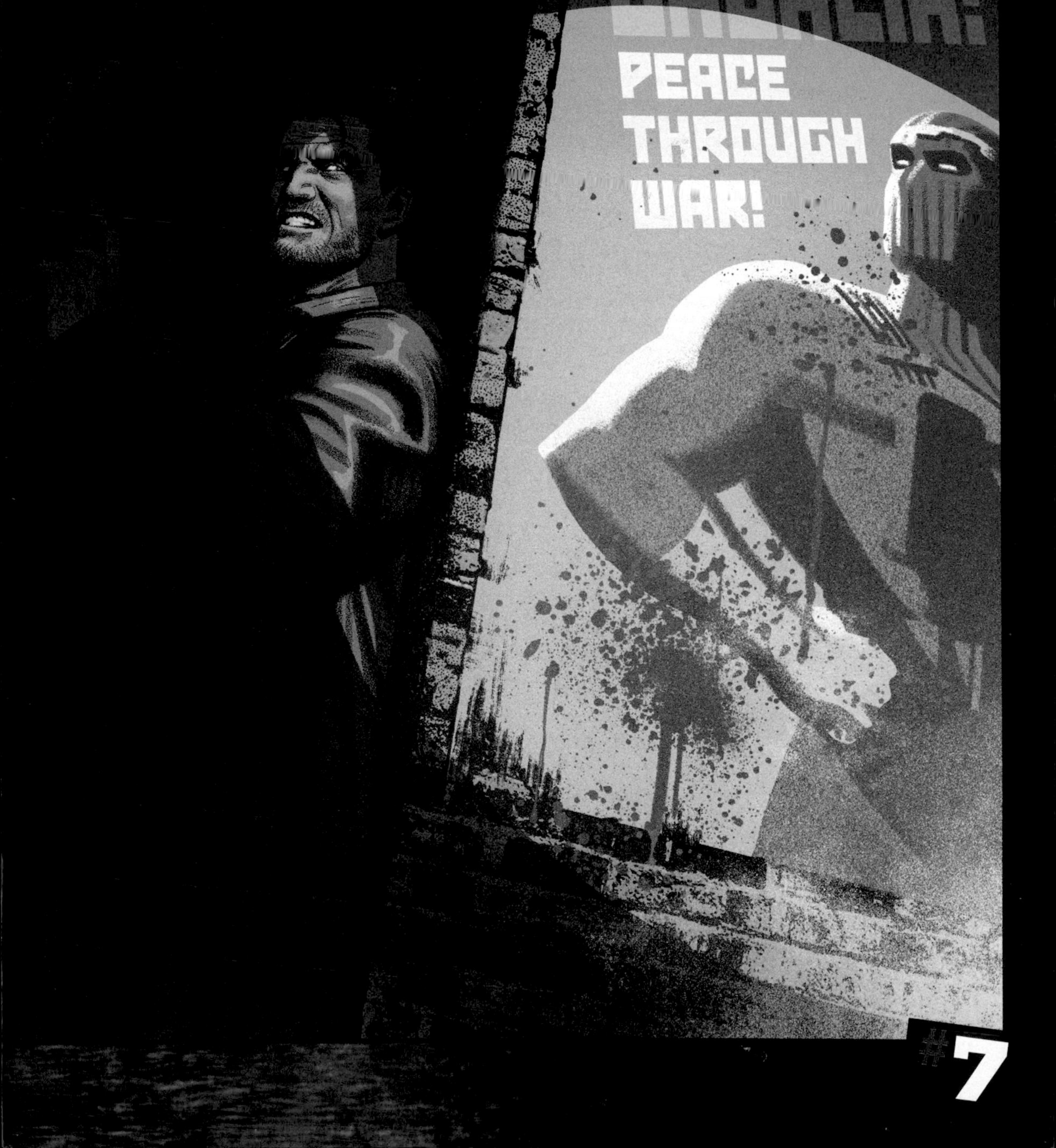
PEACE
THROUGH
WAR!
#7

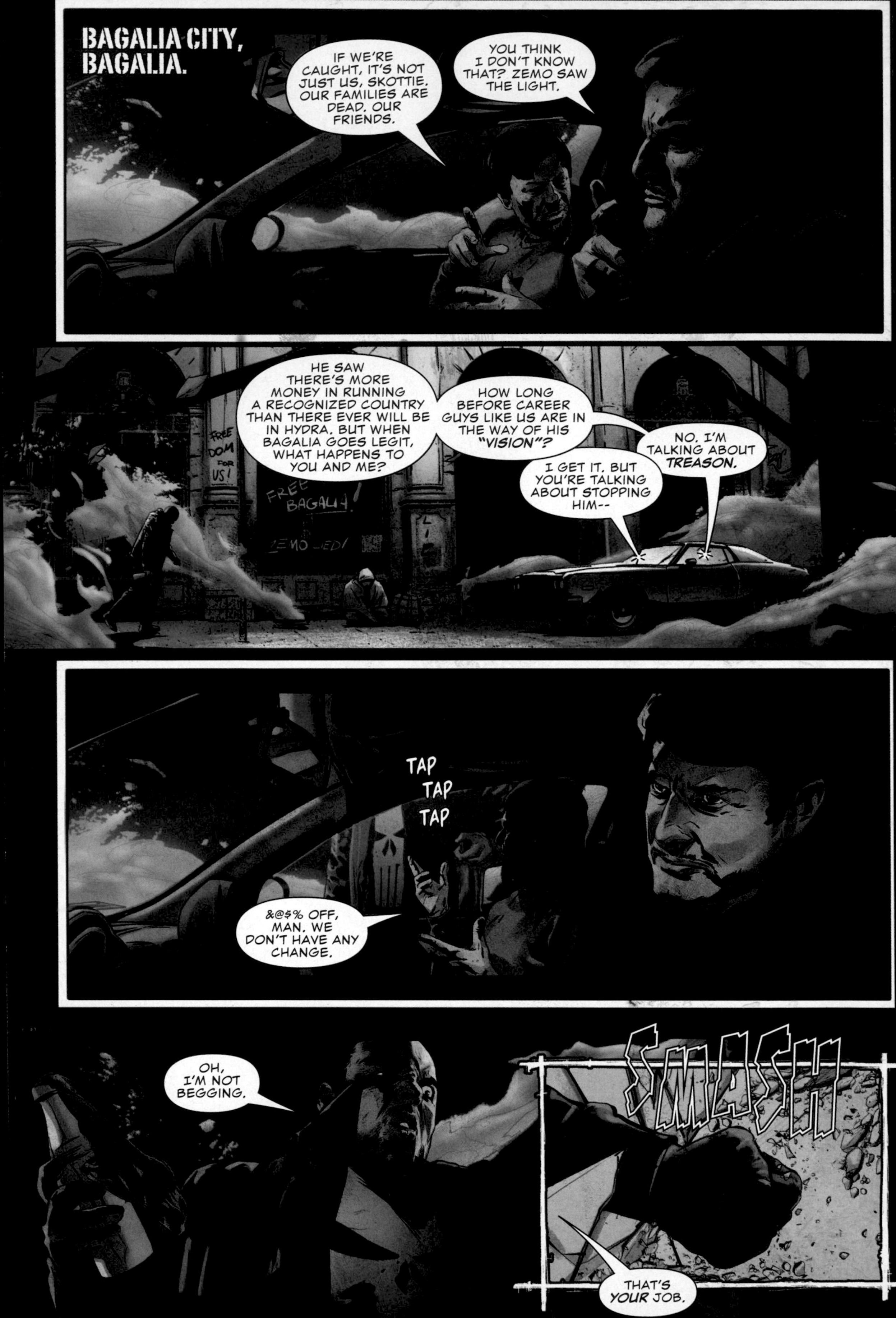
BAGALIA CITY, BAGALIA.
IF WE'RE CAUGHT, IT'S NOT JUST US, SKOTTIE. OUR FAMILIES ARE DEAD. OUR FRIENDS.
YOU THINK I DON'T KNOW THAT? ZEMO SAW THE LIGHT.
HE SAW THERE'S MORE MONEY IN RUNNING A RECOGNIZED COUNTRY THAN THERE EVER WILL BE IN HYDRA. BUT WHEN BAGALIA GOES LEGIT, WHAT HAPPENS TO YOU AND ME?
HOW LONG BEFORE CAREER GUYS LIKE US ARE IN THE WAY OF HIS "VISION"?
I GET IT. BUT YOU'RE TALKING ABOUT STOPPING HIM--
NO. I'M TALKING ABOUT TREASON.
FREE DOM FOR US!
FREE BAGALIA!
ZEMO LIED!
TAP TAP TAP
&@$% OFF, MAN. WE DON'T HAVE ANY CHANGE.
OH, I'M NOT BEGGING.
SMASH
THAT'S YOUR JOB.

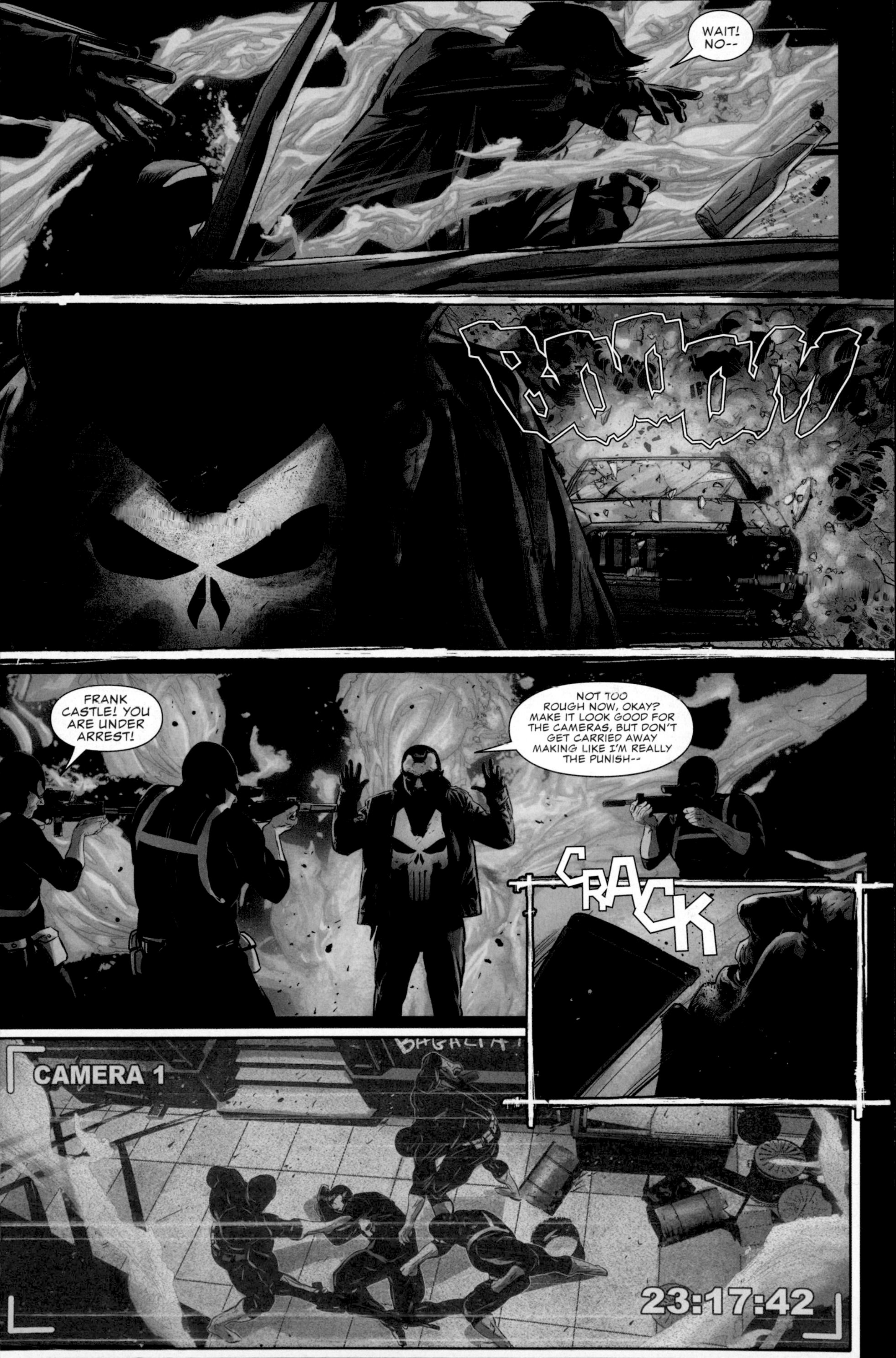
WAIT! NO--
BOOOM
FRANK CASTLE! YOU ARE UNDER ARREST!
NOT TOO ROUGH NOW, OKAY? MAKE IT LOOK GOOD FOR THE CAMERAS, BUT DON'T GET CARRIED AWAY MAKING LIKE I'M REALLY THE PUNISH--
CRACK
CAMERA 1
23:17:42

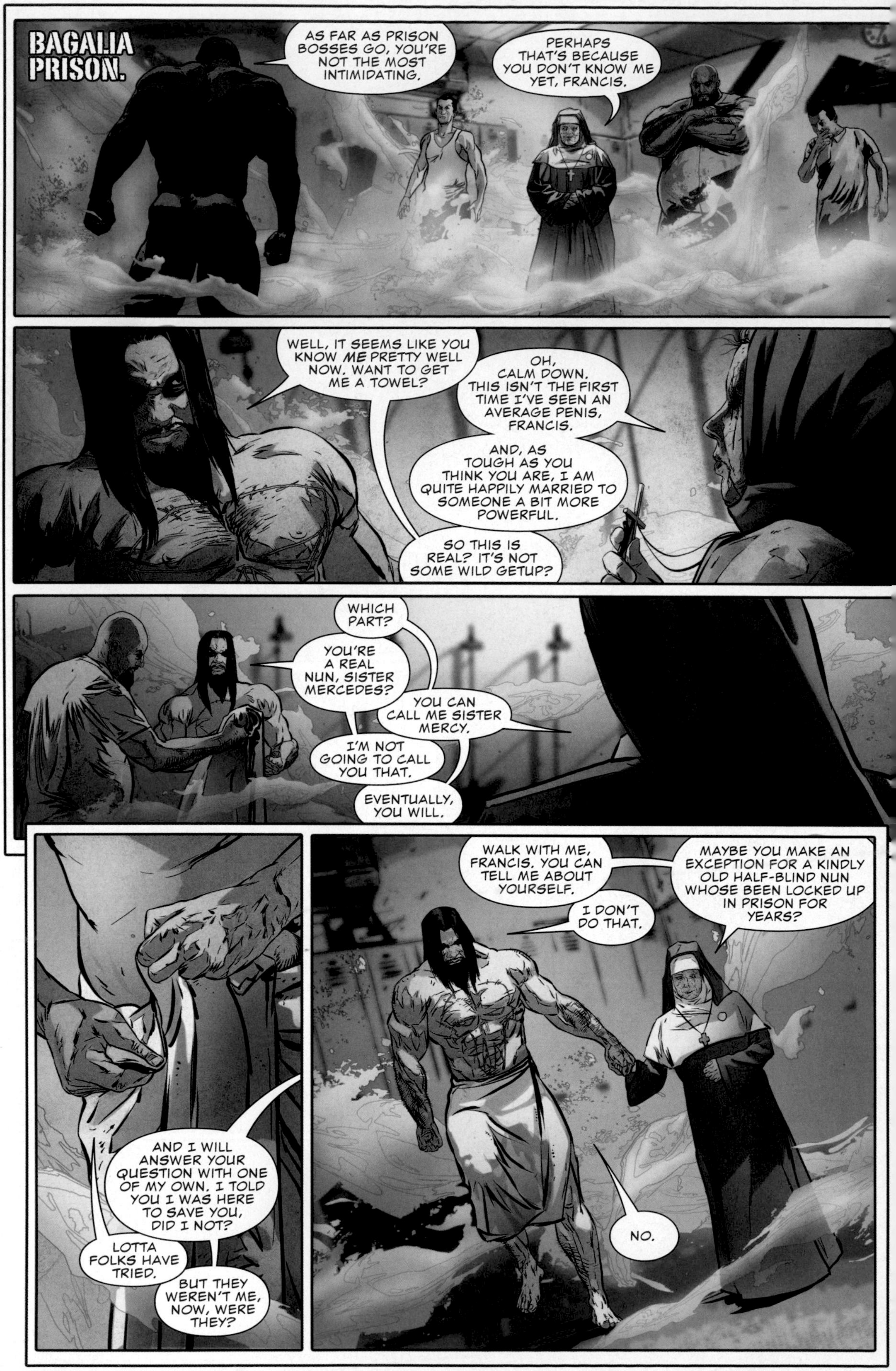
BAGALIA PRISON.
AS FAR AS PRISON BOSSES GO, YOU'RE NOT THE MOST INTIMIDATING.
PERHAPS THAT'S BECAUSE YOU DON'T KNOW ME YET, FRANCIS.
WELL, IT SEEMS LIKE YOU KNOW ME PRETTY WELL NOW. WANT TO GET ME A TOWEL?
OH, CALM DOWN. THIS ISN'T THE FIRST TIME I'VE SEEN AN AVERAGE PENIS, FRANCIS.
AND, AS TOUGH AS YOU THINK YOU ARE, I AM QUITE HAPPILY MARRIED TO SOMEONE A BIT MORE POWERFUL.
SO THIS IS REAL? IT'S NOT SOME WILD GETUP?
WHICH PART?
YOU'RE A REAL NUN, SISTER MERCEDES?
YOU CAN CALL ME SISTER MERCY.
I'M NOT GOING TO CALL YOU THAT.
EVENTUALLY, YOU WILL.
AND I WILL ANSWER YOUR QUESTION WITH ONE OF MY OWN. I TOLD YOU I WAS HERE TO SAVE YOU, DID I NOT?
LOTTA FOLKS HAVE TRIED.
BUT THEY WEREN'T ME, NOW, WERE THEY?
WALK WITH ME, FRANCIS. YOU CAN TELL ME ABOUT YOURSELF.
I DON'T DO THAT.
MAYBE YOU MAKE AN EXCEPTION FOR A KINDLY OLD HALF-BLIND NUN WHOSE BEEN LOCKED UP IN PRISON FOR YEARS?
NO.

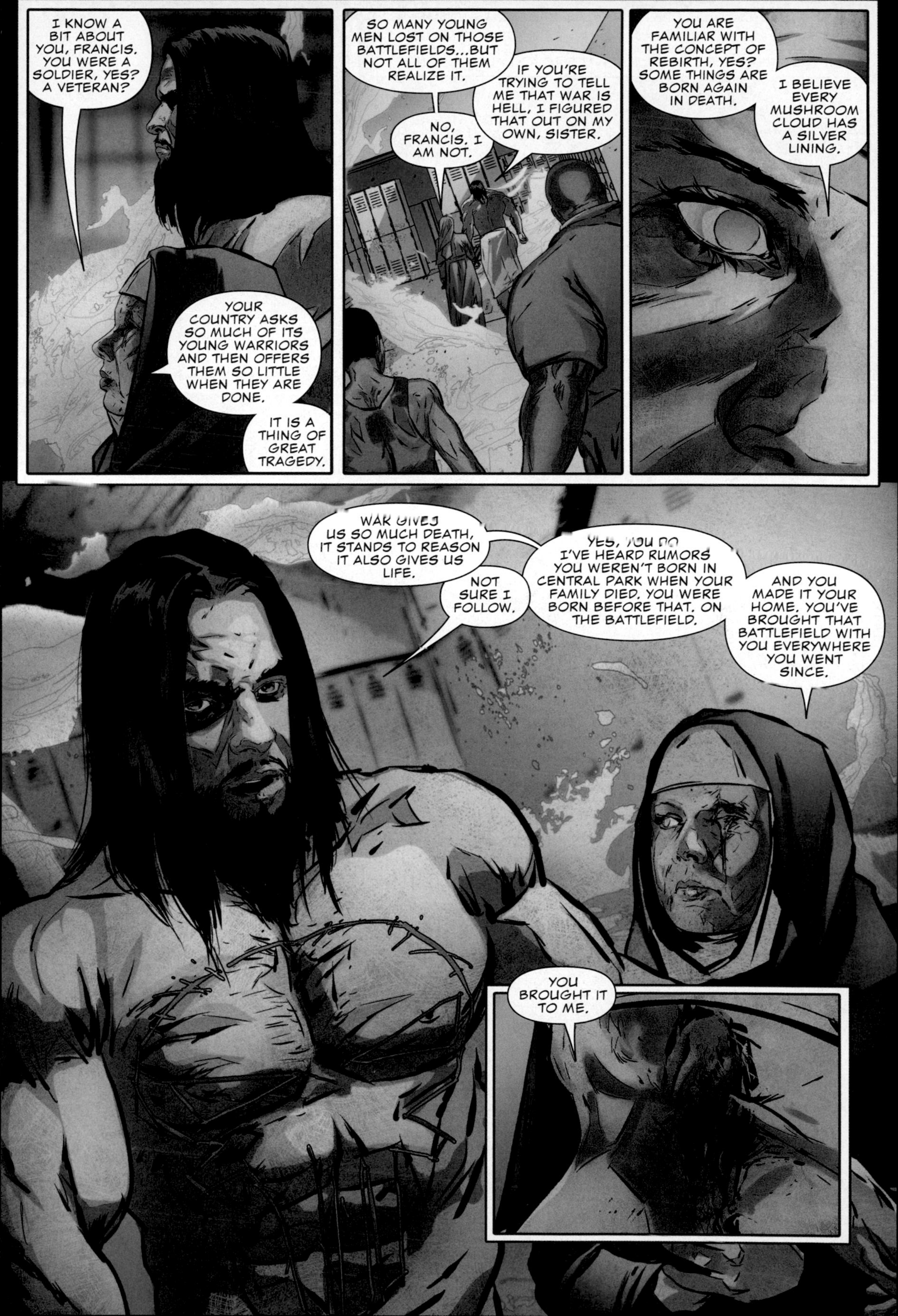
I KNOW A BIT ABOUT YOU, FRANCIS. YOU WERE A SOLDIER, YES? A VETERAN?
YOUR COUNTRY ASKS SO MUCH OF ITS YOUNG WARRIORS AND THEN OFFERS THEM SO LITTLE WHEN THEY ARE DONE.
IT IS A THING OF GREAT TRAGEDY.
SO MANY YOUNG MEN LOST ON THOSE BATTLEFIELDS...BUT NOT ALL OF THEM REALIZE IT.
IF YOU'RE TRYING TO TELL ME THAT WAR IS HELL, I FIGURED THAT OUT ON MY OWN, SISTER.
NO, FRANCIS. I AM NOT.
YOU ARE FAMILIAR WITH THE CONCEPT OF REBIRTH, YES? SOME THINGS ARE BORN AGAIN IN DEATH.
I BELIEVE EVERY MUSHROOM CLOUD HAS A SILVER LINING.
US SO MUCH DEATH, IT STANDS TO REASON IT ALSO GIVES US LIFE.
NOT SURE I FOLLOW.
I'VE HEARD RUMORS YOU WEREN'T BORN IN CENTRAL PARK WHEN YOUR FAMILY DIED. YOU WERE BORN BEFORE THAT. ON THE BATTLEFIELD.
AND YOU MADE IT YOUR HOME. YOU'VE BROUGHT THAT BATTLEFIELD WITH YOU EVERYWHERE YOU WENT SINCE.
YOU BROUGHT IT TO ME.

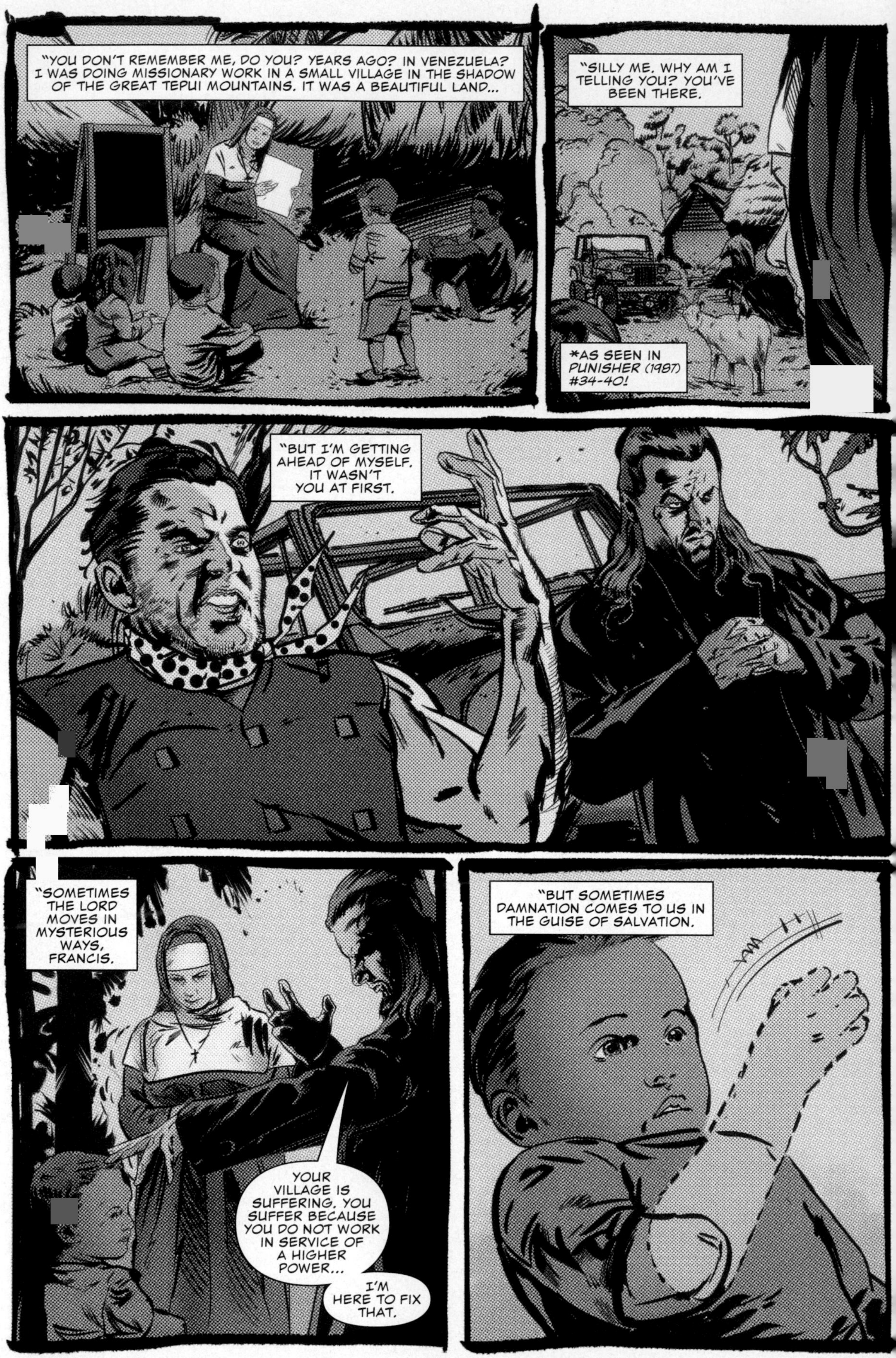
"YOU DON'T REMEMBER ME, DO YOU? YEARS AGO? IN VENEZUELA? I WAS DOING MISSIONARY WORK IN A SMALL VILLAGE IN THE SHADOW OF THE GREAT TEPUI MOUNTAINS. IT WAS A BEAUTIFUL LAND...
"SILLY ME. WHY AM I TELLING YOU? YOU'VE BEEN THERE.
*AS SEEN IN PUNISHER (1987) #34-40!
"BUT I'M GETTING AHEAD OF MYSELF. IT WASN'T YOU AT FIRST.
"SOMETIMES THE LORD MOVES IN MYSTERIOUS WAYS, FRANCIS.
YOUR VILLAGE IS SUFFERING. YOU SUFFER BECAUSE YOU DO NOT WORK IN SERVICE OF A HIGHER POWER...
I'M HERE TO FIX THAT.
"BUT SOMETIMES DAMNATION COMES TO US IN THE GUISE OF SALVATION.

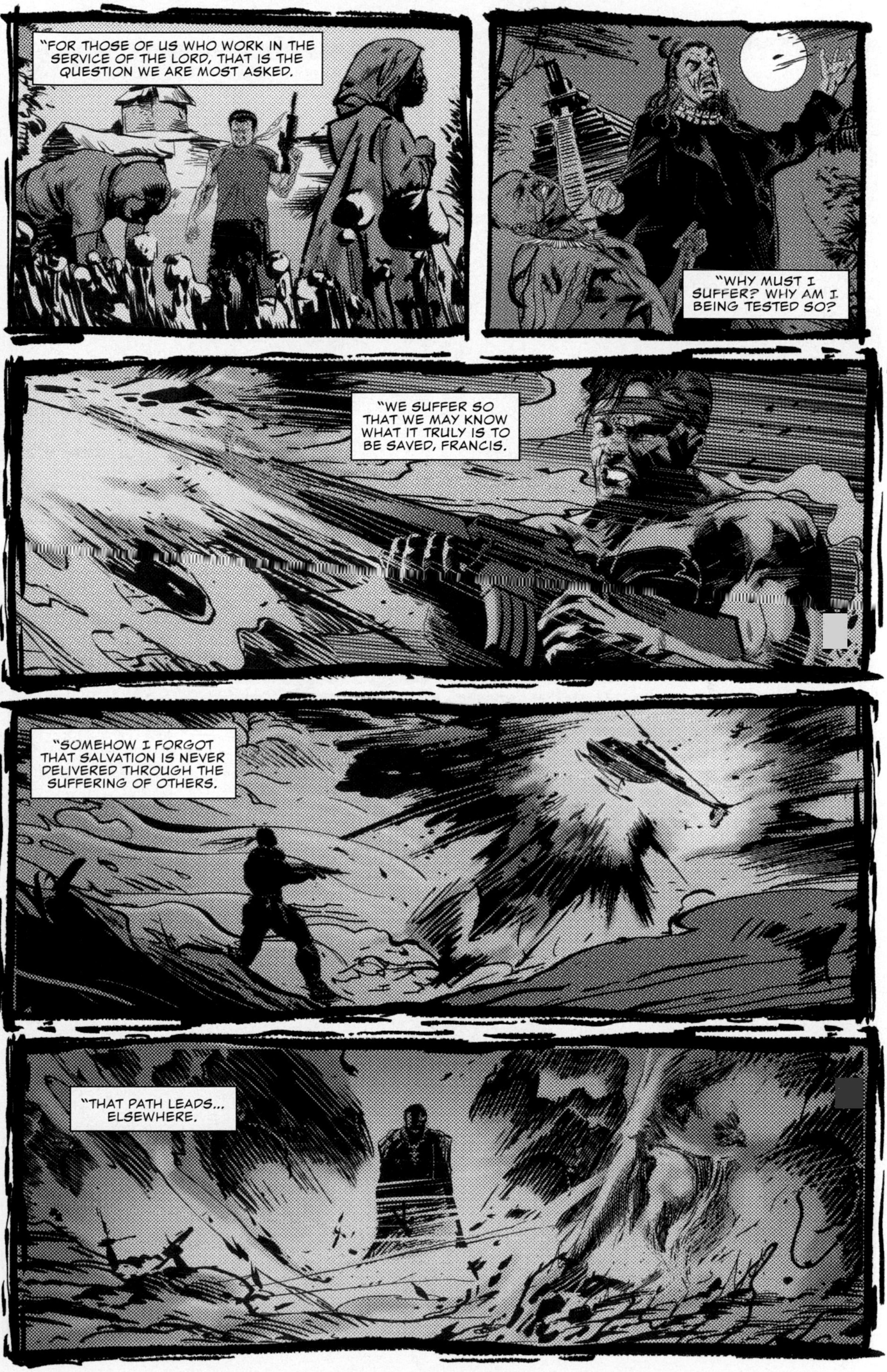
"FOR THOSE OF US WHO WORK IN THE SERVICE OF THE LORD, THAT IS THE QUESTION WE ARE MOST ASKED.
"WHY MUST I SUFFER? WHY AM I BEING TESTED SO?
"WE SUFFER SO THAT WE MAY KNOW WHAT IT TRULY IS TO BE SAVED, FRANCIS.
"SOMEHOW I FORGOT THAT SALVATION IS NEVER DELIVERED THROUGH THE SUFFERING OF OTHERS.
"THAT PATH LEADS... ELSEWHERE.

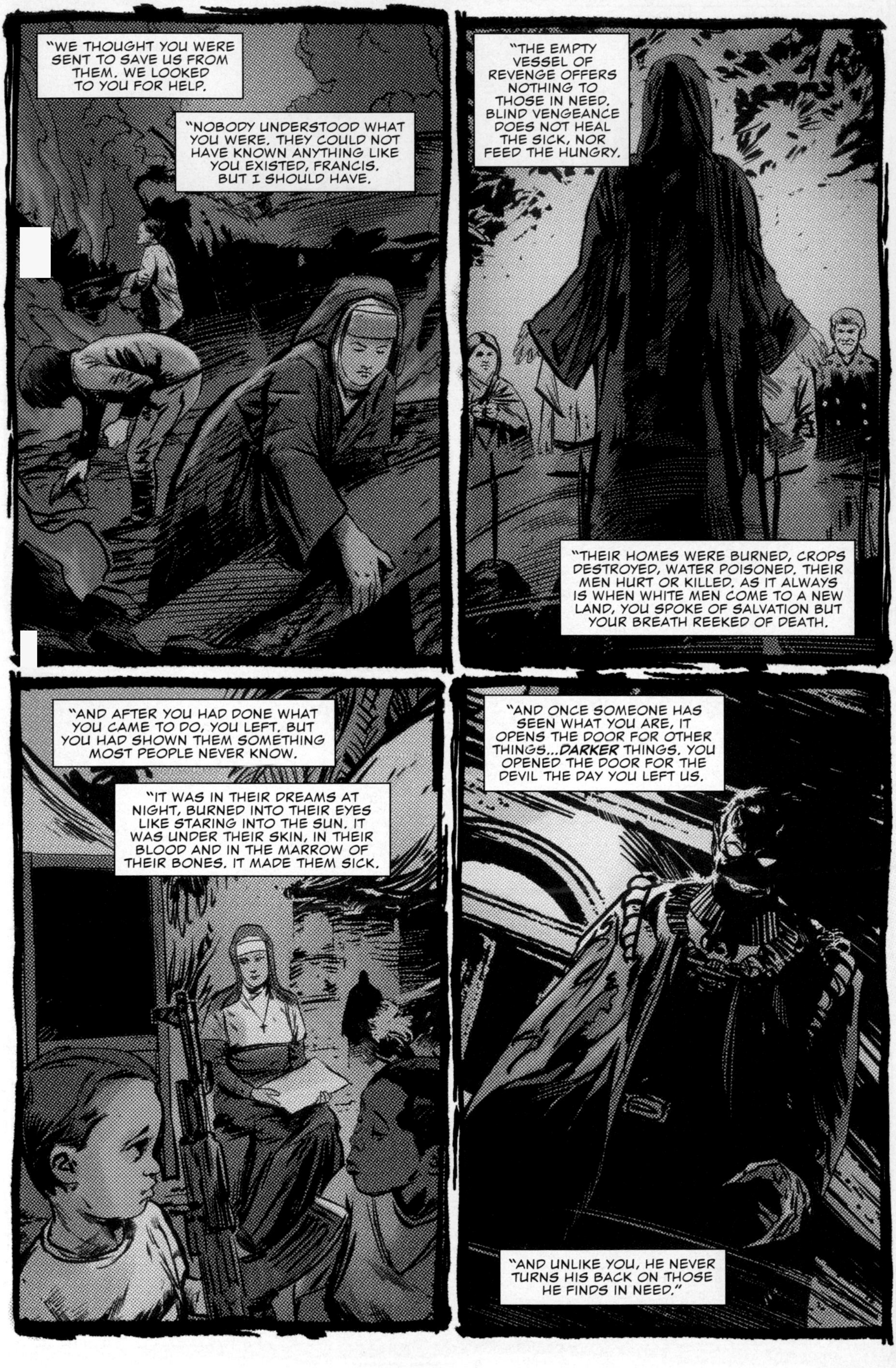
"WE THOUGHT YOU WERE SENT TO SAVE US FROM THEM. WE LOOKED TO YOU FOR HELP.
"NOBODY UNDERSTOOD WHAT YOU WERE. THEY COULD NOT HAVE KNOWN ANYTHING LIKE YOU EXISTED, FRANCIS. BUT I SHOULD HAVE.
"THE EMPTY VESSEL OF REVENGE OFFERS NOTHING TO THOSE IN NEED. BLIND VENGEANCE DOES NOT HEAL THE SICK, NOR FEED THE HUNGRY.
"THEIR HOMES WERE BURNED, CROPS DESTROYED, WATER POISONED. THEIR MEN HURT OR KILLED. AS IT ALWAYS IS WHEN WHITE MEN COME TO A NEW LAND, YOU SPOKE OF SALVATION BUT YOUR BREATH REEKED OF DEATH.
"AND AFTER YOU HAD DONE WHAT YOU CAME TO DO, YOU LEFT. BUT YOU HAD SHOWN THEM SOMETHING MOST PEOPLE NEVER KNOW.
"IT WAS IN THEIR DREAMS AT NIGHT, BURNED INTO THEIR EYES LIKE STARING INTO THE SUN. IT WAS UNDER THEIR SKIN, IN THEIR BLOOD AND IN THE MARROW OF THEIR BONES. IT MADE THEM SICK.
"AND ONCE SOMEONE HAS SEEN WHAT YOU ARE, IT OPENS THE DOOR FOR OTHER THINGS...*DARKER* THINGS. YOU OPENED THE DOOR FOR THE DEVIL THE DAY YOU LEFT US.
"AND UNLIKE YOU, HE NEVER TURNS HIS BACK ON THOSE HE FINDS IN NEED."

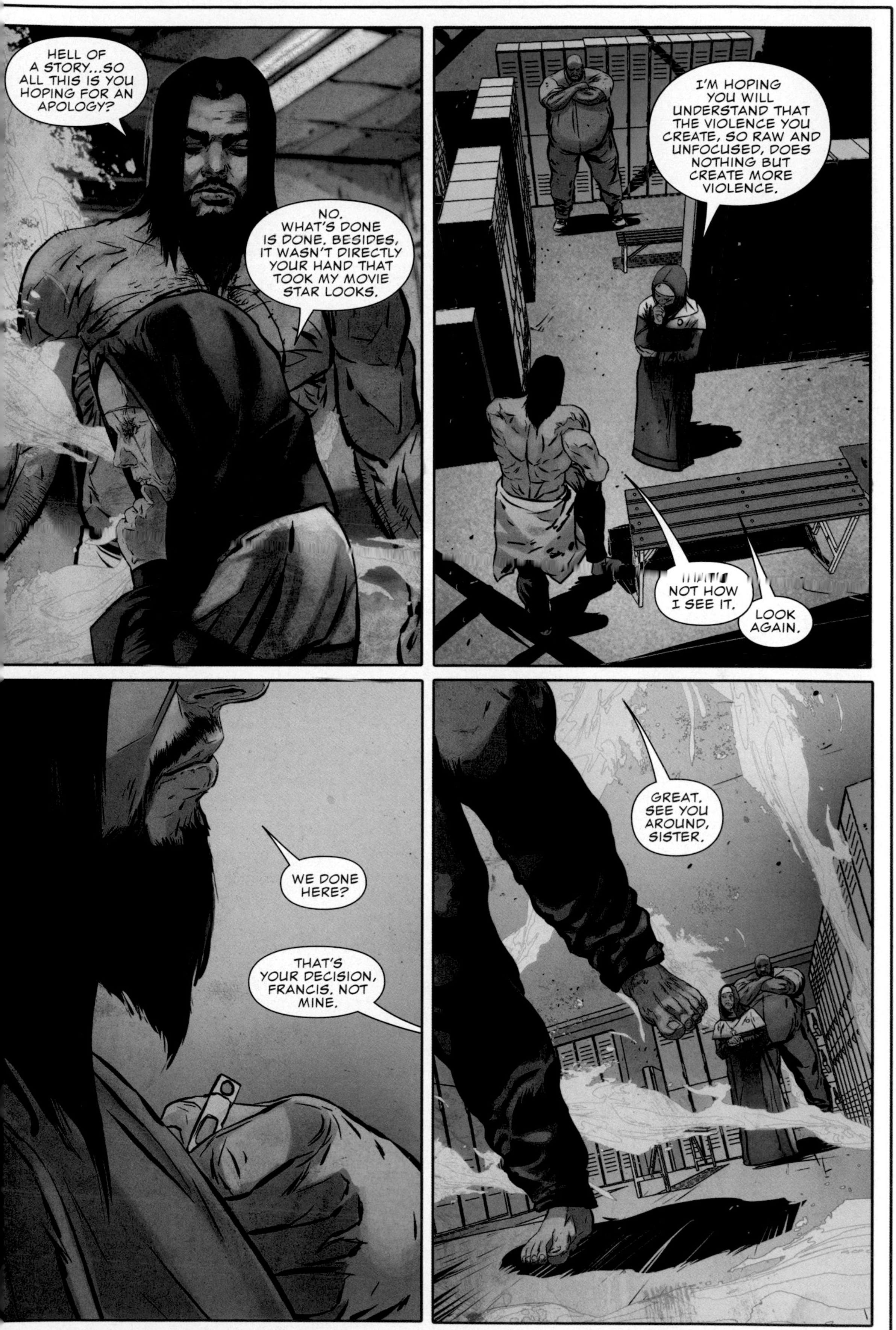
HELL OF A STORY...SO ALL THIS IS YOU HOPING FOR AN APOLOGY?
NO. WHAT'S DONE IS DONE. BESIDES, IT WASN'T DIRECTLY YOUR HAND THAT TOOK MY MOVIE STAR LOOKS.
I'M HOPING YOU WILL UNDERSTAND THAT THE VIOLENCE YOU CREATE, SO RAW AND UNFOCUSED, DOES NOTHING BUT CREATE MORE VIOLENCE.
NOT HOW I SEE IT.
LOOK AGAIN.
WE DONE HERE?
THAT'S YOUR DECISION, FRANCIS. NOT MINE.
GREAT. SEE YOU AROUND, SISTER.

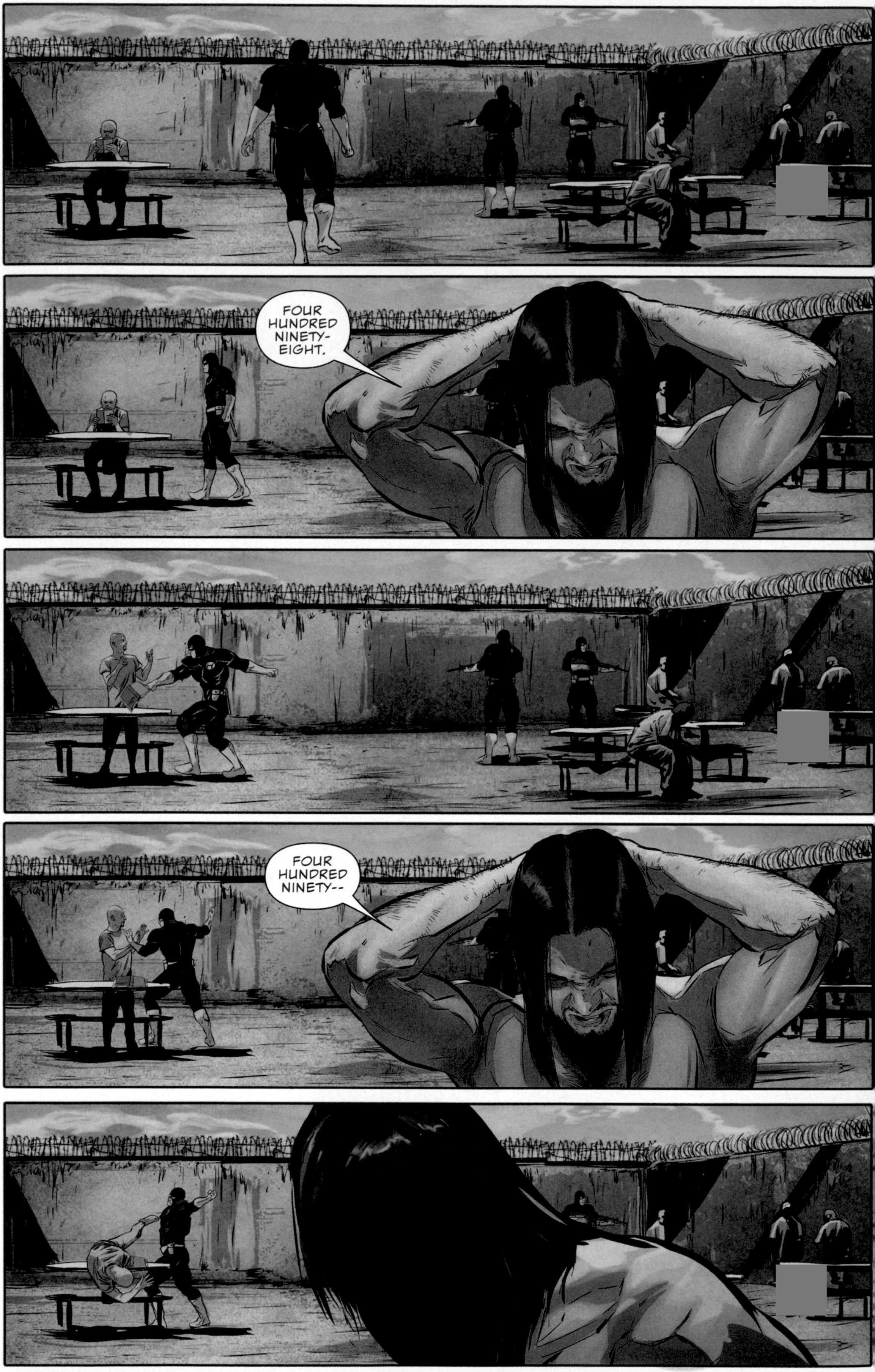
FOUR HUNDRED NINETY-EIGHT.
FOUR HUNDRED NINETY--

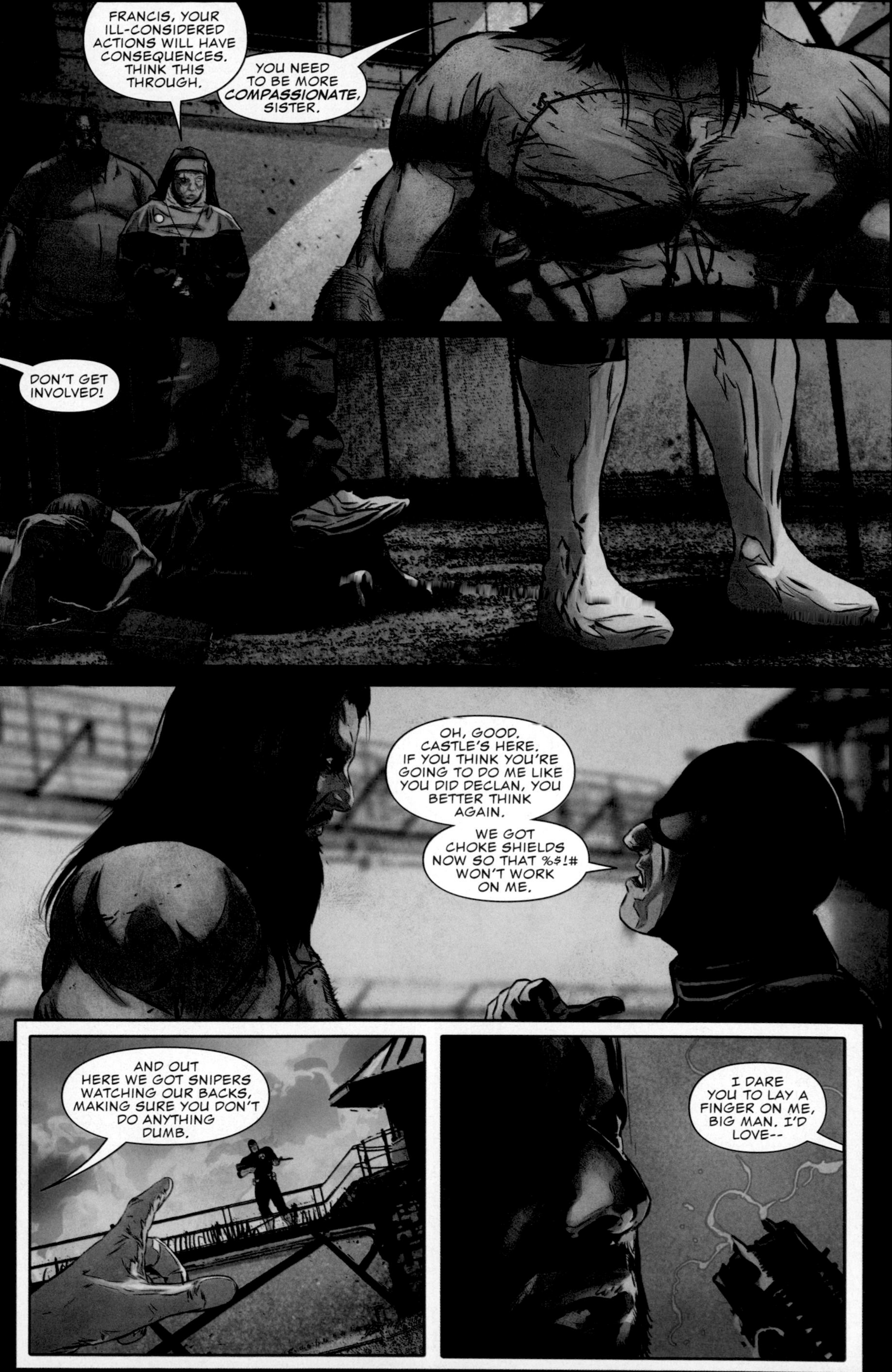
FRANCIS, YOUR ILL-CONSIDERED ACTIONS WILL HAVE CONSEQUENCES. THINK THIS THROUGH.
YOU NEED TO BE MORE COMPASSIONATE, SISTER.
DON'T GET INVOLVED!
OH, GOOD. CASTLE'S HERE. IF YOU THINK YOU'RE GOING TO DO ME LIKE YOU DID DECLAN, YOU BETTER THINK AGAIN.
WE GOT CHOKE SHIELDS NOW SO THAT %$!# WON'T WORK ON ME.
AND OUT HERE WE GOT SNIPERS WATCHING OUR BACKS, MAKING SURE YOU DON'T DO ANYTHING DUMB.
I DARE YOU TO LAY A FINGER ON ME, BIG MAN. I'D LOVE--

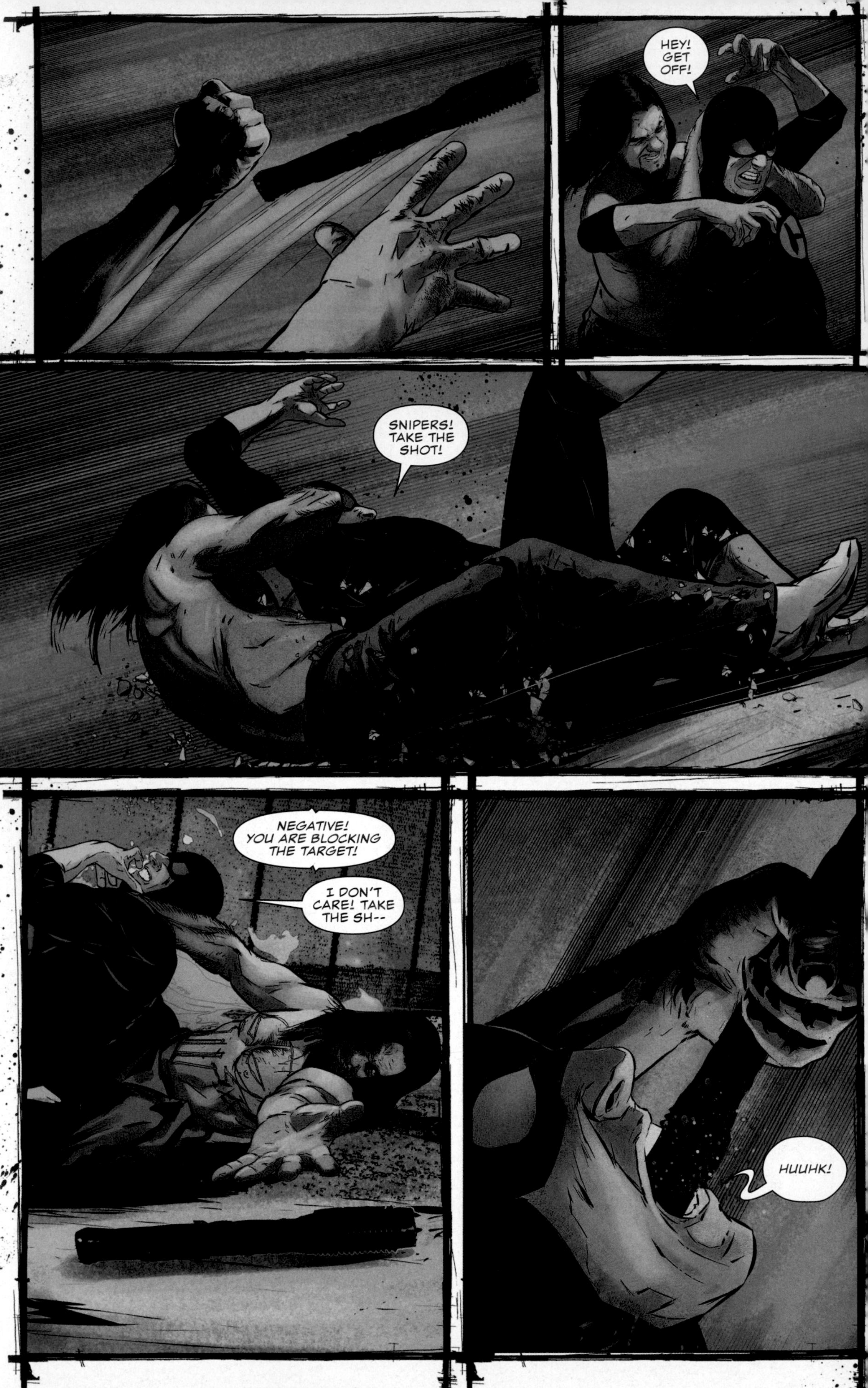
HEY! GET OFF!
SNIPERS! TAKE THE SHOT!
NEGATIVE! YOU ARE BLOCKING THE TARGET!
I DON'T CARE! TAKE THE SH--
HUUHK!

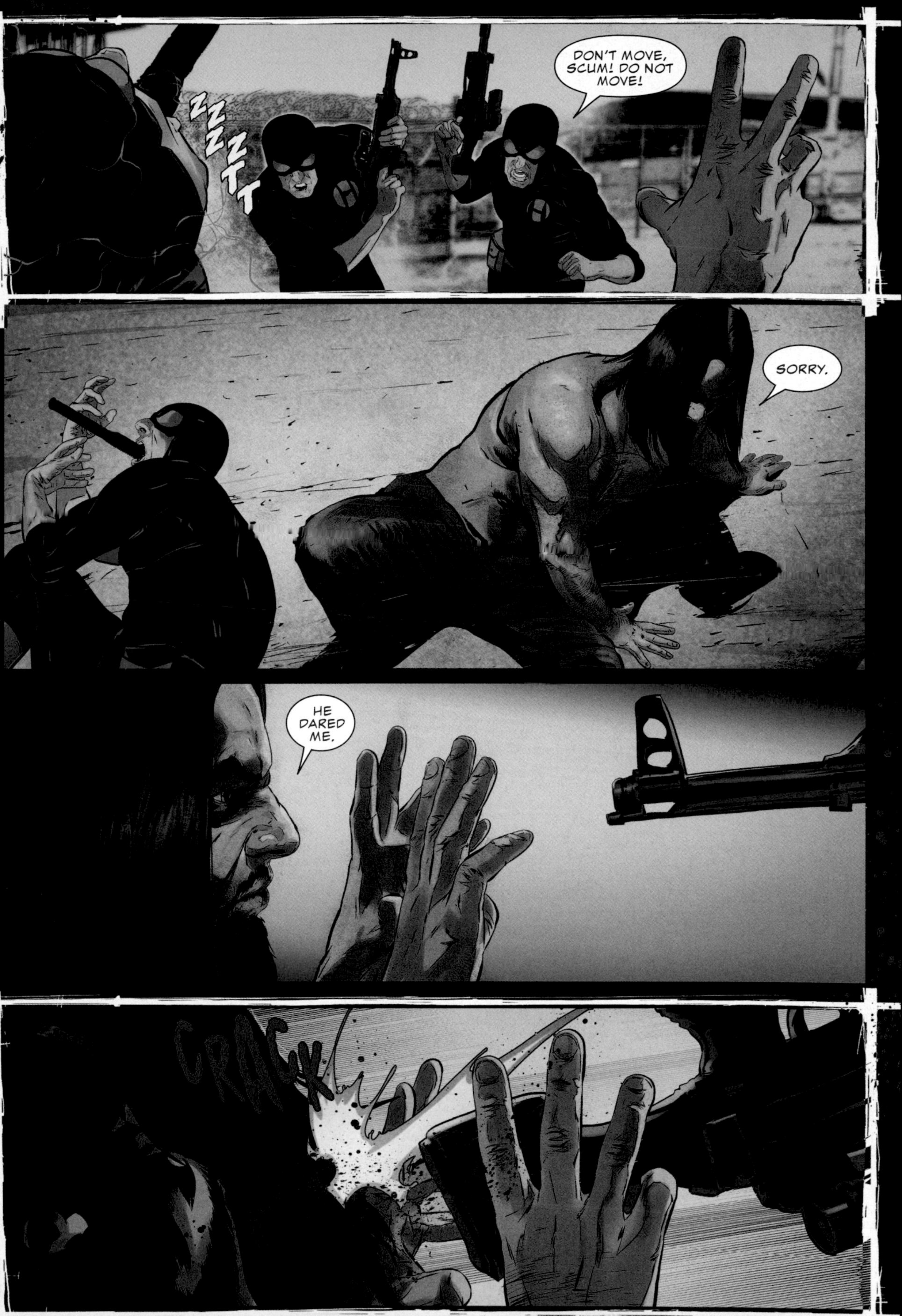
ZZZZTT
DON'T MOVE, SCUM! DO NOT MOVE!
SORRY.
HE DARED ME.
CRACK

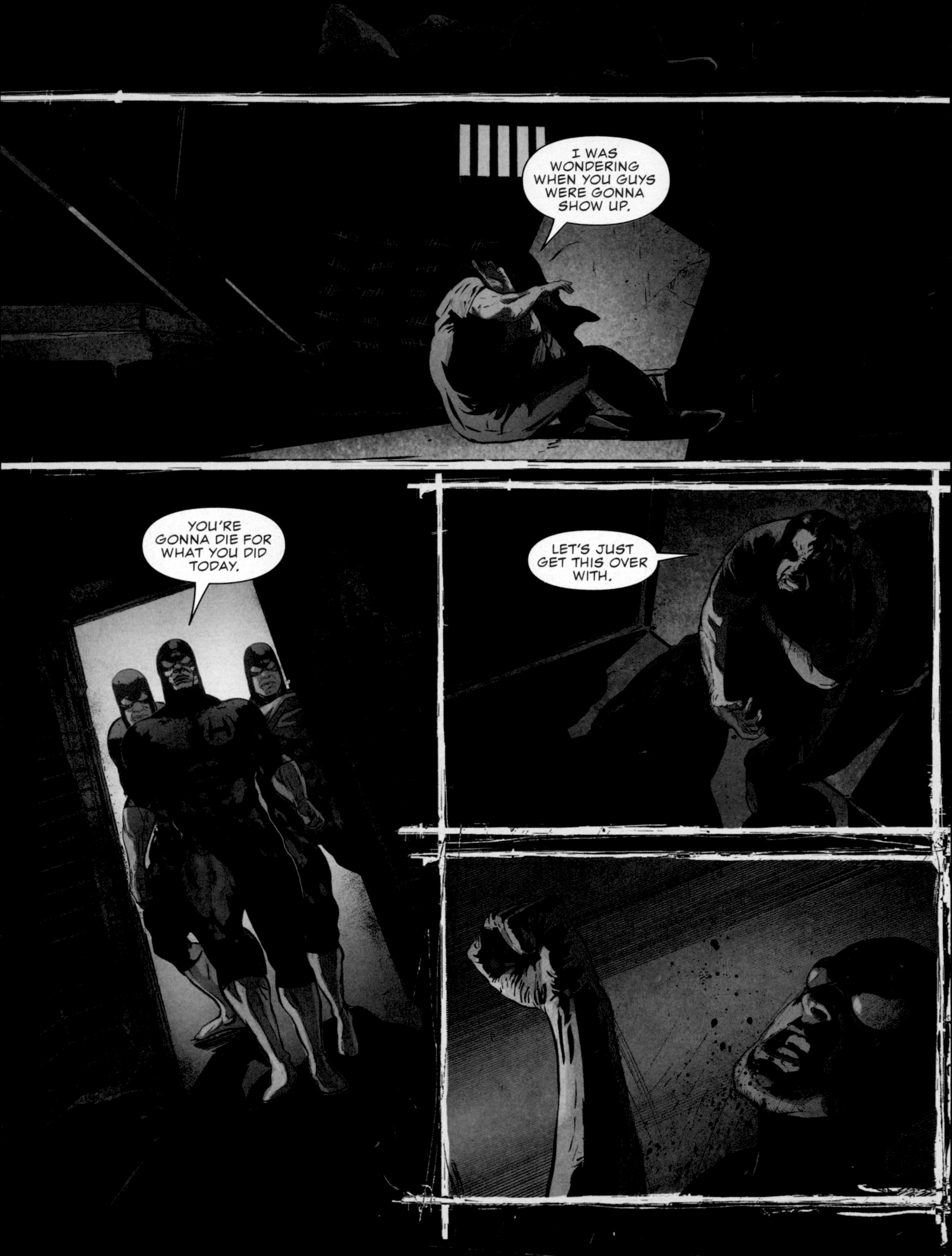
I WAS WONDERING WHEN YOU GUYS WERE GONNA SHOW UP.
YOU'RE GONNA DIE FOR WHAT YOU DID TODAY.
LET'S JUST GET THIS OVER WITH.

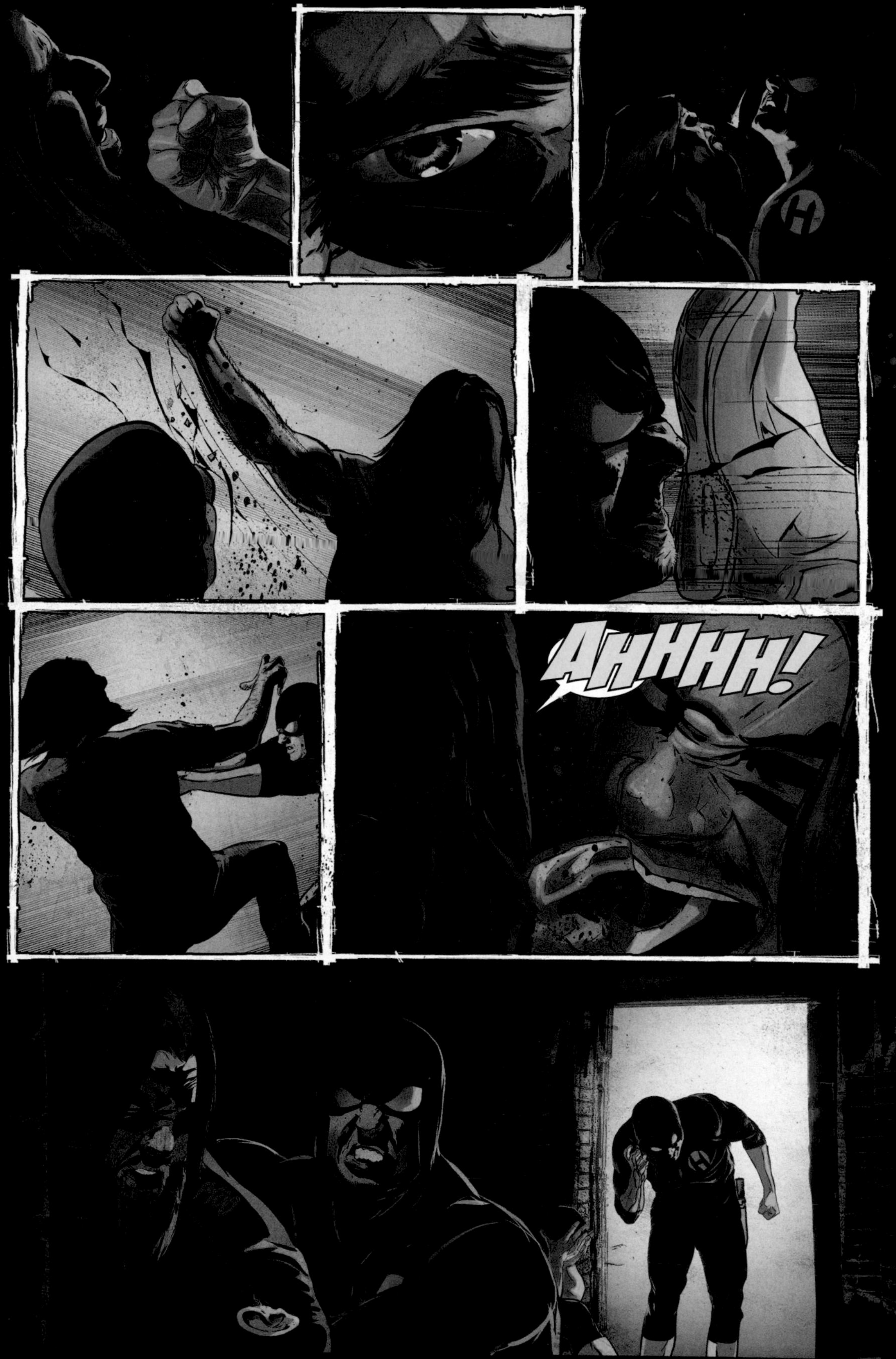
AHHHH!

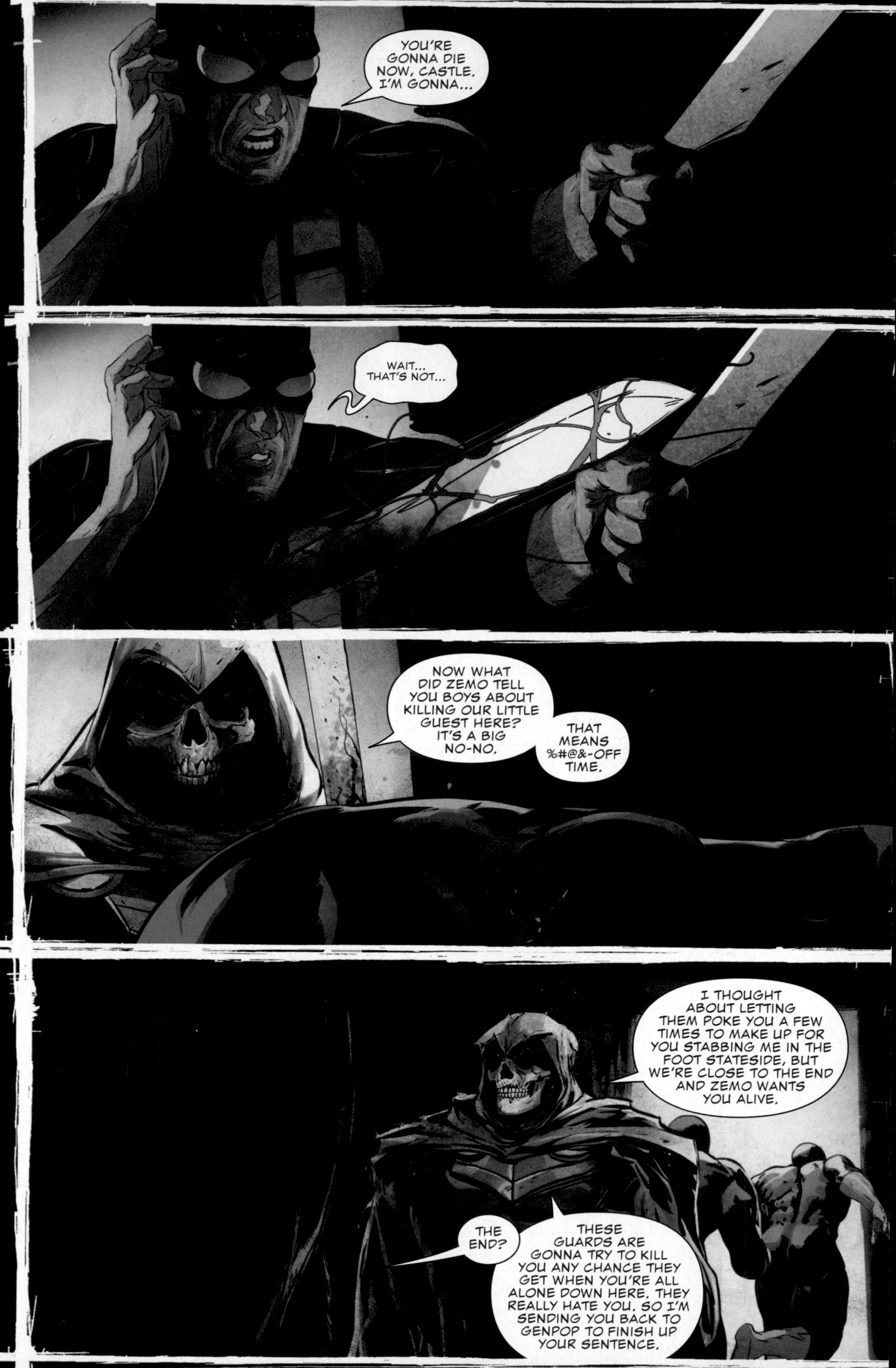
YOU'RE GONNA DIE NOW, CASTLE. I'M GONNA...
WAIT... THAT'S NOT...
NOW WHAT DID ZEMO TELL YOU BOYS ABOUT KILLING OUR LITTLE GUEST HERE? IT'S A BIG NO-NO.
THAT MEANS %#@&-OFF TIME.
I THOUGHT ABOUT LETTING THEM POKE YOU A FEW TIMES TO MAKE UP FOR YOU STABBING ME IN THE FOOT STATESIDE, BUT WE'RE CLOSE TO THE END AND ZEMO WANTS YOU ALIVE.
THE END?
THESE GUARDS ARE GONNA TRY TO KILL YOU ANY CHANCE THEY GET WHEN YOU'RE ALL ALONE DOWN HERE. THEY REALLY HATE YOU. SO I'M SENDING YOU BACK TO GENPOP TO FINISH UP YOUR SENTENCE.

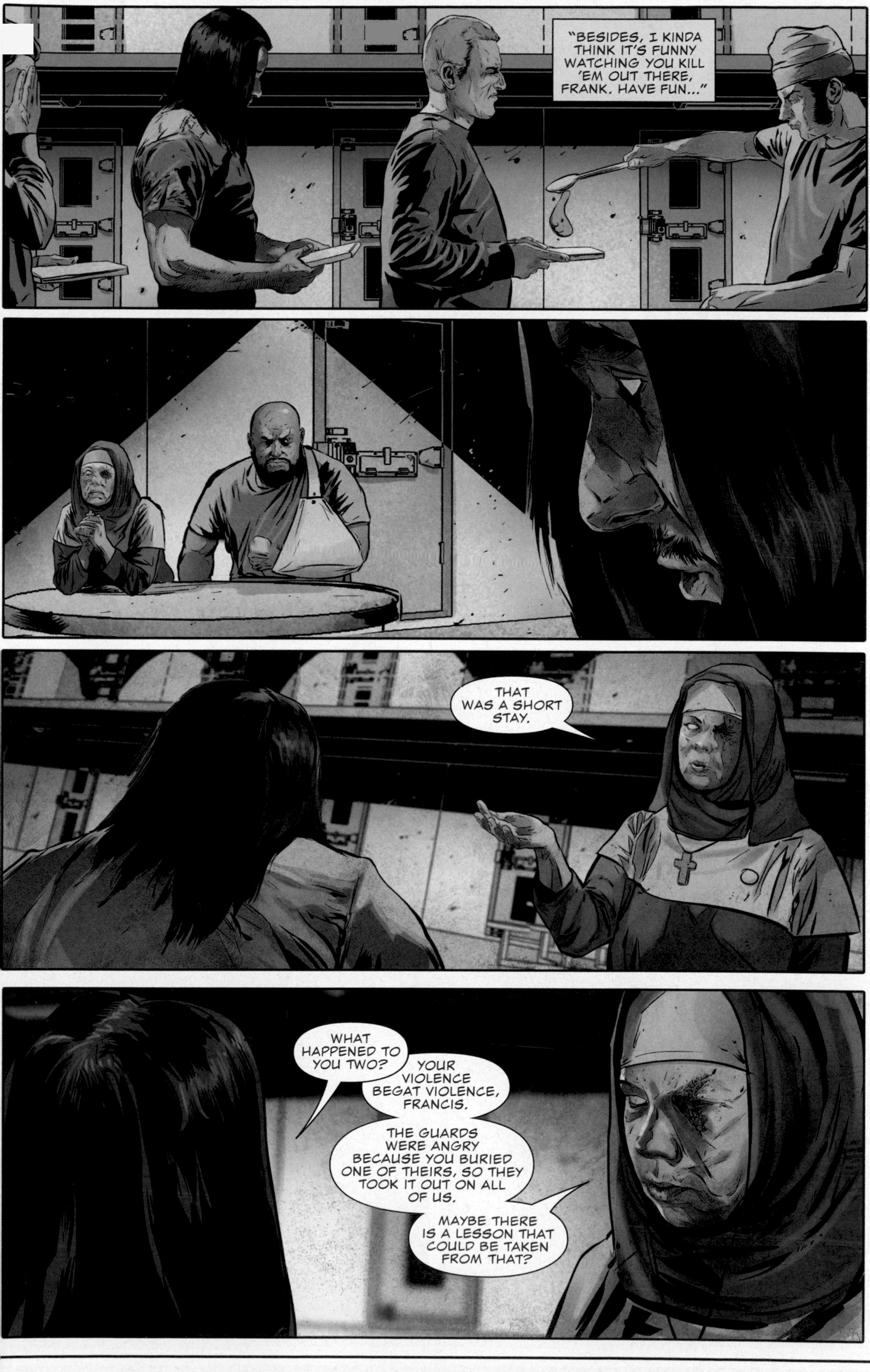
"BESIDES, I KINDA THINK IT'S FUNNY WATCHING YOU KILL 'EM OUT THERE, FRANK. HAVE FUN..."
THAT WAS A SHORT STAY.
WHAT HAPPENED TO YOU TWO?
YOUR VIOLENCE BEGAT VIOLENCE, FRANCIS.
THE GUARDS WERE ANGRY BECAUSE YOU BURIED ONE OF THEIRS, SO THEY TOOK IT OUT ON ALL OF US.
MAYBE THERE IS A LESSON THAT COULD BE TAKEN FROM THAT?

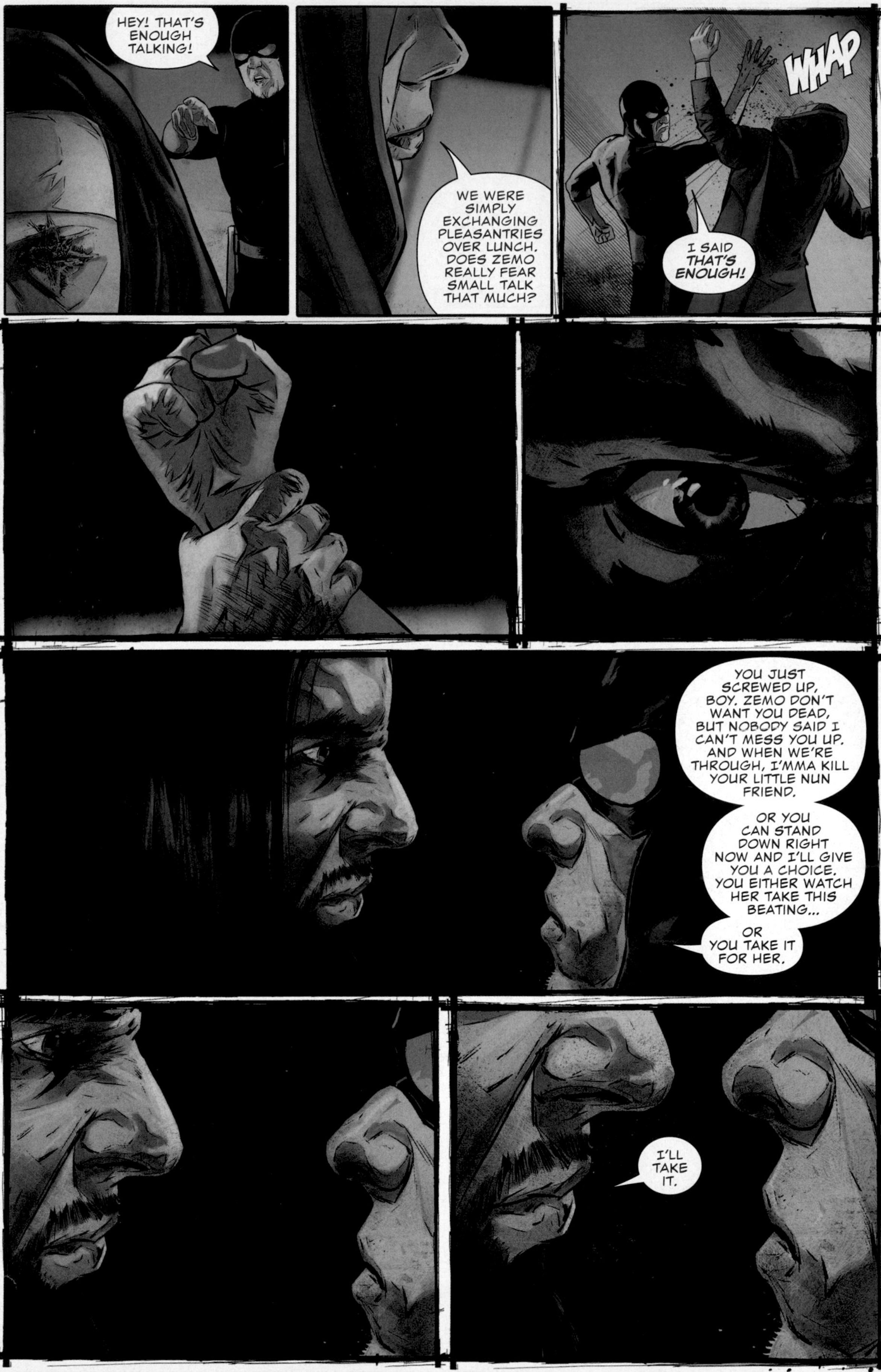
HEY! THAT'S ENOUGH TALKING!
WE WERE SIMPLY EXCHANGING PLEASANTRIES OVER LUNCH. DOES ZEMO REALLY FEAR SMALL TALK THAT MUCH?
WHAP
I SAID *THAT'S ENOUGH!*
YOU JUST SCREWED UP, BOY. ZEMO DON'T WANT YOU DEAD, BUT NOBODY SAID I CAN'T MESS YOU UP. AND WHEN WE'RE THROUGH, I'MMA KILL YOUR LITTLE NUN FRIEND.
OR YOU CAN STAND DOWN RIGHT NOW AND I'LL GIVE YOU A CHOICE. YOU EITHER WATCH HER TAKE THIS BEATING...
OR YOU TAKE IT FOR HER.
I'LL TAKE IT.

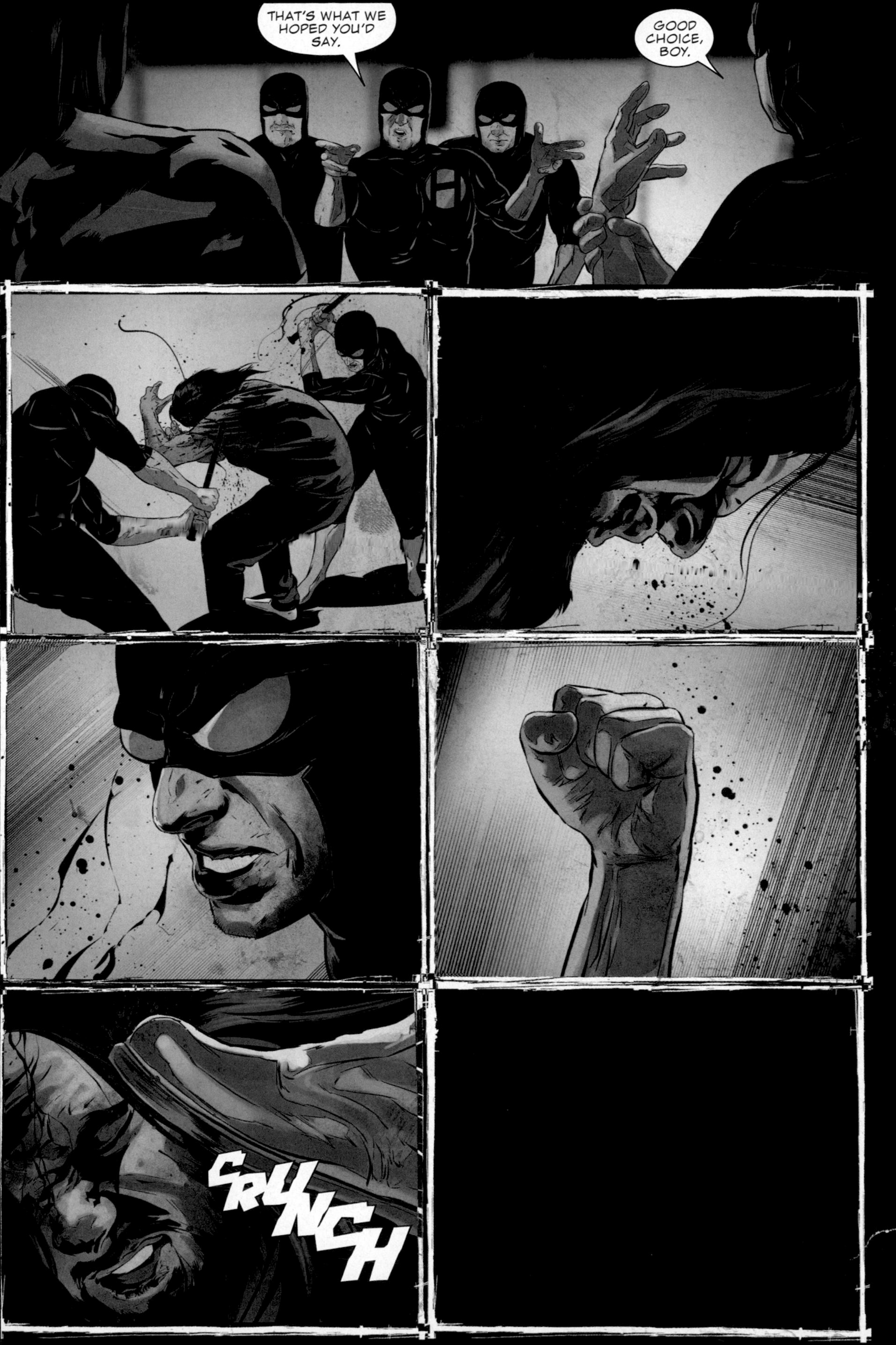
THAT'S WHAT WE HOPED YOU'D SAY.
GOOD CHOICE, BOY.
CRUNCH

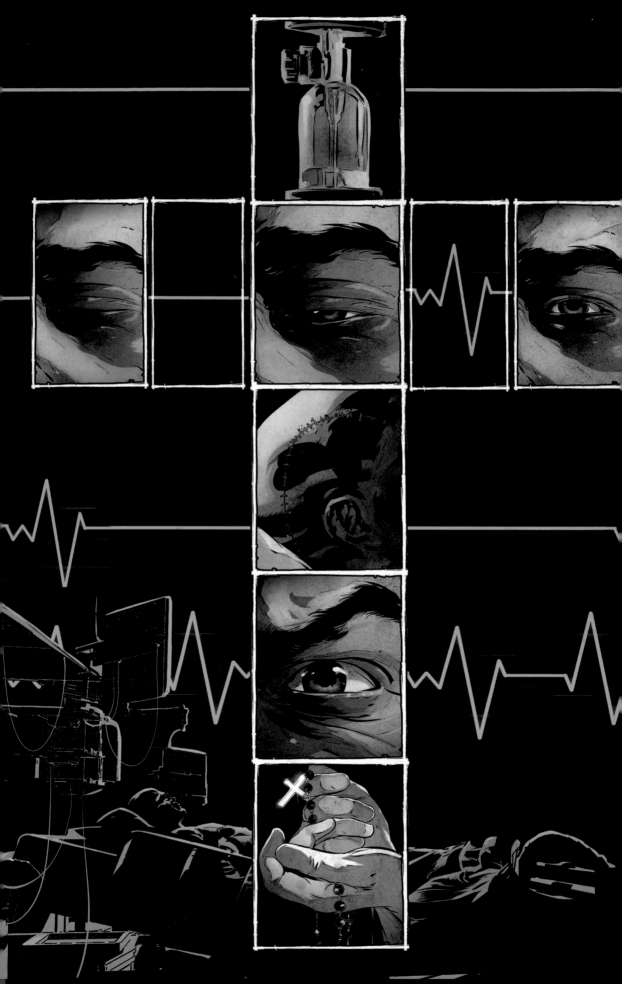

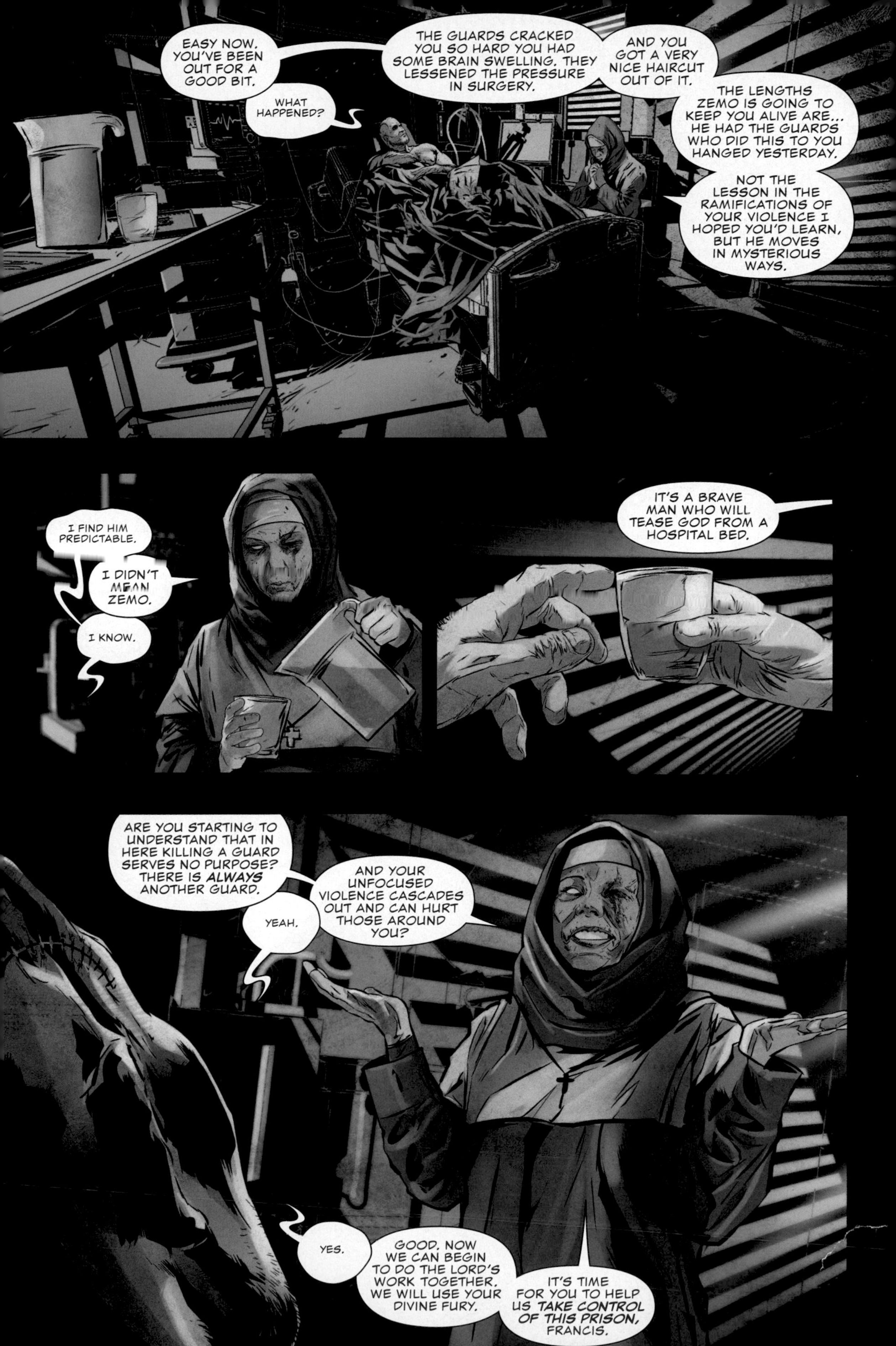
EASY NOW. YOU'VE BEEN OUT FOR A GOOD BIT.
WHAT HAPPENED?
THE GUARDS CRACKED YOU SO HARD YOU HAD SOME BRAIN SWELLING. THEY LESSENED THE PRESSURE IN SURGERY.
AND YOU GOT A VERY NICE HAIRCUT OUT OF IT.
THE LENGTHS ZEMO IS GOING TO KEEP YOU ALIVE ARE... HE HAD THE GUARDS WHO DID THIS TO YOU HANGED YESTERDAY.
NOT THE LESSON IN THE RAMIFICATIONS OF YOUR VIOLENCE I HOPED YOU'D LEARN, BUT HE MOVES IN MYSTERIOUS WAYS.
I FIND HIM PREDICTABLE.
I DIDN'T MEAN ZEMO.
I KNOW.
IT'S A BRAVE MAN WHO WILL TEASE GOD FROM A HOSPITAL BED.
ARE YOU STARTING TO UNDERSTAND THAT IN HERE KILLING A GUARD SERVES NO PURPOSE? THERE IS *ALWAYS* ANOTHER GUARD.
YEAH.
AND YOUR UNFOCUSED VIOLENCE CASCADES OUT AND CAN HURT THOSE AROUND YOU?
YES.
GOOD. NOW WE CAN BEGIN TO DO THE LORD'S WORK TOGETHER. WE WILL USE YOUR DIVINE FURY.
IT'S TIME FOR YOU TO HELP US *TAKE CONTROL OF THIS PRISON,* FRANCIS.

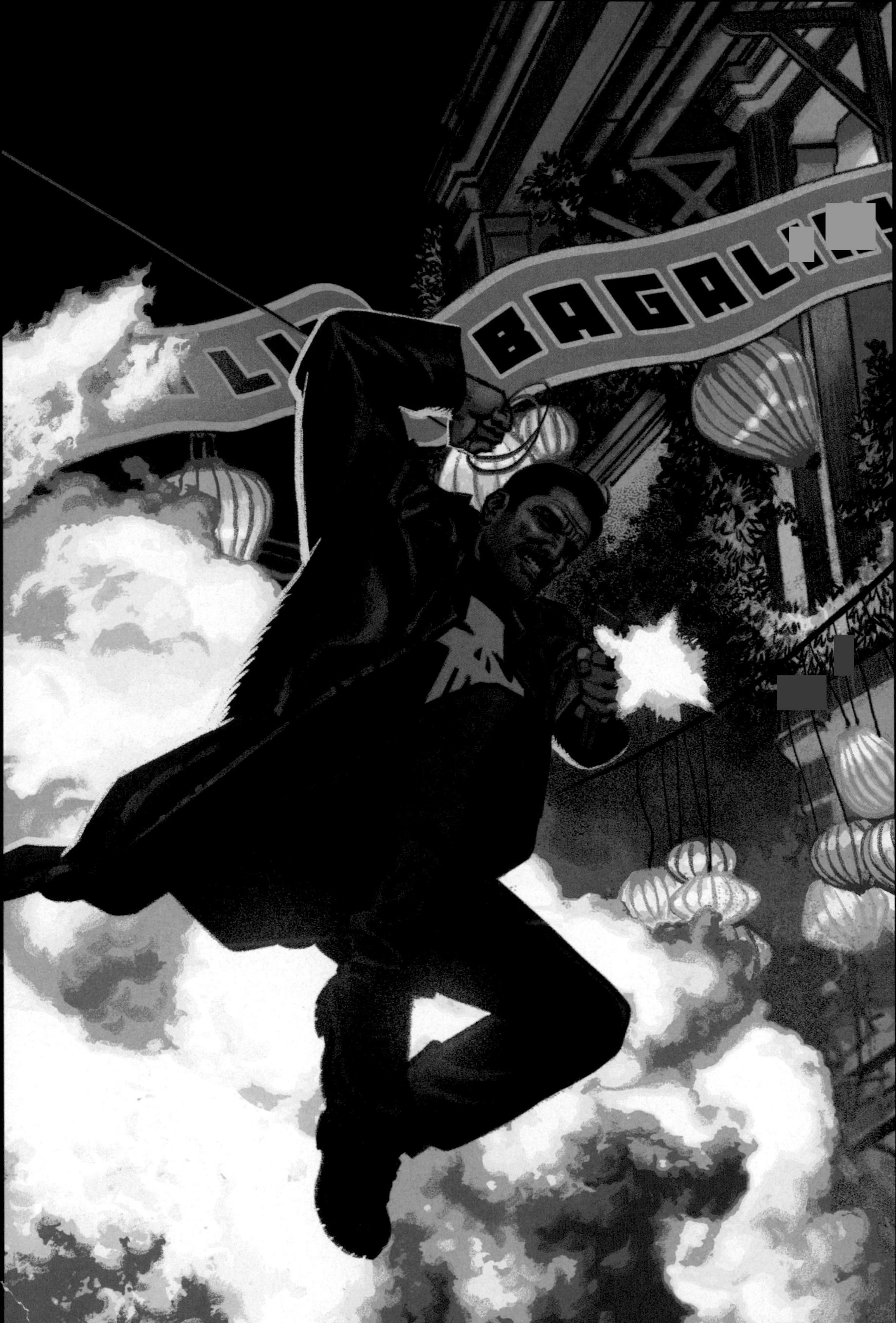

#8

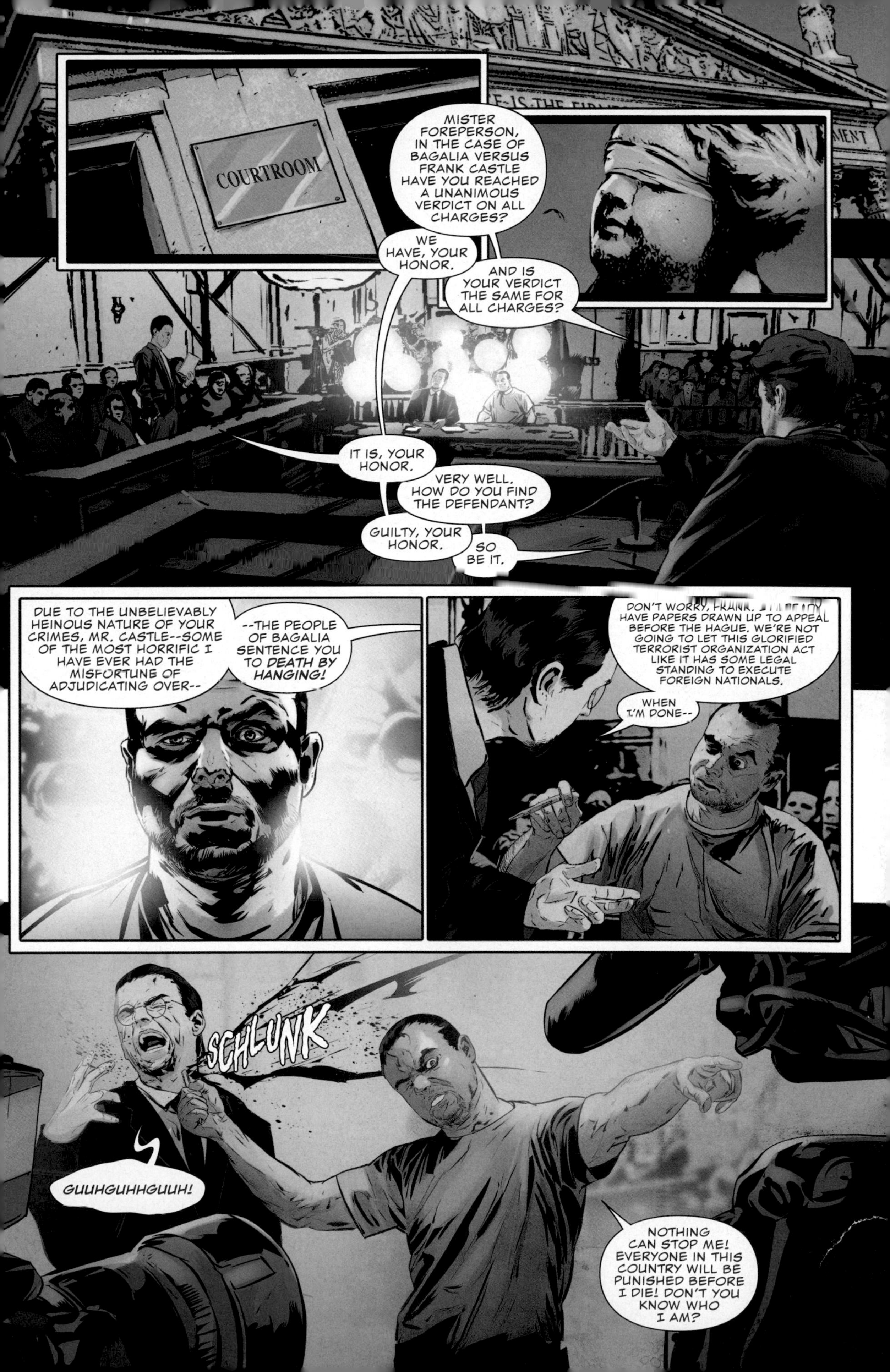

COURTROOM
MISTER FOREPERSON, IN THE CASE OF BAGALIA VERSUS FRANK CASTLE HAVE YOU REACHED A UNANIMOUS VERDICT ON ALL CHARGES?
WE HAVE, YOUR HONOR.
AND IS YOUR VERDICT THE SAME FOR ALL CHARGES?
IT IS, YOUR HONOR.
VERY WELL. HOW DO YOU FIND THE DEFENDANT?
GUILTY, YOUR HONOR.
SO BE IT.
DUE TO THE UNBELIEVABLY HEINOUS NATURE OF YOUR CRIMES, MR. CASTLE--SOME OF THE MOST HORRIFIC I HAVE EVER HAD THE MISFORTUNE OF ADJUDICATING OVER--
--THE PEOPLE OF BAGALIA SENTENCE YOU TO *DEATH BY HANGING!*
DON'T WORRY, FRANK.
HAVE PAPERS DRAWN UP TO APPEAL BEFORE THE HAGUE. WE'RE NOT GOING TO LET THIS GLORIFIED TERRORIST ORGANIZATION ACT LIKE IT HAS SOME LEGAL STANDING TO EXECUTE FOREIGN NATIONALS.
WHEN I'M DONE--
SCHLUNK
GUUHGUHHGUUH!
NOTHING CAN STOP ME! EVERYONE IN THIS COUNTRY WILL BE PUNISHED BEFORE I DIE! DON'T YOU KNOW WHO I AM?

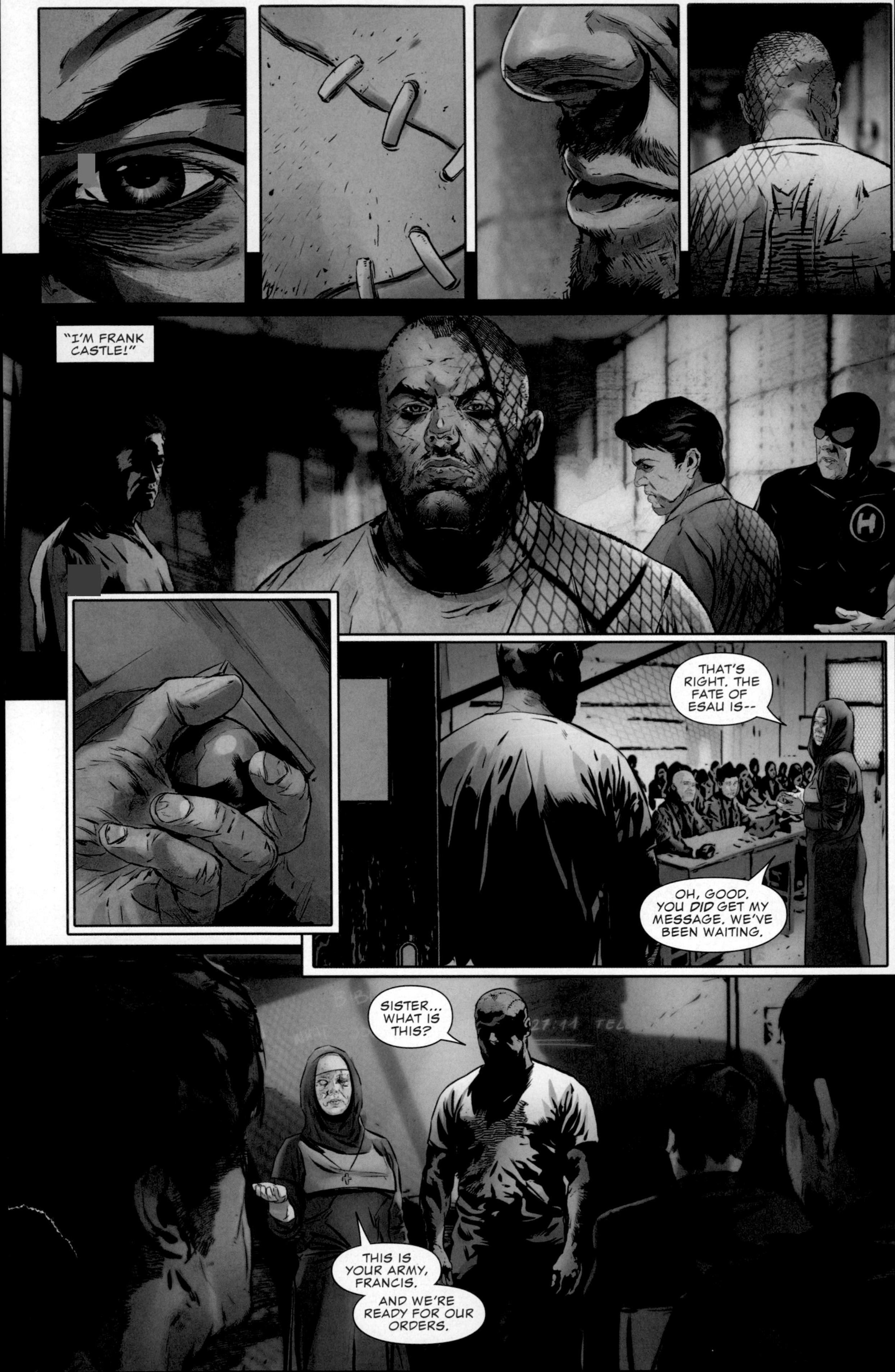
"I'M FRANK CASTLE!"
THAT'S RIGHT. THE FATE OF ESAU IS--
OH, GOOD. YOU *DID* GET MY MESSAGE. WE'VE BEEN WAITING.
SISTER... WHAT IS THIS?
THIS IS YOUR ARMY, FRANCIS.
AND WE'RE READY FOR OUR ORDERS.

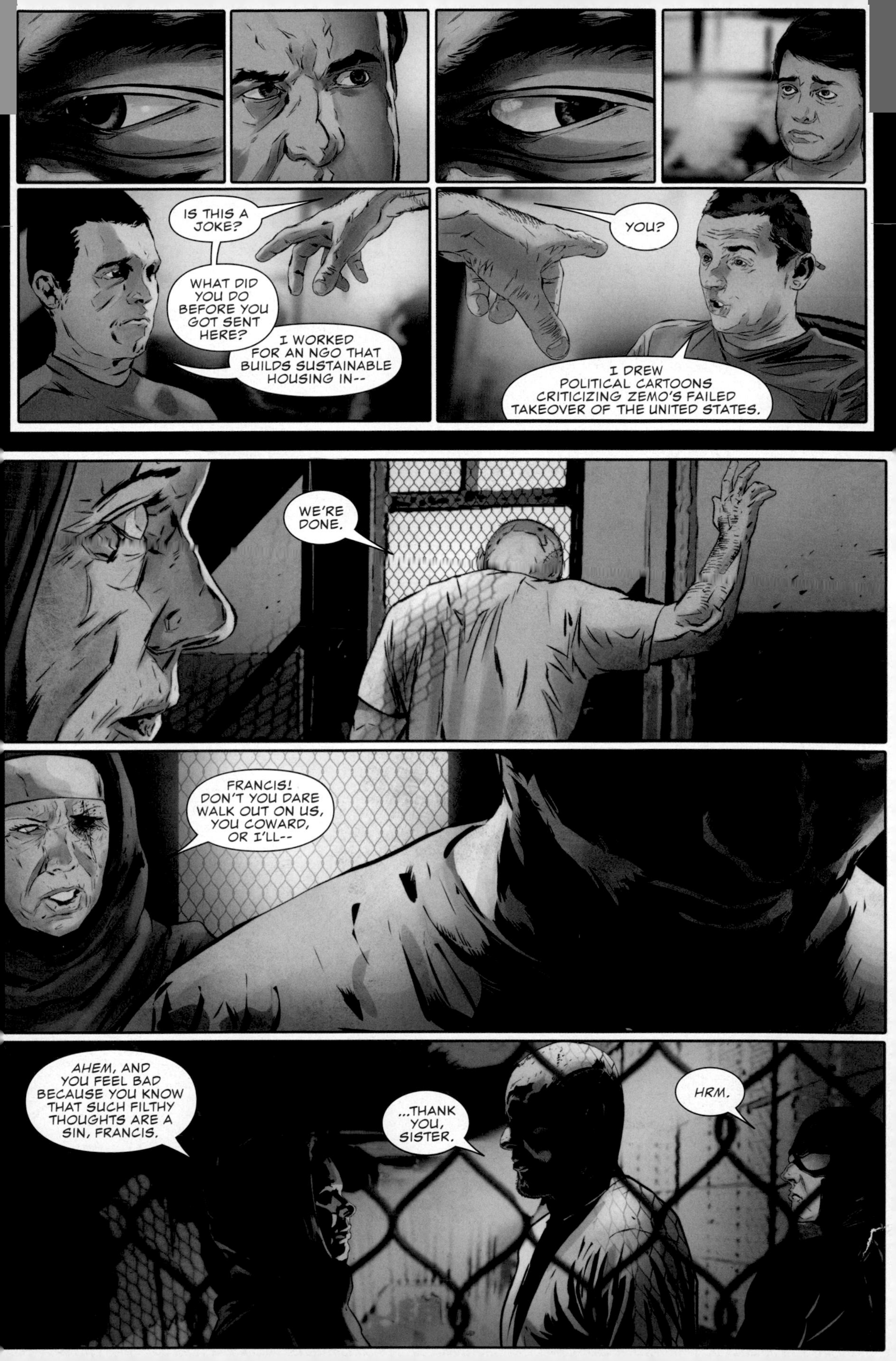
IS THIS A JOKE?
WHAT DID YOU DO BEFORE YOU GOT SENT HERE?
I WORKED FOR AN NGO THAT BUILDS SUSTAINABLE HOUSING IN--
YOU?
I DREW POLITICAL CARTOONS CRITICIZING ZEMO'S FAILED TAKEOVER OF THE UNITED STATES.
WE'RE DONE.
FRANCIS! DON'T YOU DARE WALK OUT ON US, YOU COWARD, OR I'LL--
AHEM, AND YOU FEEL BAD BECAUSE YOU KNOW THAT SUCH FILTHY THOUGHTS ARE A SIN, FRANCIS.
...THANK YOU, SISTER.
HRM.

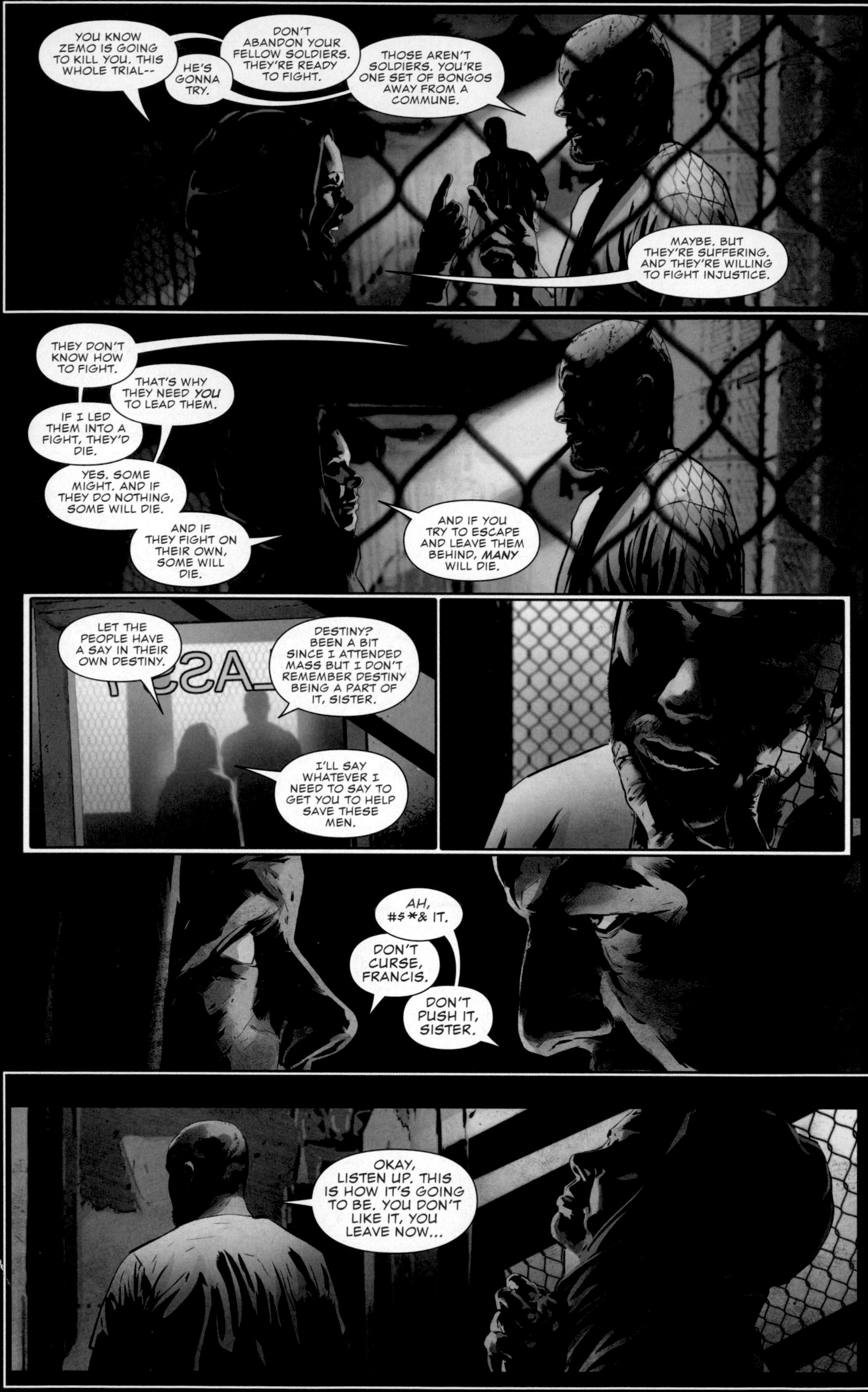

YOU KNOW ZEMO IS GOING TO KILL YOU. THIS WHOLE TRIAL--
HE'S GONNA TRY.
DON'T ABANDON YOUR FELLOW SOLDIERS. THEY'RE READY TO FIGHT.
THOSE AREN'T SOLDIERS. YOU'RE ONE SET OF BONGOS AWAY FROM A COMMUNE.
MAYBE. BUT THEY'RE SUFFERING. AND THEY'RE WILLING TO FIGHT INJUSTICE.
THEY DON'T KNOW HOW TO FIGHT.
THAT'S WHY THEY NEED *YOU* TO LEAD THEM.
IF I LED THEM INTO A FIGHT, THEY'D DIE.
YES. SOME MIGHT. AND IF THEY DO NOTHING, SOME WILL DIE.
AND IF THEY FIGHT ON THEIR OWN, SOME WILL DIE.
AND IF YOU TRY TO ESCAPE AND LEAVE THEM BEHIND, *MANY* WILL DIE.
LET THE PEOPLE HAVE A SAY IN THEIR OWN DESTINY.
DESTINY? BEEN A BIT SINCE I ATTENDED MASS BUT I DON'T REMEMBER DESTINY BEING A PART OF IT, SISTER.
I'LL SAY WHATEVER I NEED TO SAY TO GET YOU TO HELP SAVE THESE MEN.
AH, #$*& IT.
DON'T CURSE, FRANCIS.
DON'T PUSH IT, SISTER.
OKAY, LISTEN UP. THIS IS HOW IT'S GOING TO BE. YOU DON'T LIKE IT, YOU LEAVE NOW...

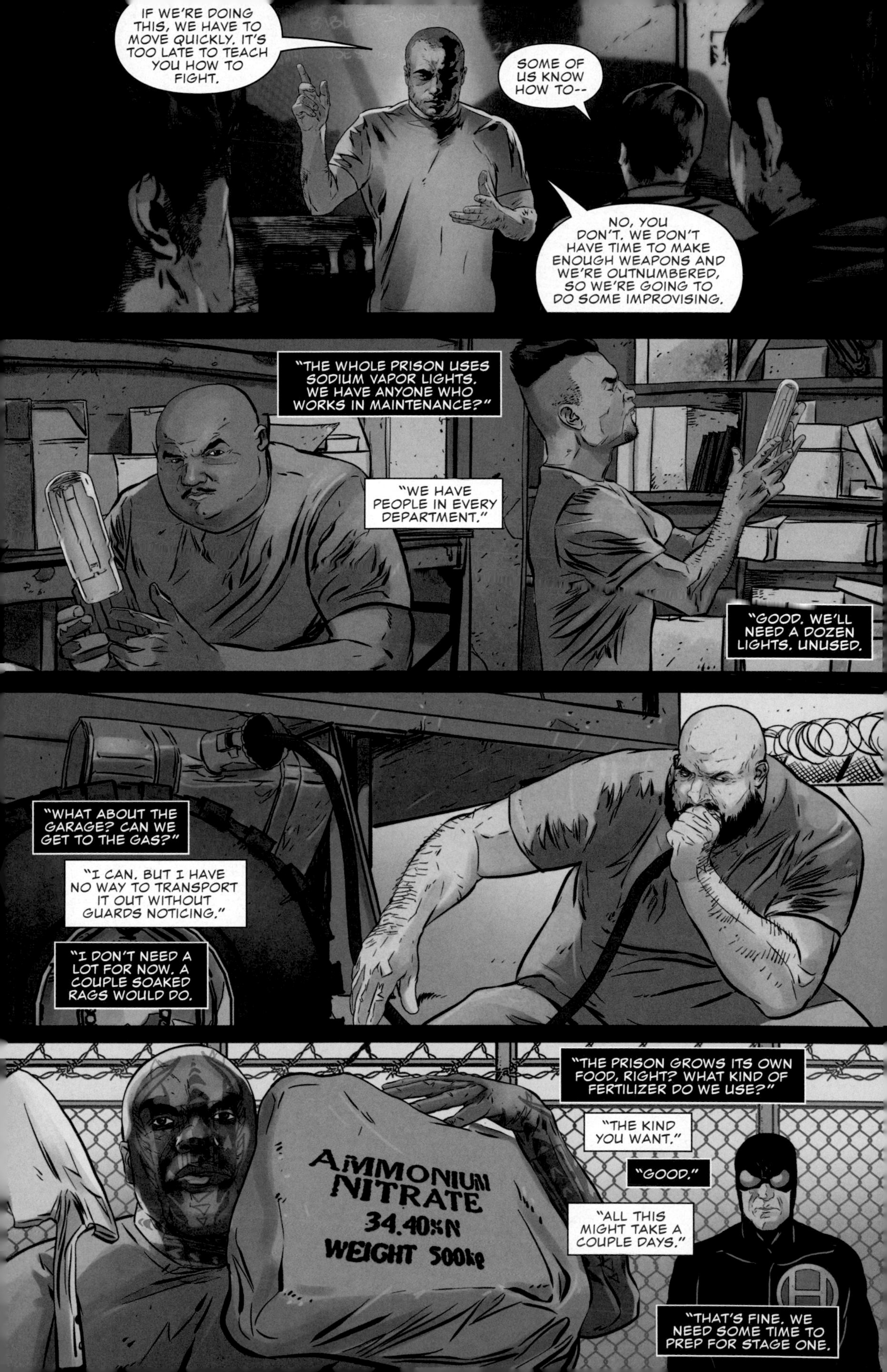
IF WE'RE DOING THIS, WE HAVE TO MOVE QUICKLY. IT'S TOO LATE TO TEACH YOU HOW TO FIGHT.
SOME OF US KNOW HOW TO--
NO, YOU DON'T. WE DON'T HAVE TIME TO MAKE ENOUGH WEAPONS AND WE'RE OUTNUMBERED, SO WE'RE GOING TO DO SOME IMPROVISING.
"THE WHOLE PRISON USES SODIUM VAPOR LIGHTS. WE HAVE ANYONE WHO WORKS IN MAINTENANCE?"
"WE HAVE PEOPLE IN EVERY DEPARTMENT."
"GOOD. WE'LL NEED A DOZEN LIGHTS. UNUSED.
"WHAT ABOUT THE GARAGE? CAN WE GET TO THE GAS?"
"I CAN. BUT I HAVE NO WAY TO TRANSPORT IT OUT WITHOUT GUARDS NOTICING."
"I DON'T NEED A LOT FOR NOW. A COUPLE SOAKED RAGS WOULD DO.
AMMONIUM NITRATE
34.40%N
WEIGHT 500kg
"THE PRISON GROWS ITS OWN FOOD, RIGHT? WHAT KIND OF FERTILIZER DO WE USE?"
"THE KIND YOU WANT."
"GOOD."
"ALL THIS MIGHT TAKE A COUPLE DAYS."
"THAT'S FINE. WE NEED SOME TIME TO PREP FOR STAGE ONE.

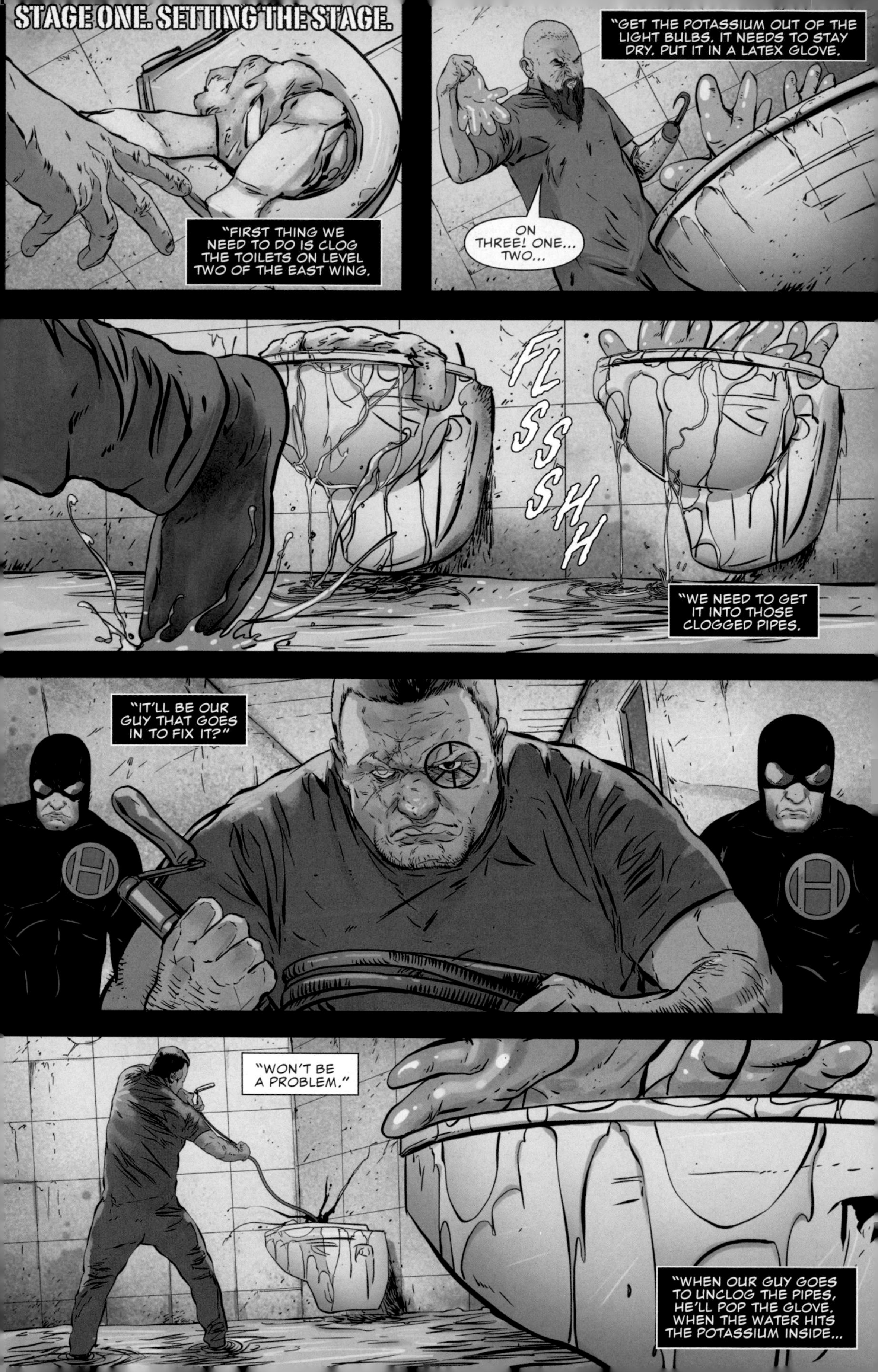
STAGE ONE. SETTING THE STAGE.
"FIRST THING WE NEED TO DO IS CLOG THE TOILETS ON LEVEL TWO OF THE EAST WING.
"GET THE POTASSIUM OUT OF THE LIGHT BULBS. IT NEEDS TO STAY DRY. PUT IT IN A LATEX GLOVE.
ON THREE! ONE... TWO...
FLSSSHH
"WE NEED TO GET IT INTO THOSE CLOGGED PIPES.
"IT'LL BE OUR GUY THAT GOES IN TO FIX IT?"
"WON'T BE A PROBLEM."
"WHEN OUR GUY GOES TO UNCLOG THE PIPES, HE'LL POP THE GLOVE. WHEN THE WATER HITS THE POTASSIUM INSIDE...

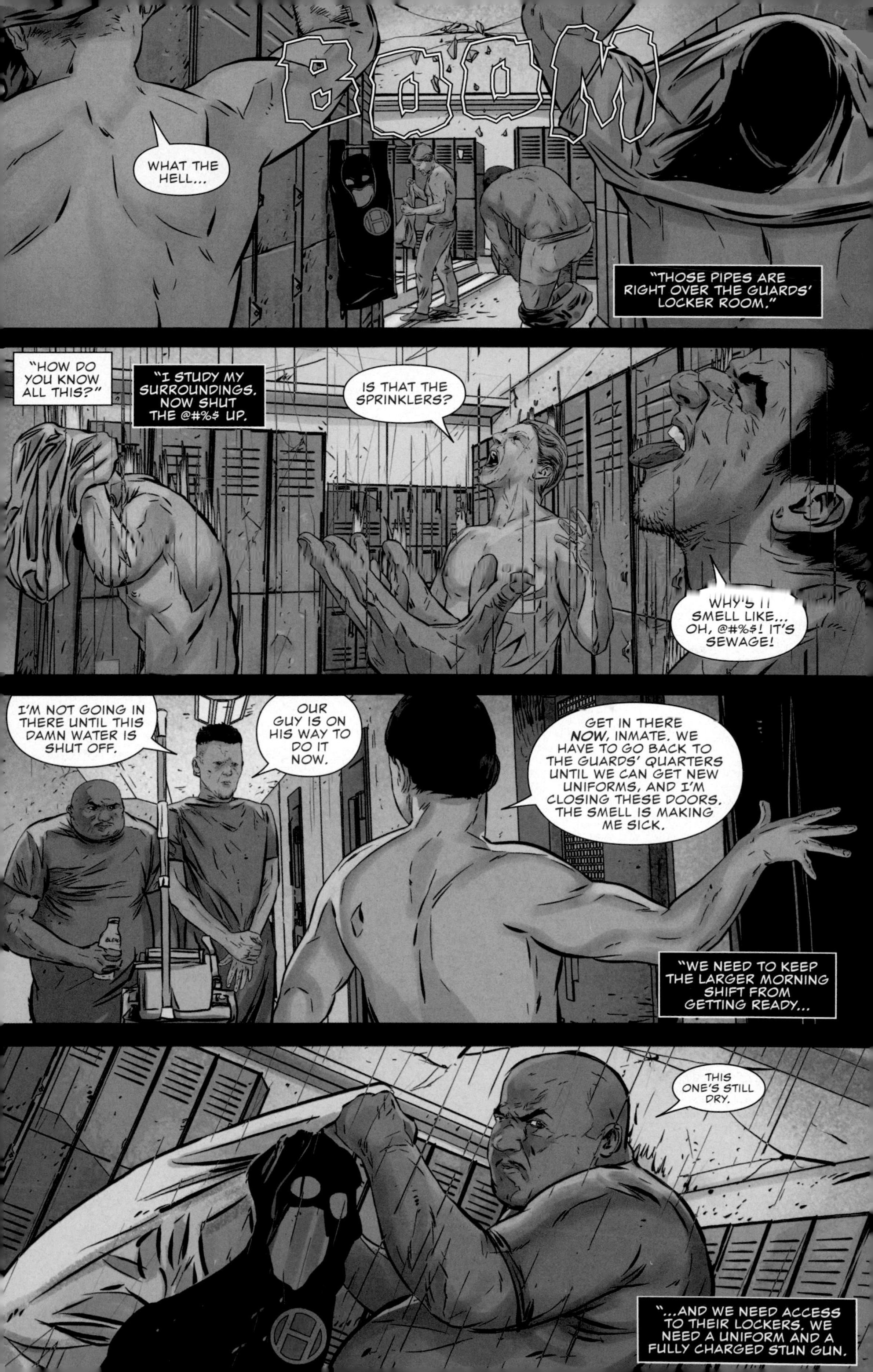
BOOM
WHAT THE HELL...
"THOSE PIPES ARE RIGHT OVER THE GUARDS' LOCKER ROOM."
"HOW DO YOU KNOW ALL THIS?"
"I STUDY MY SURROUNDINGS. NOW SHUT THE @#%$ UP.
IS THAT THE SPRINKLERS?
WHY'S IT SMELL LIKE... OH, @#%$! IT'S SEWAGE!
I'M NOT GOING IN THERE UNTIL THIS DAMN WATER IS SHUT OFF.
OUR GUY IS ON HIS WAY TO DO IT NOW.
GET IN THERE NOW, INMATE. WE HAVE TO GO BACK TO THE GUARDS' QUARTERS UNTIL WE CAN GET NEW UNIFORMS, AND I'M CLOSING THESE DOORS. THE SMELL IS MAKING ME SICK.
"WE NEED TO KEEP THE LARGER MORNING SHIFT FROM GETTING READY...
THIS ONE'S STILL DRY.
"...AND WE NEED ACCESS TO THEIR LOCKERS. WE NEED A UNIFORM AND A FULLY CHARGED STUN GUN.

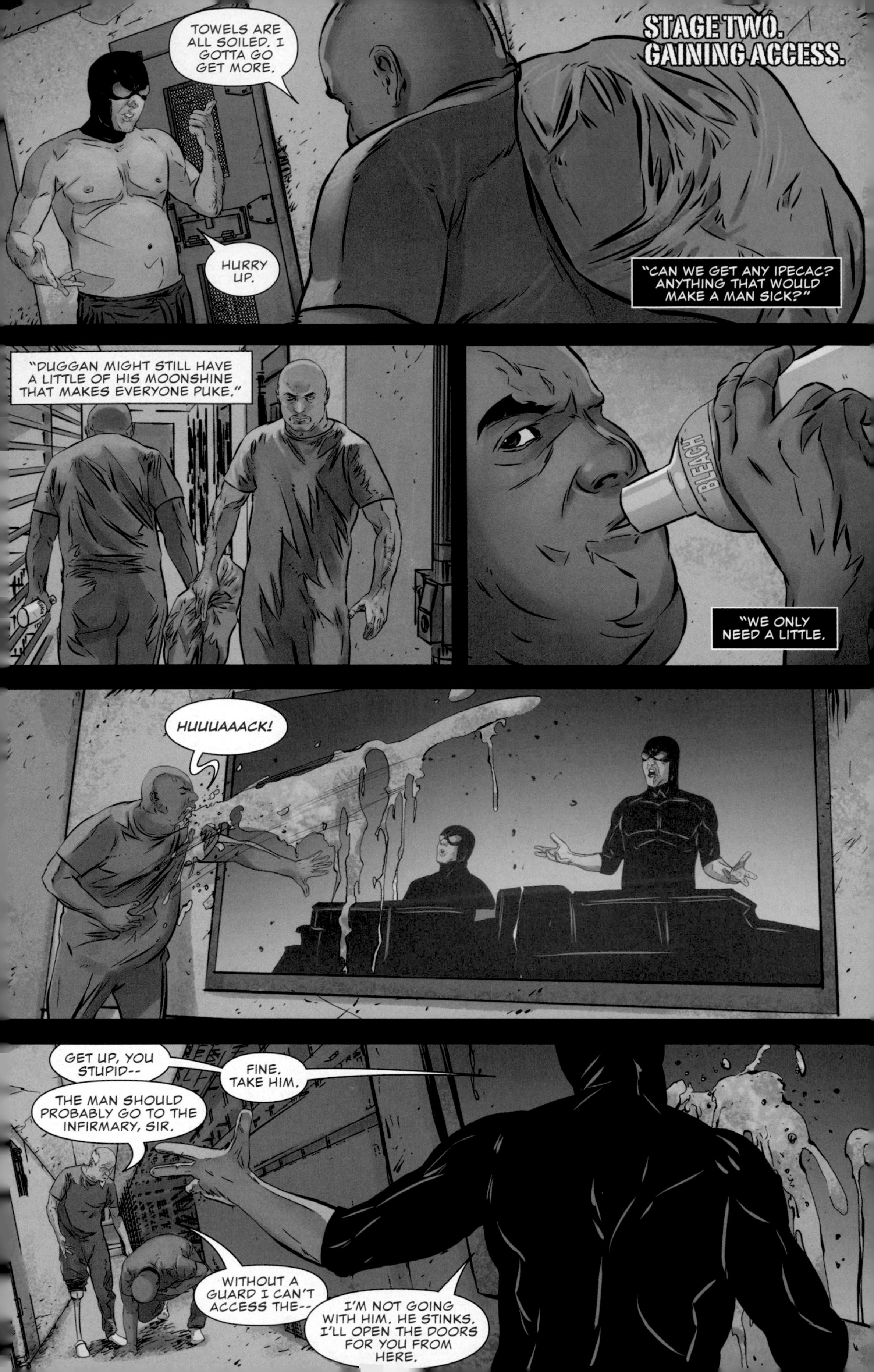
STAGE TWO. GAINING ACCESS.
TOWELS ARE ALL SOILED. I GOTTA GO GET MORE.
HURRY UP.
"CAN WE GET ANY IPECAC? ANYTHING THAT WOULD MAKE A MAN SICK?"
"DUGGAN MIGHT STILL HAVE A LITTLE OF HIS MOONSHINE THAT MAKES EVERYONE PUKE."
BLEACH
"WE ONLY NEED A LITTLE.
HUUUAAACK!
GET UP, YOU STUPID--
THE MAN SHOULD PROBABLY GO TO THE INFIRMARY, SIR.
FINE. TAKE HIM.
WITHOUT A GUARD I CAN'T ACCESS THE--
I'M NOT GOING WITH HIM. HE STINKS. I'LL OPEN THE DOORS FOR YOU FROM HERE.

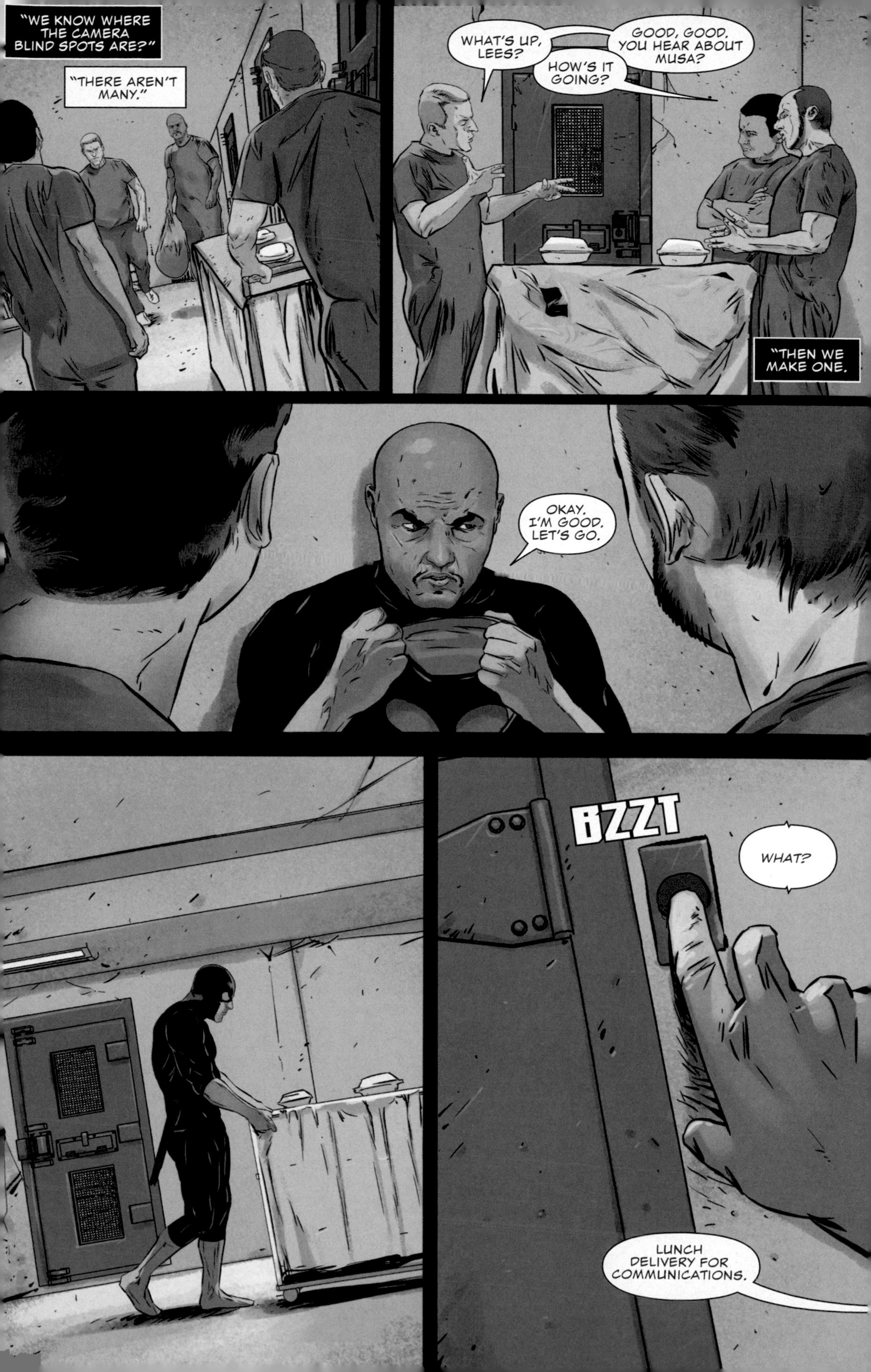
"WE KNOW WHERE THE CAMERA BLIND SPOTS ARE?"
"THERE AREN'T MANY."
WHAT'S UP, LEES?
GOOD, GOOD. YOU HEAR ABOUT MUSA?
HOW'S IT GOING?
"THEN WE MAKE ONE.
OKAY. I'M GOOD. LET'S GO.
BZZT
WHAT?
LUNCH DELIVERY FOR COMMUNICATIONS.

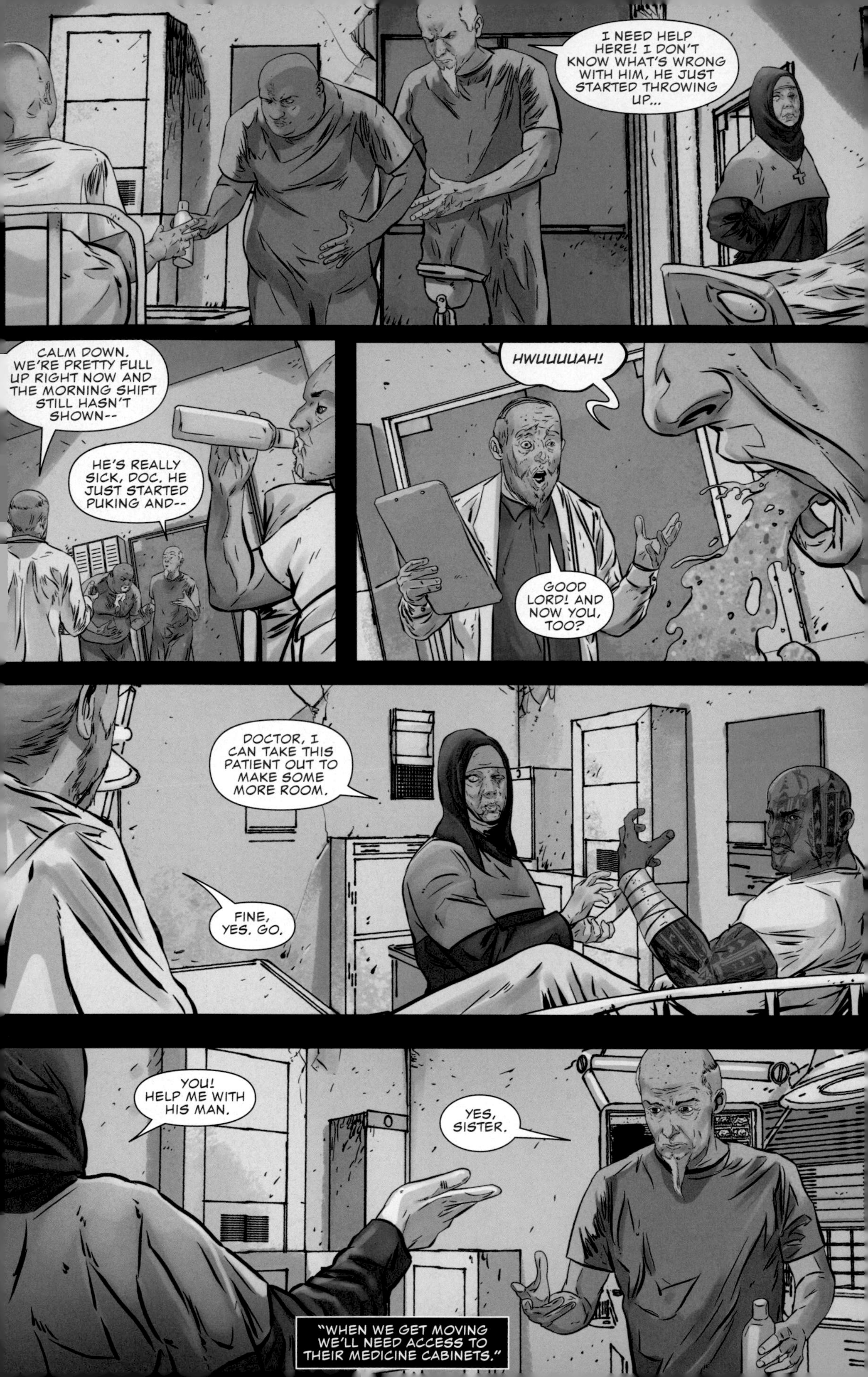
I NEED HELP HERE! I DON'T KNOW WHAT'S WRONG WITH HIM, HE JUST STARTED THROWING UP...
CALM DOWN. WE'RE PRETTY FULL UP RIGHT NOW AND THE MORNING SHIFT STILL HASN'T SHOWN--
HE'S REALLY SICK, DOC. HE JUST STARTED PUKING AND--
HWUUUUAH!
GOOD LORD! AND NOW YOU, TOO?
DOCTOR, I CAN TAKE THIS PATIENT OUT TO MAKE SOME MORE ROOM.
FINE, YES. GO.
YOU! HELP ME WITH HIS MAN.
YES, SISTER.
"WHEN WE GET MOVING WE'LL NEED ACCESS TO THEIR MEDICINE CABINETS."

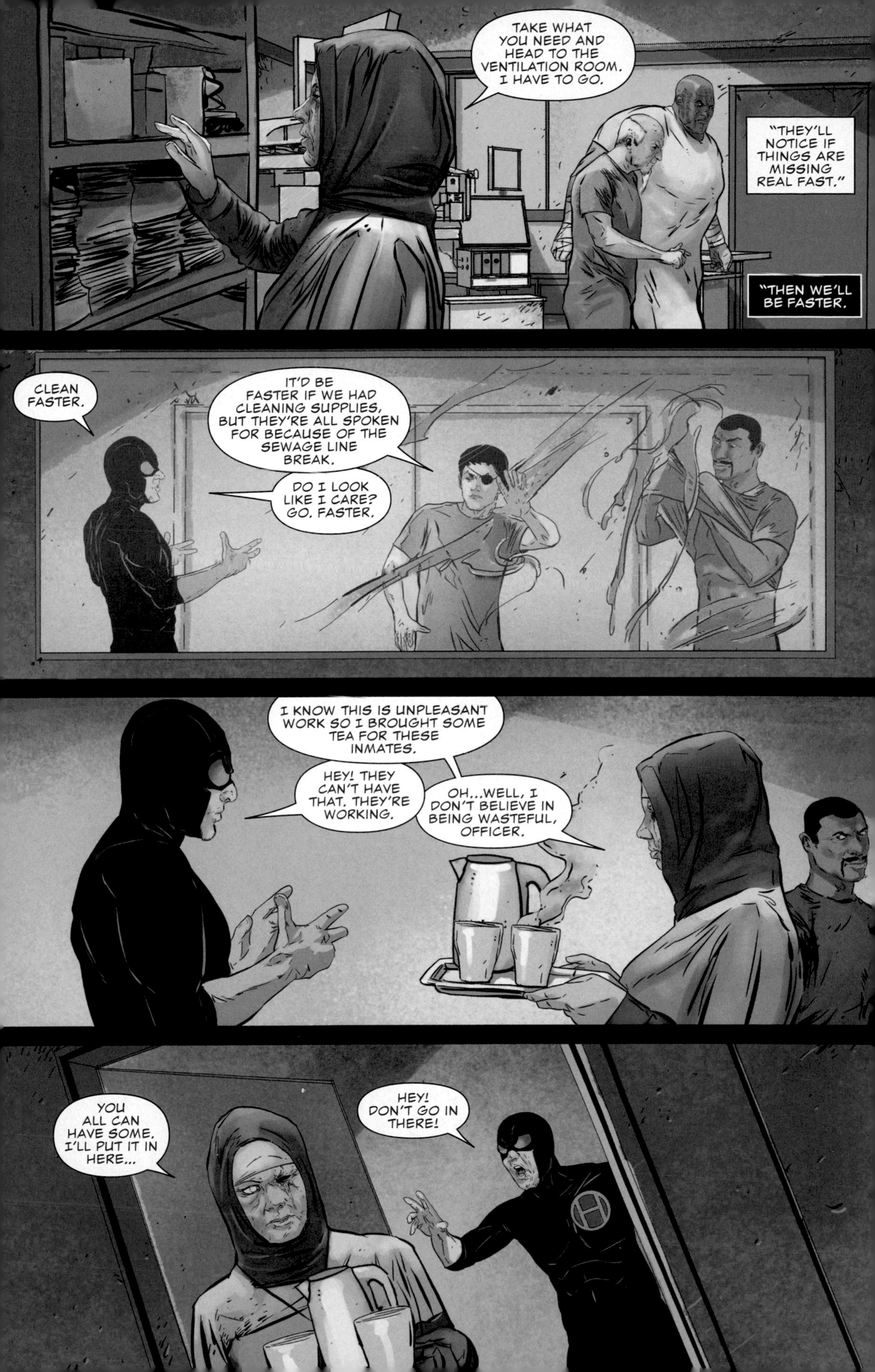
TAKE WHAT YOU NEED AND HEAD TO THE VENTILATION ROOM. I HAVE TO GO.
"THEY'LL NOTICE IF THINGS ARE MISSING REAL FAST."
"THEN WE'LL BE FASTER.
CLEAN FASTER.
IT'D BE FASTER IF WE HAD CLEANING SUPPLIES, BUT THEY'RE ALL SPOKEN FOR BECAUSE OF THE SEWAGE LINE BREAK.
DO I LOOK LIKE I CARE? GO. FASTER.
I KNOW THIS IS UNPLEASANT WORK SO I BROUGHT SOME TEA FOR THESE INMATES.
HEY! THEY CAN'T HAVE THAT. THEY'RE WORKING.
OH...WELL, I DON'T BELIEVE IN BEING WASTEFUL, OFFICER.
YOU ALL CAN HAVE SOME. I'LL PUT IT IN HERE...
HEY! DON'T GO IN THERE!

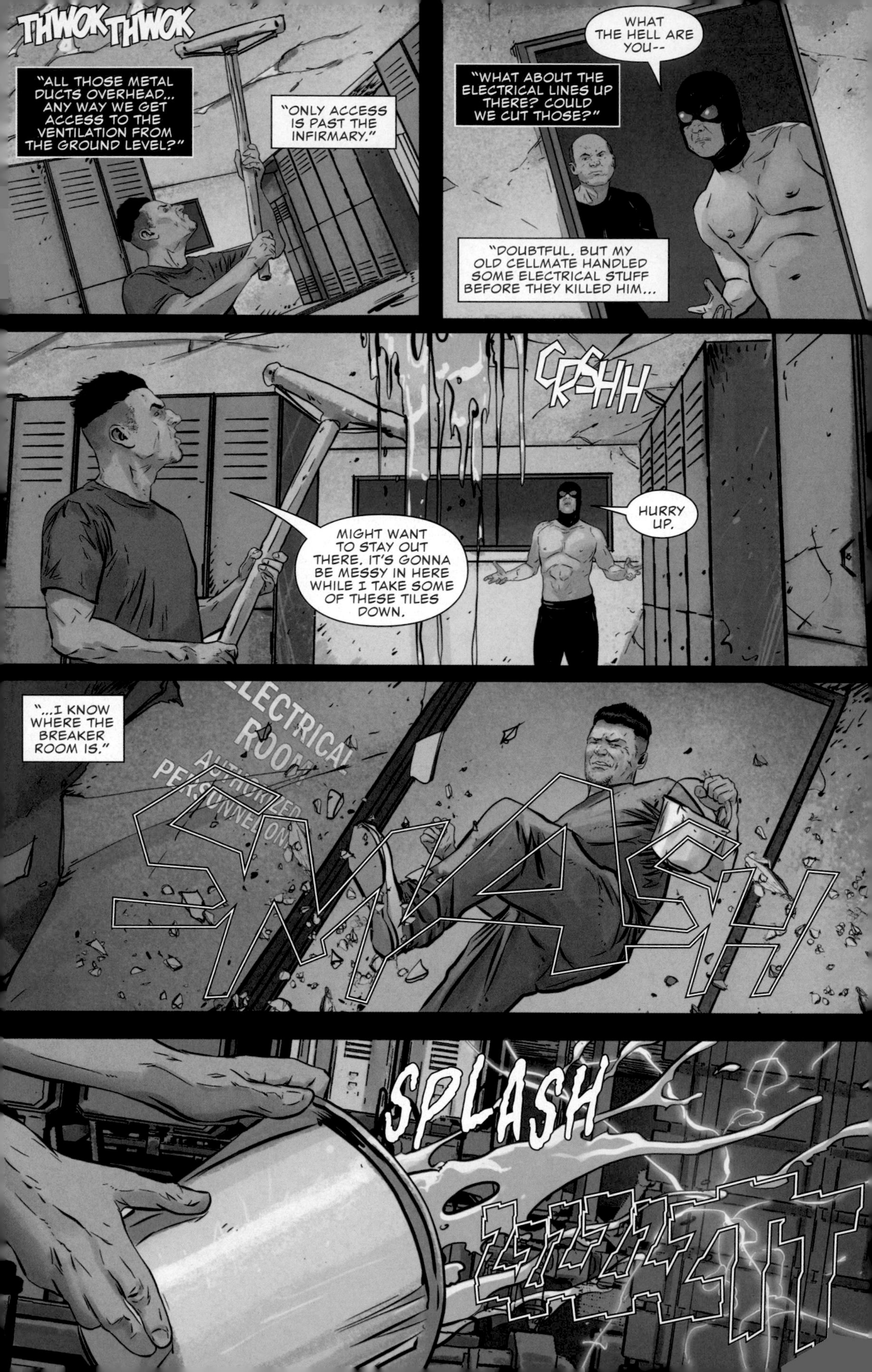
THWOK THWOK
"ALL THOSE METAL DUCTS OVERHEAD... ANY WAY WE GET ACCESS TO THE VENTILATION FROM THE GROUND LEVEL?"
"ONLY ACCESS IS PAST THE INFIRMARY."
"WHAT ABOUT THE ELECTRICAL LINES UP THERE? COULD WE CUT THOSE?"
WHAT THE HELL ARE YOU--
"DOUBTFUL. BUT MY OLD CELLMATE HANDLED SOME ELECTRICAL STUFF BEFORE THEY KILLED HIM...
CRSHH
MIGHT WANT TO STAY OUT THERE. IT'S GONNA BE MESSY IN HERE WHILE I TAKE SOME OF THESE TILES DOWN.
HURRY UP.
"...I KNOW WHERE THE BREAKER ROOM IS."
ELECTRICAL ROOM
AUTHORIZED PERSONNEL ONLY
SMASH
SPLASH

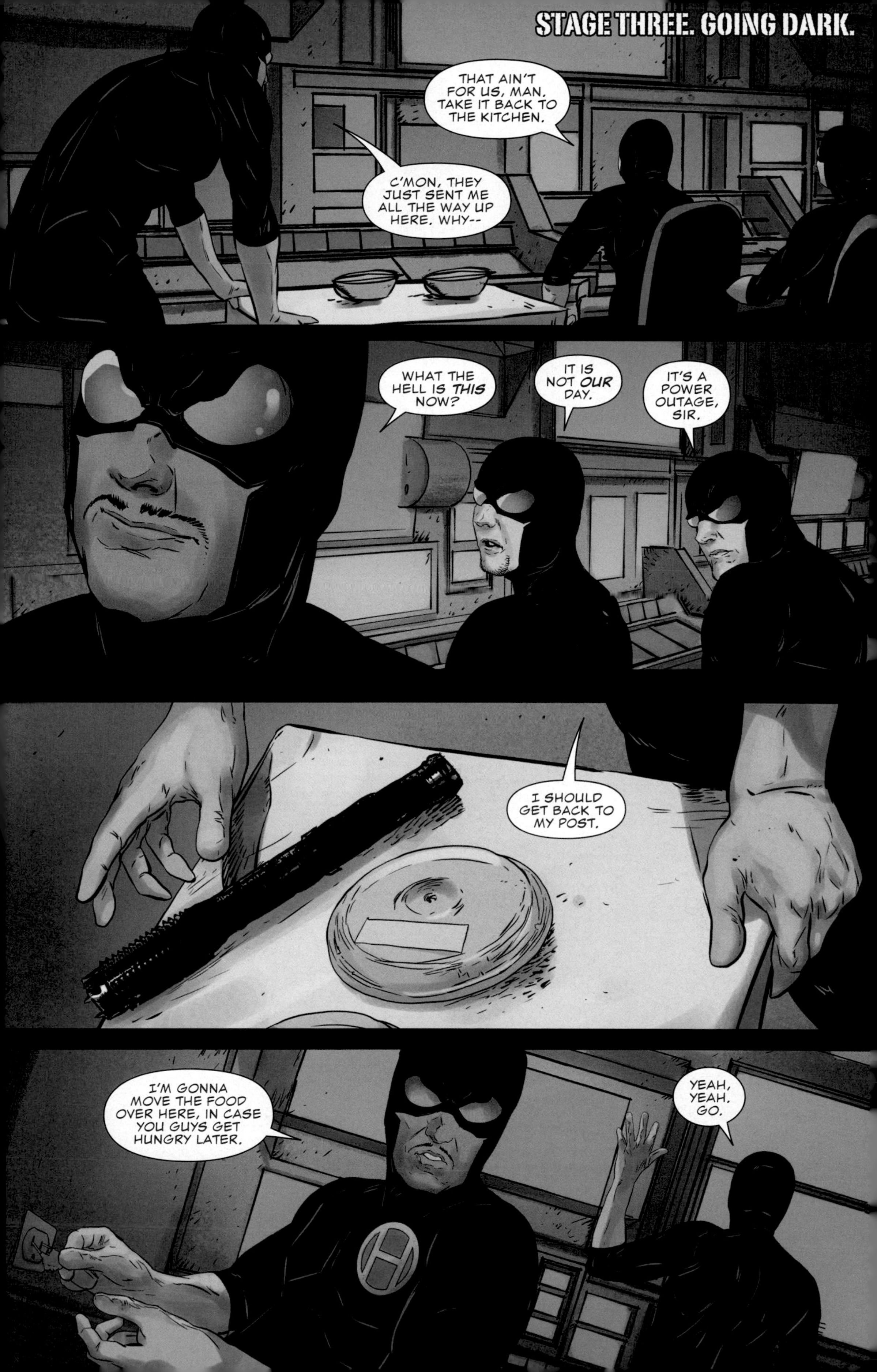
STAGE THREE. GOING DARK.
THAT AIN'T FOR US, MAN. TAKE IT BACK TO THE KITCHEN.
C'MON, THEY JUST SENT ME ALL THE WAY UP HERE. WHY--
WHAT THE HELL IS THIS NOW?
IT IS NOT OUR DAY.
IT'S A POWER OUTAGE, SIR.
I SHOULD GET BACK TO MY POST.
I'M GONNA MOVE THE FOOD OVER HERE, IN CASE YOU GUYS GET HUNGRY LATER.
YEAH, YEAH. GO.

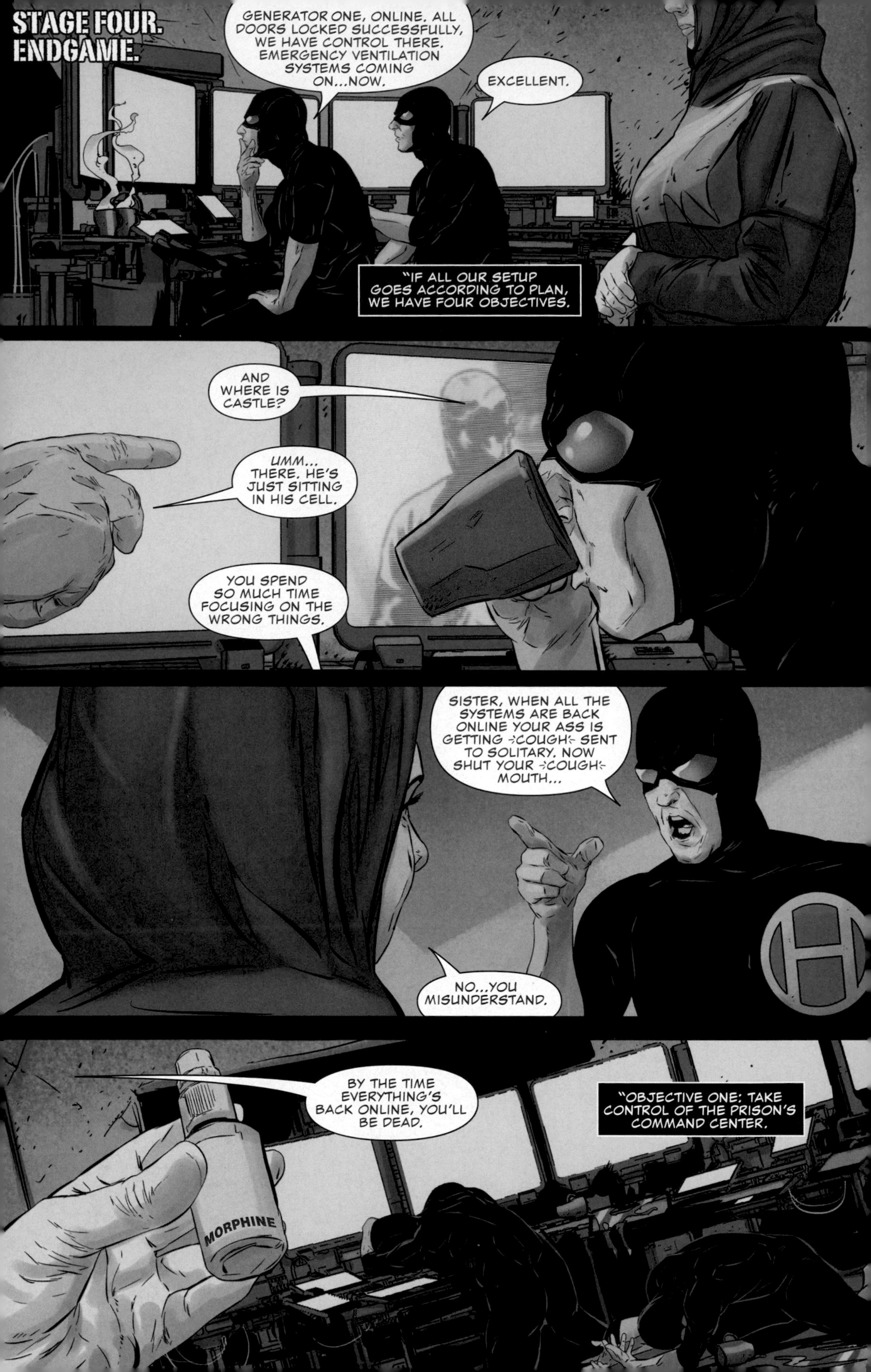
STAGE FOUR. ENDGAME.
GENERATOR ONE, ONLINE. ALL DOORS LOCKED SUCCESSFULLY, WE HAVE CONTROL THERE. EMERGENCY VENTILATION SYSTEMS COMING ON...NOW.
EXCELLENT.
"IF ALL OUR SETUP GOES ACCORDING TO PLAN, WE HAVE FOUR OBJECTIVES.
AND WHERE IS CASTLE?
UMM... THERE. HE'S JUST SITTING IN HIS CELL.
YOU SPEND SO MUCH TIME FOCUSING ON THE WRONG THINGS.
SISTER, WHEN ALL THE SYSTEMS ARE BACK ONLINE YOUR ASS IS GETTING -COUGH- SENT TO SOLITARY. NOW SHUT YOUR -COUGH- MOUTH...
NO...YOU MISUNDERSTAND.
BY THE TIME EVERYTHING'S BACK ONLINE, YOU'LL BE DEAD.
"OBJECTIVE ONE: TAKE CONTROL OF THE PRISON'S COMMAND CENTER.
MORPHINE

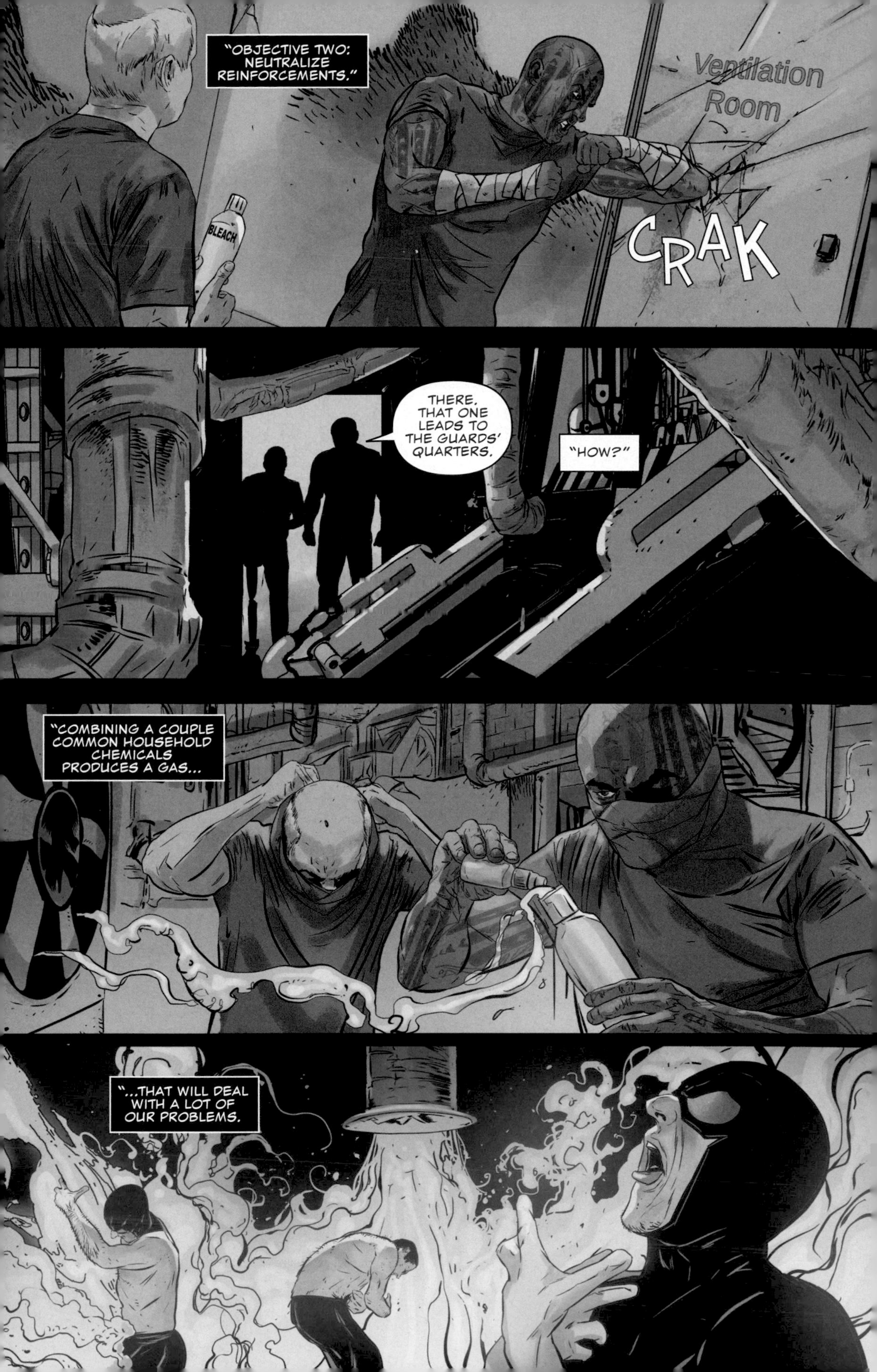
"OBJECTIVE TWO: NEUTRALIZE REINFORCEMENTS."
BLEACH
Ventilation Room
CRAK
THERE. THAT ONE LEADS TO THE GUARDS' QUARTERS.
"HOW?"
"COMBINING A COUPLE COMMON HOUSEHOLD CHEMICALS PRODUCES A GAS...
"...THAT WILL DEAL WITH A LOT OF OUR PROBLEMS.

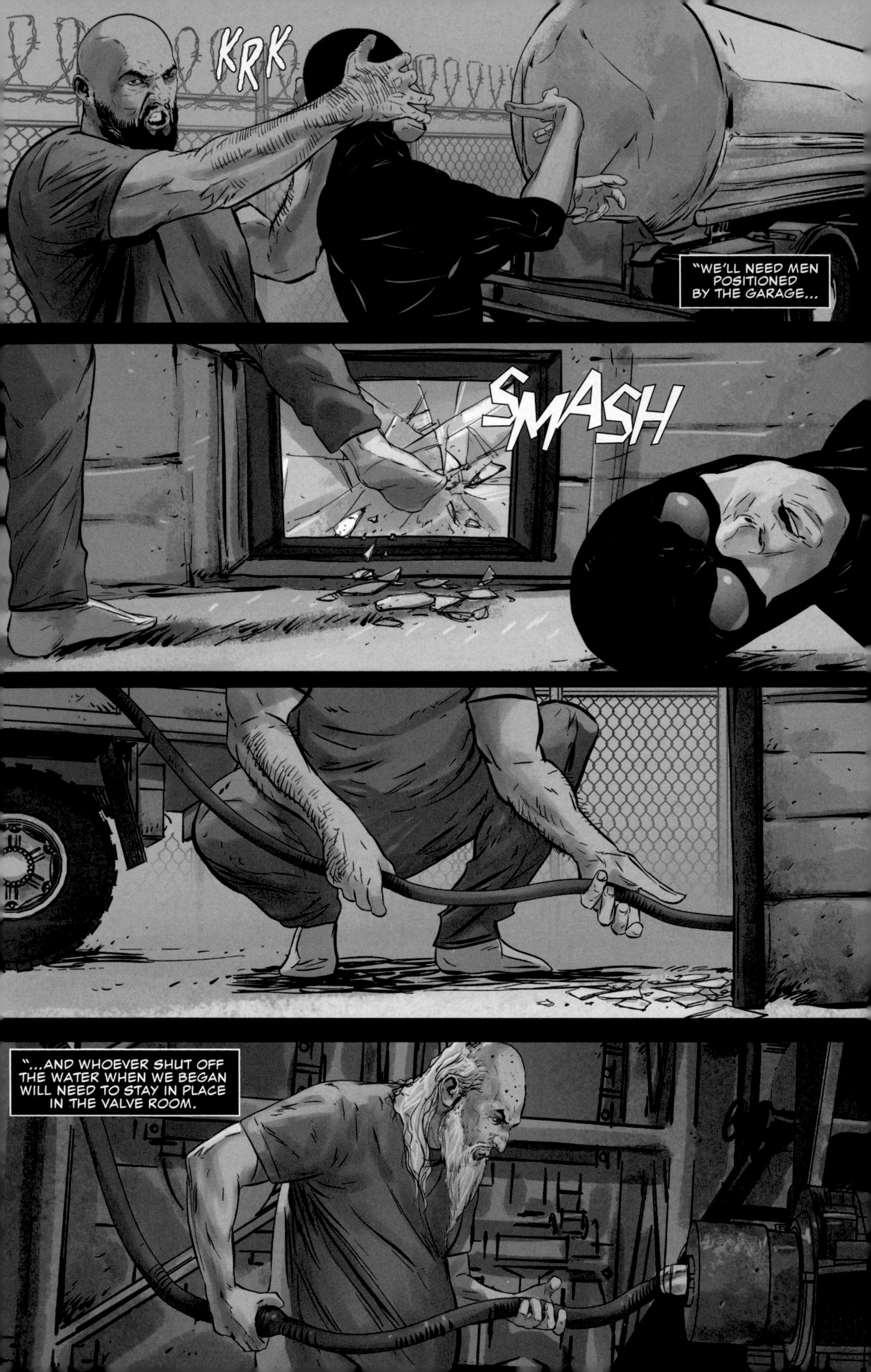
KRK
"WE'LL NEED MEN POSITIONED BY THE GARAGE...
SMASH
"...AND WHOEVER SHUT OFF THE WATER WHEN WE BEGAN WILL NEED TO STAY IN PLACE IN THE VALVE ROOM.

BACKUP GENERATOR IS BACK ONLINE.

GOOD. RAISE HYDRA COMMAND ON THE COMMS. I WANT A BATTALION OF REINFORCEMENTS HERE UNTIL WE HAVE A HANDLE ON--

"OBJECTIVE THREE: CUT OFF COMMUNICATION WITH THE OUTSIDE WORLD."

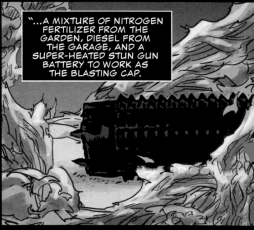

"AND HOW DO WE DO THAT?"

WHAT THE--

"A CLOTH DRIZZLED IN GAS...

"...A MIXTURE OF NITROGEN FERTILIZER FROM THE GARDEN, DIESEL FROM THE GARAGE, AND A SUPER-HEATED STUN GUN BATTERY TO WORK AS THE BLASTING CAP.

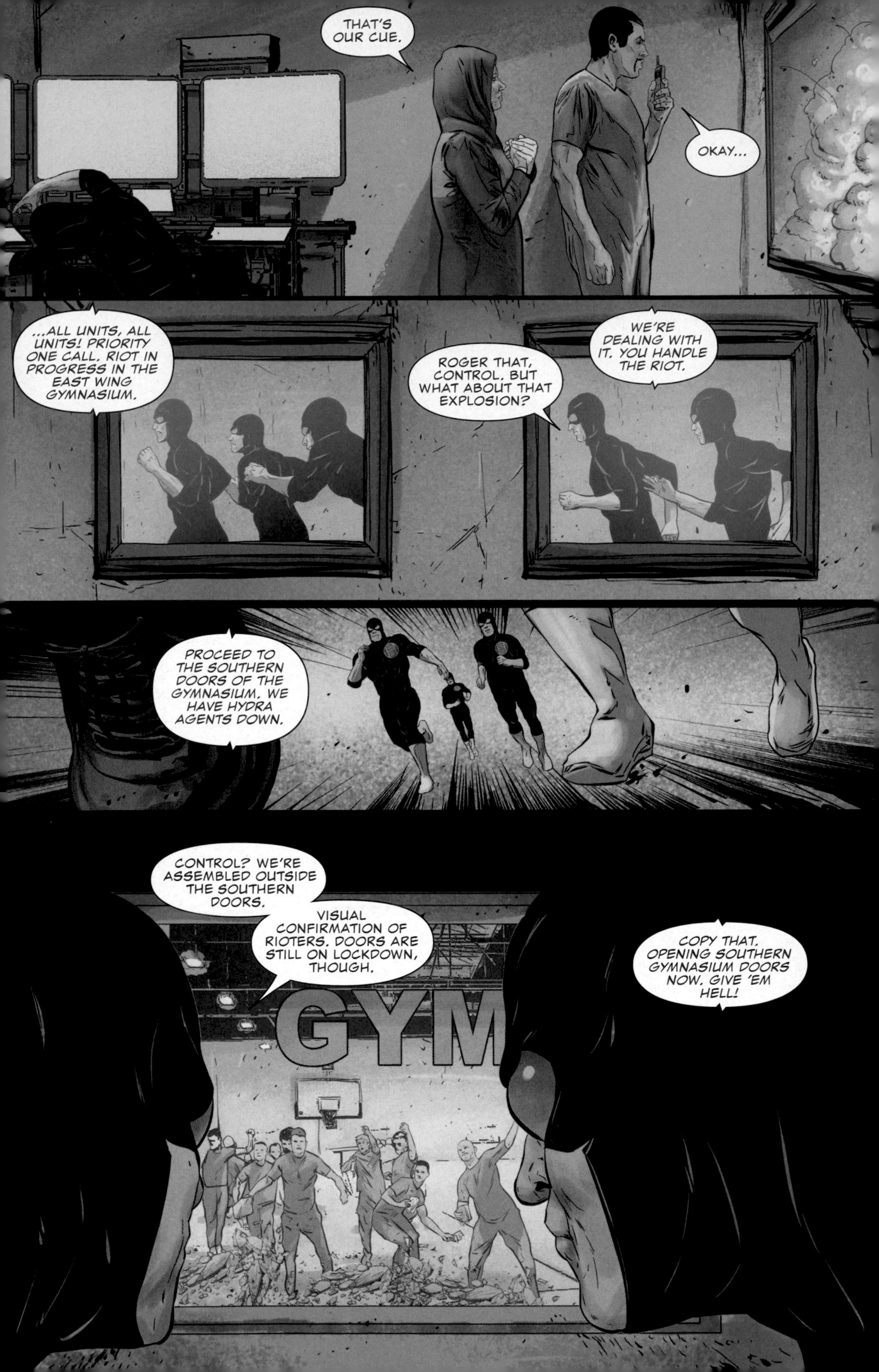
THAT'S OUR CUE.
OKAY...
...ALL UNITS, ALL UNITS! PRIORITY ONE CALL. RIOT IN PROGRESS IN THE EAST WING GYMNASIUM.
ROGER THAT, CONTROL, BUT WHAT ABOUT THAT EXPLOSION?
WE'RE DEALING WITH IT. YOU HANDLE THE RIOT.
PROCEED TO THE SOUTHERN DOORS OF THE GYMNASIUM. WE HAVE HYDRA AGENTS DOWN.
CONTROL? WE'RE ASSEMBLED OUTSIDE THE SOUTHERN DOORS.
VISUAL CONFIRMATION OF RIOTERS. DOORS ARE STILL ON LOCKDOWN, THOUGH.
COPY THAT. OPENING SOUTHERN GYMNASIUM DOORS NOW. GIVE 'EM HELL!
GYM

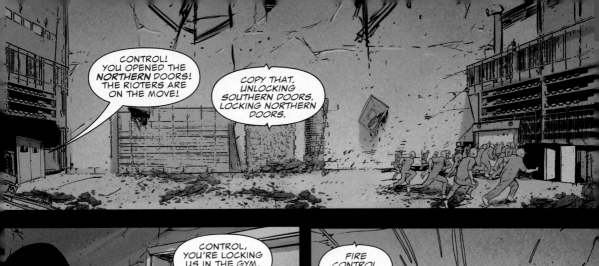

CONTROL! YOU OPENED THE *NORTHERN* DOORS! THE RIOTERS ARE ON THE MOVE!

COPY THAT. UNLOCKING SOUTHERN DOORS. LOCKING NORTHERN DOORS.

CONTROL, YOU'RE LOCKING US IN THE GYM. REPEAT, YOU--

WHY'D THEY ALL RUN OUT TOGETHER?

COPY THAT, LOCKING SOUTHERN DOORS.

FIRE CONTROL MEASURES INITIATED.

CONTROL, WHAT THE #*@$ ARE YOU DOING?!

THERE'S NO FIRE!

WHAT'S GOING ON?!

THIS... THIS ISN'T WATER...

NO, IT'S NOT.

IT'S GASOLINE.

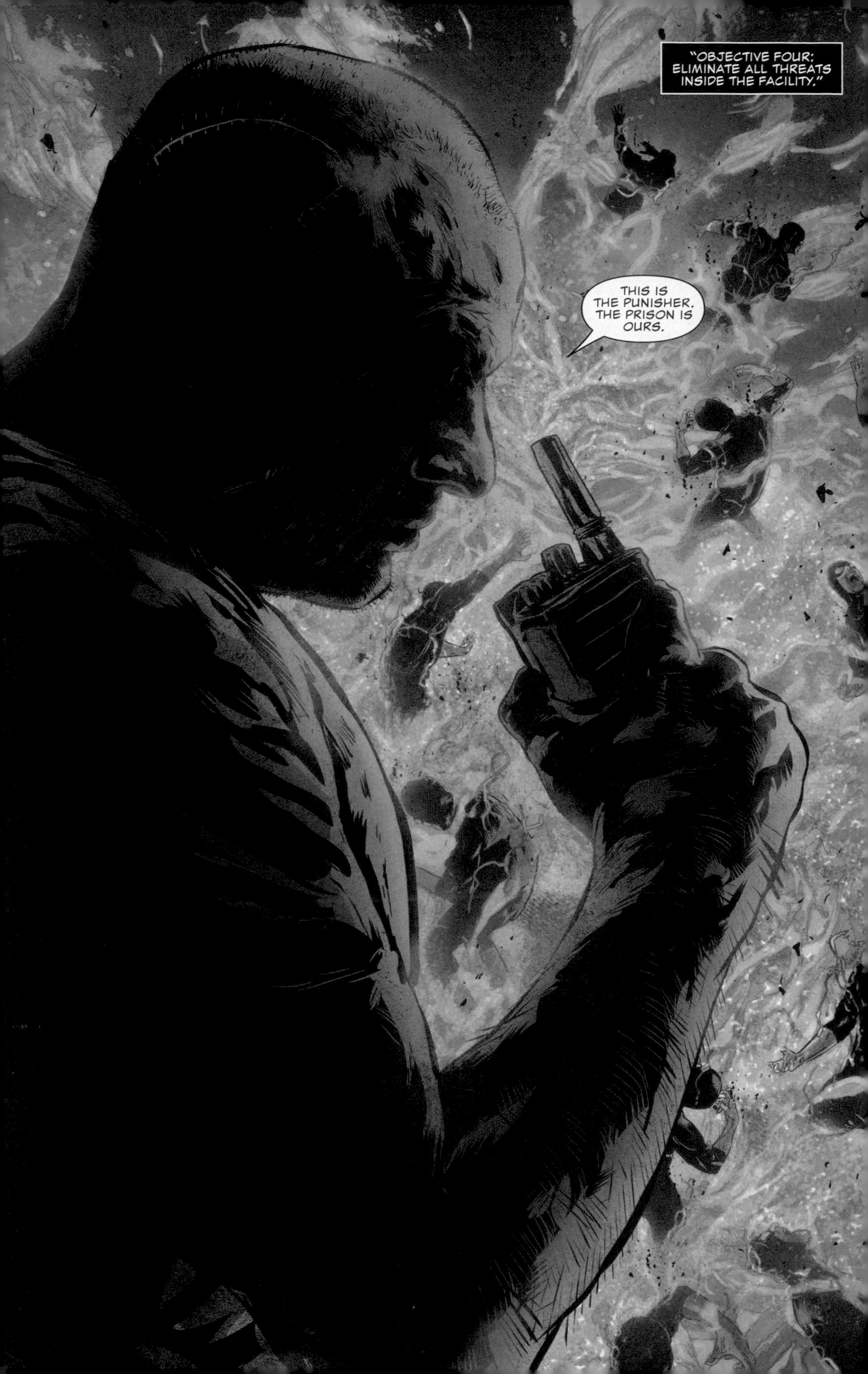
"OBJECTIVE FOUR: ELIMINATE ALL THREATS INSIDE THE FACILITY."
THIS IS THE PUNISHER. THE PRISON IS OURS.

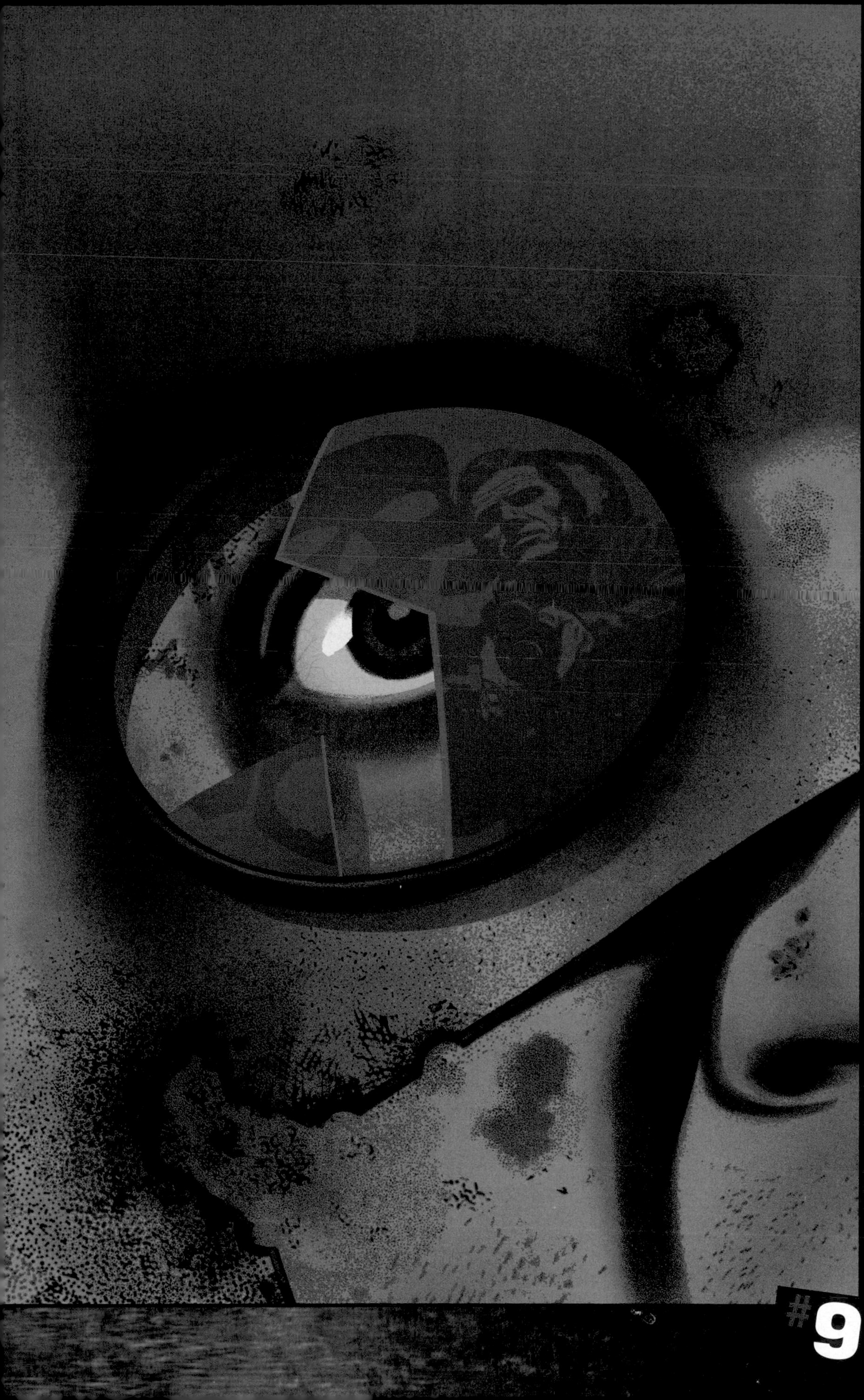
#9

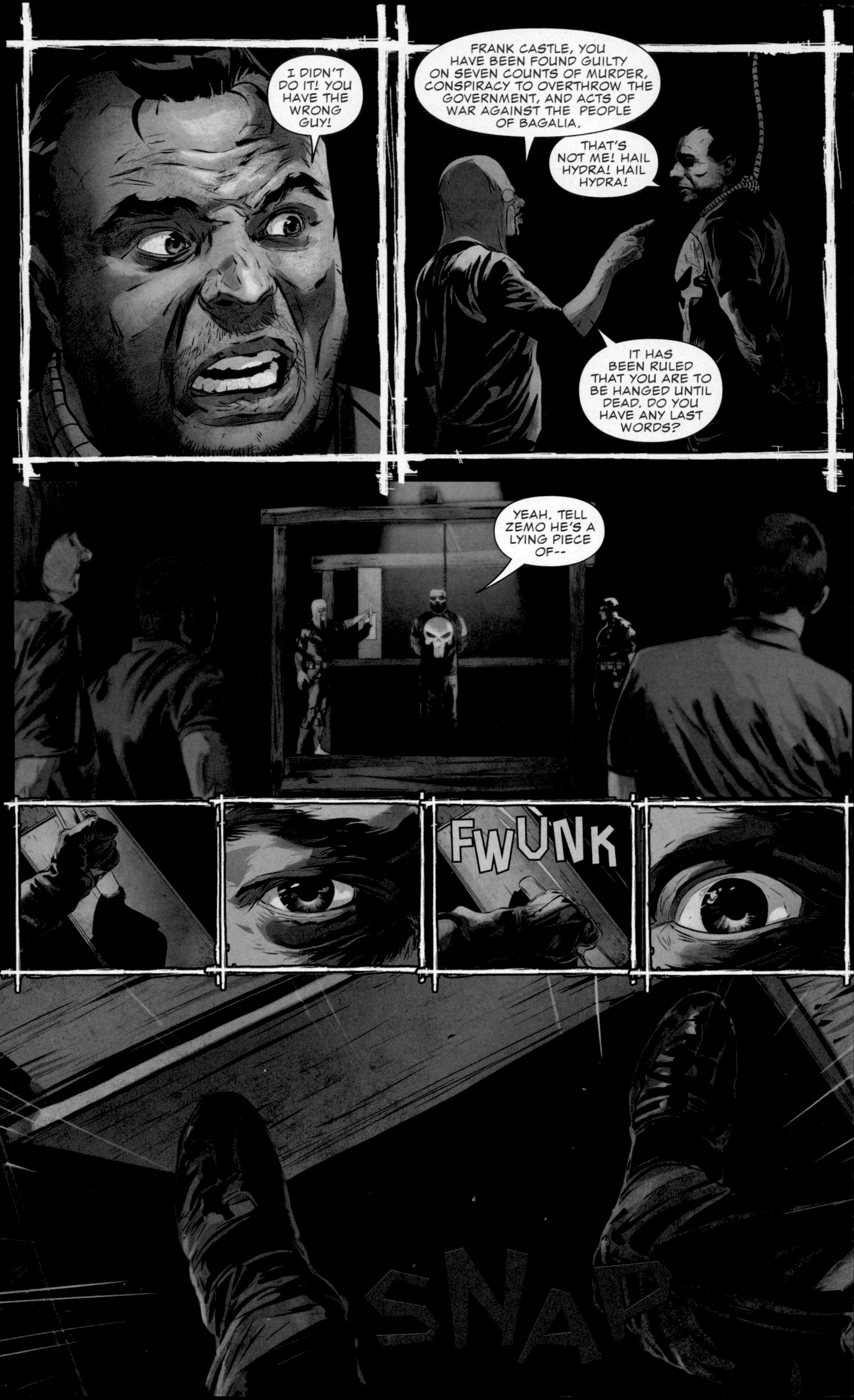
I DIDN'T DO IT! YOU HAVE THE WRONG GUY!
FRANK CASTLE, YOU HAVE BEEN FOUND GUILTY ON SEVEN COUNTS OF MURDER, CONSPIRACY TO OVERTHROW THE GOVERNMENT, AND ACTS OF WAR AGAINST THE PEOPLE OF BAGALIA.
THAT'S NOT ME! HAIL HYDRA! HAIL HYDRA!
IT HAS BEEN RULED THAT YOU ARE TO BE HANGED UNTIL DEAD. DO YOU HAVE ANY LAST WORDS?
YEAH. TELL ZEMO HE'S A LYING PIECE OF--
FWUNK
SNAP

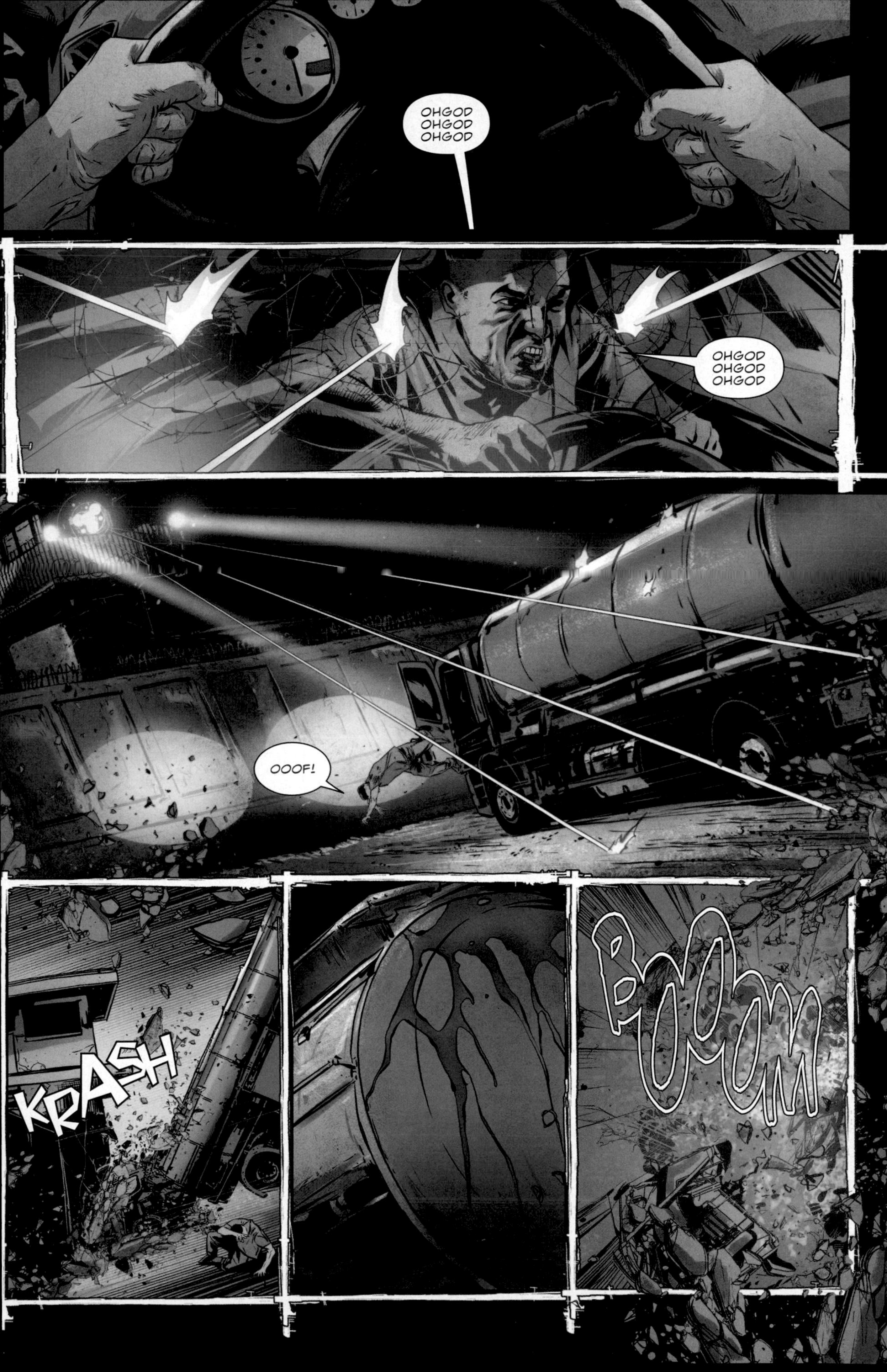
OHGOD
OHGOD
OHGOD
OHGOD
OHGOD
OHGOD
OOOF!
KRASH
BOOOM

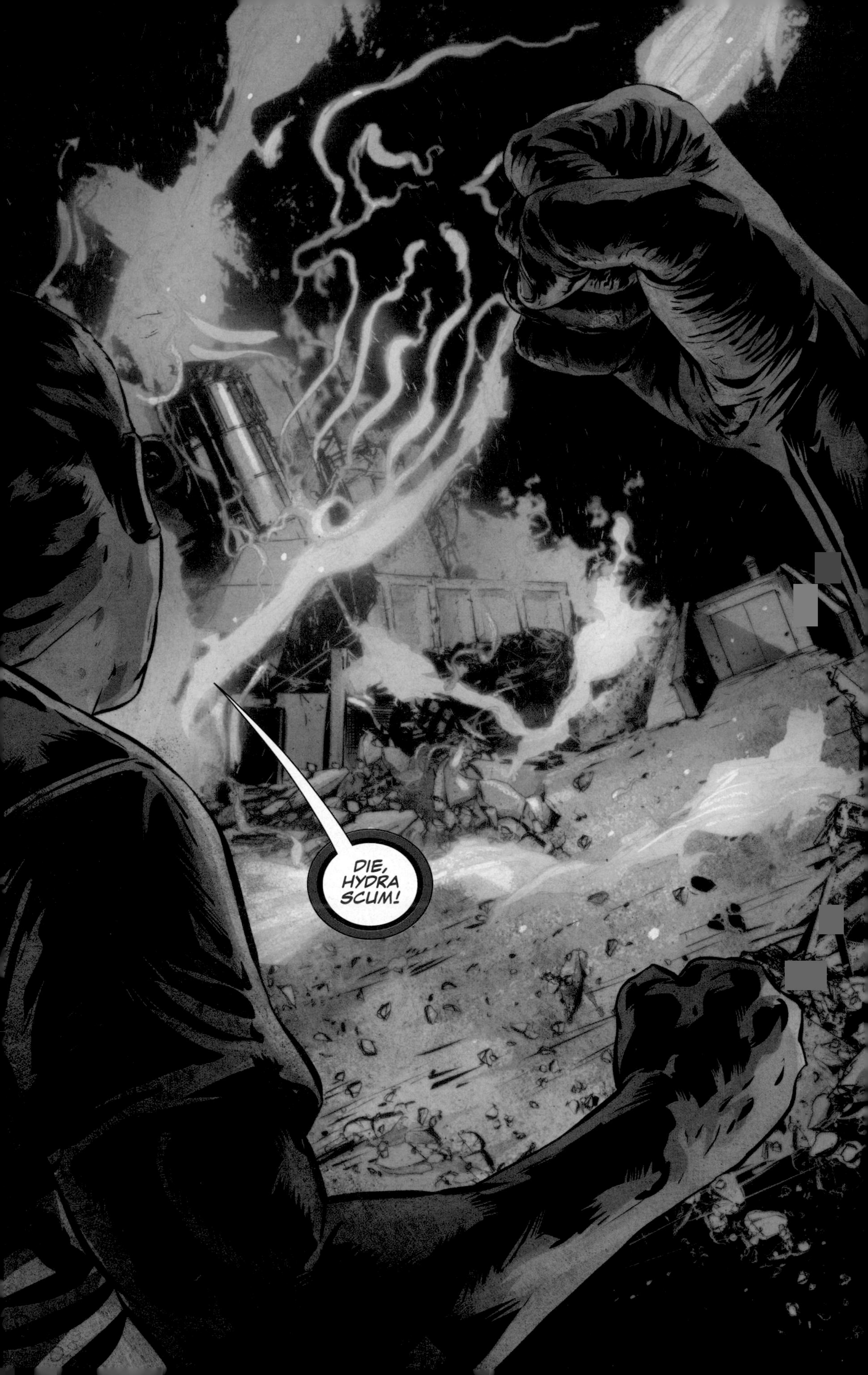
DIE, HYDRA SCUM!

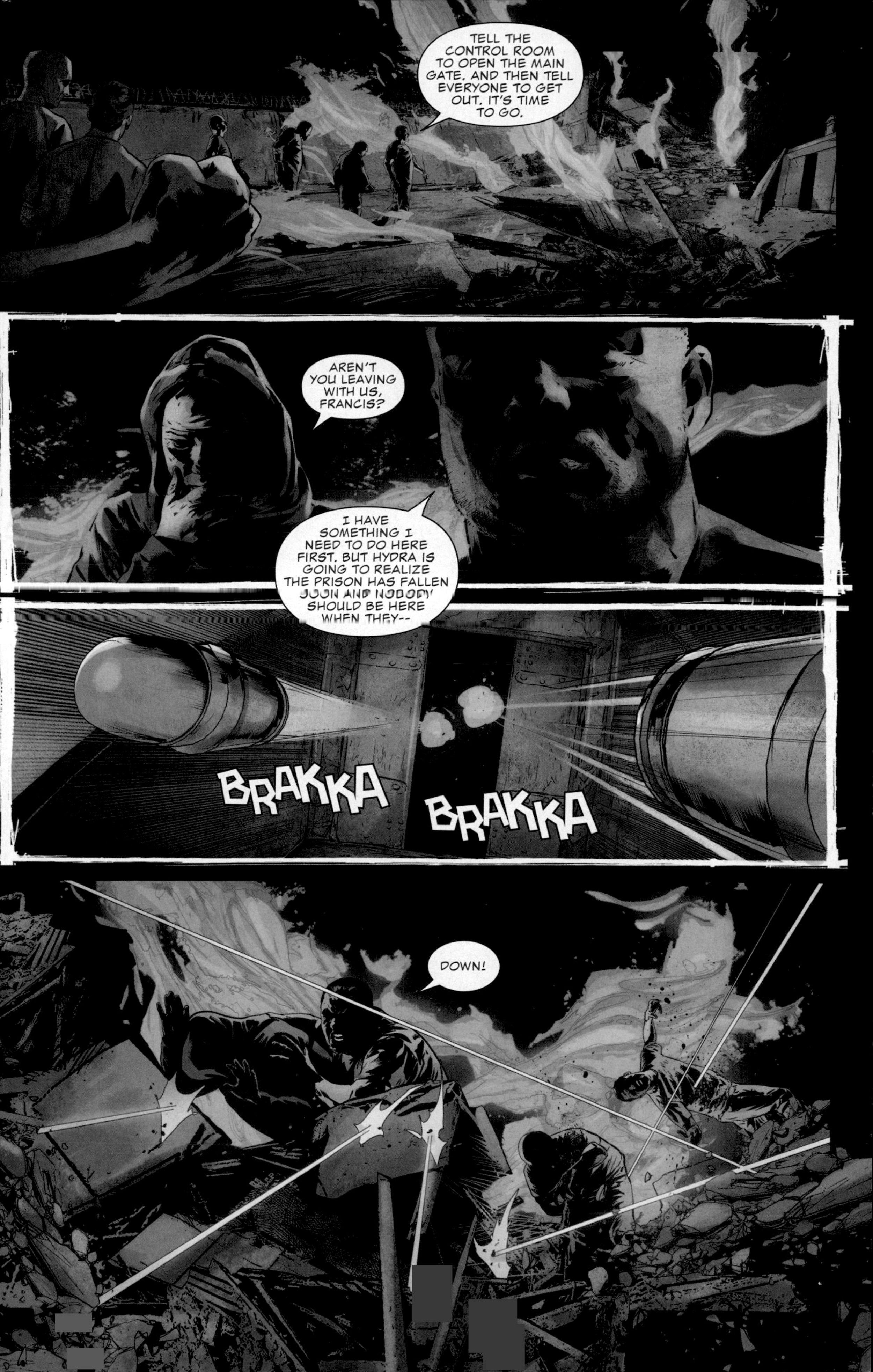
TELL THE CONTROL ROOM TO OPEN THE MAIN GATE. AND THEN TELL EVERYONE TO GET OUT. IT'S TIME TO GO.
AREN'T YOU LEAVING WITH US, FRANCIS?
I HAVE SOMETHING I NEED TO DO HERE FIRST. BUT HYDRA IS GOING TO REALIZE THE PRISON HAS FALLEN SOON AND NOBODY SHOULD BE HERE WHEN THEY--
BRAKKA
BRAKKA
DOWN!

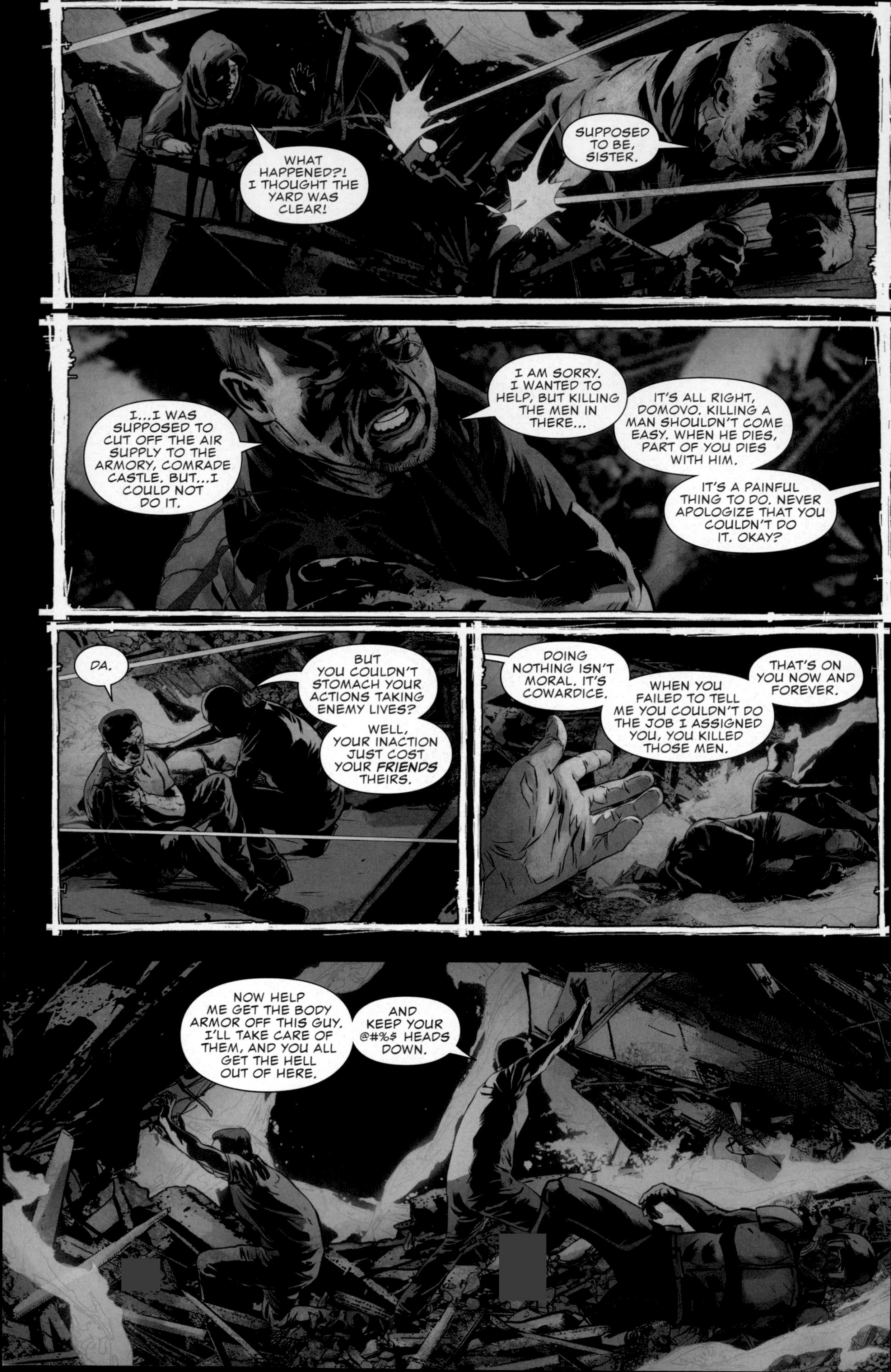
WHAT HAPPENED?! I THOUGHT THE YARD WAS CLEAR!
SUPPOSED TO BE, SISTER.
I...I WAS SUPPOSED TO CUT OFF THE AIR SUPPLY TO THE ARMORY, COMRADE CASTLE. BUT...I COULD NOT DO IT.
I AM SORRY. I WANTED TO HELP, BUT KILLING THE MEN IN THERE...
IT'S ALL RIGHT, DOMOVO. KILLING A MAN SHOULDN'T COME EASY. WHEN HE DIES, PART OF YOU DIES WITH HIM.
IT'S A PAINFUL THING TO DO. NEVER APOLOGIZE THAT YOU COULDN'T DO IT. OKAY?
DA.
BUT YOU COULDN'T STOMACH YOUR ACTIONS TAKING ENEMY LIVES?
WELL, YOUR INACTION JUST COST YOUR FRIENDS THEIRS.
DOING NOTHING ISN'T MORAL. IT'S COWARDICE.
WHEN YOU FAILED TO TELL ME YOU COULDN'T DO THE JOB I ASSIGNED YOU, YOU KILLED THOSE MEN.
THAT'S ON YOU NOW AND FOREVER.
NOW HELP ME GET THE BODY ARMOR OFF THIS GUY. I'LL TAKE CARE OF THEM, AND YOU ALL GET THE HELL OUT OF HERE.
AND KEEP YOUR @#%$ HEADS DOWN.

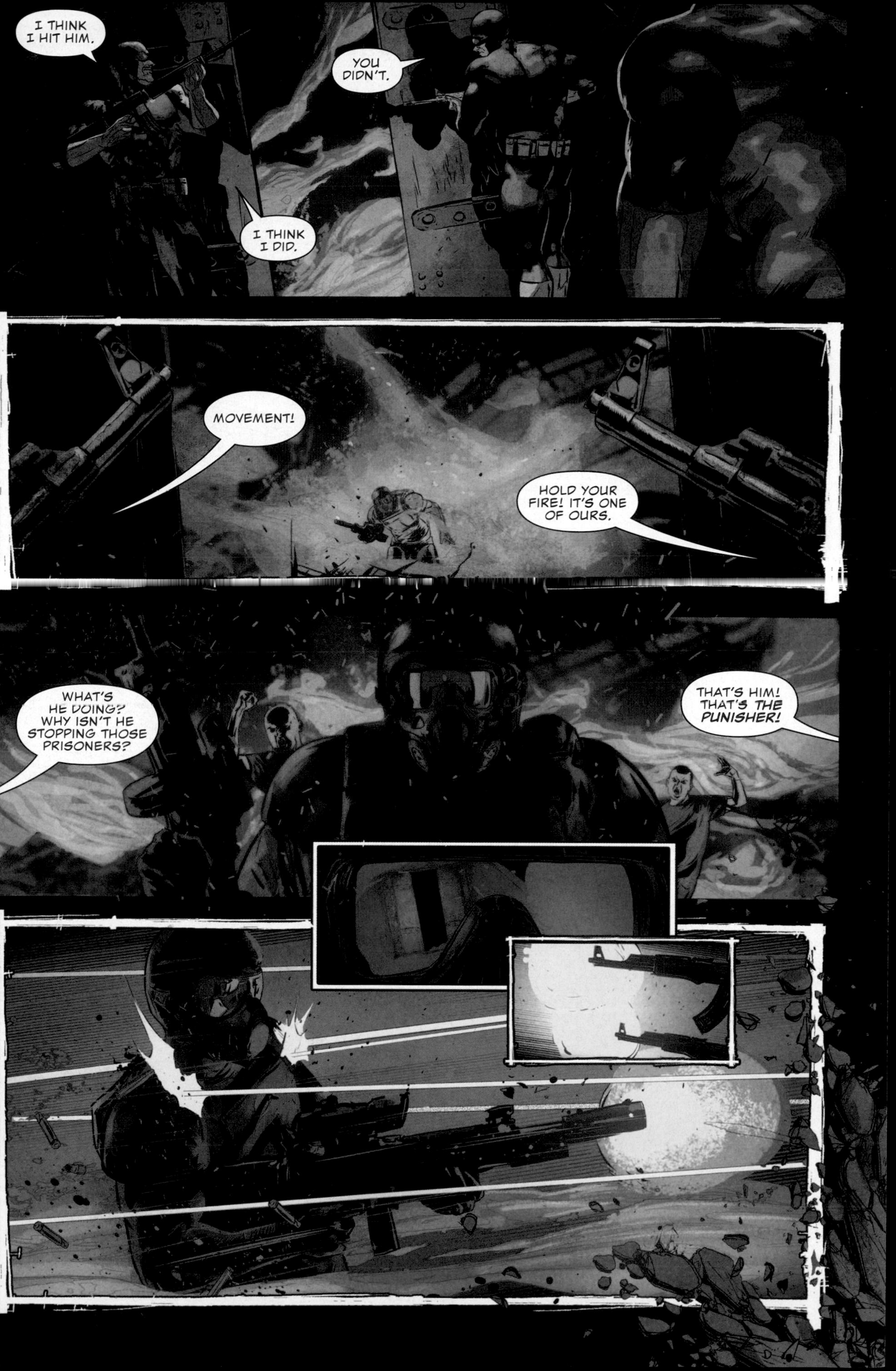
I THINK I HIT HIM.
YOU DIDN'T.
I THINK I DID.
MOVEMENT!
HOLD YOUR FIRE! IT'S ONE OF OURS.
WHAT'S HE DOING? WHY ISN'T HE STOPPING THOSE PRISONERS?
THAT'S HIM! THAT'S *THE PUNISHER!*

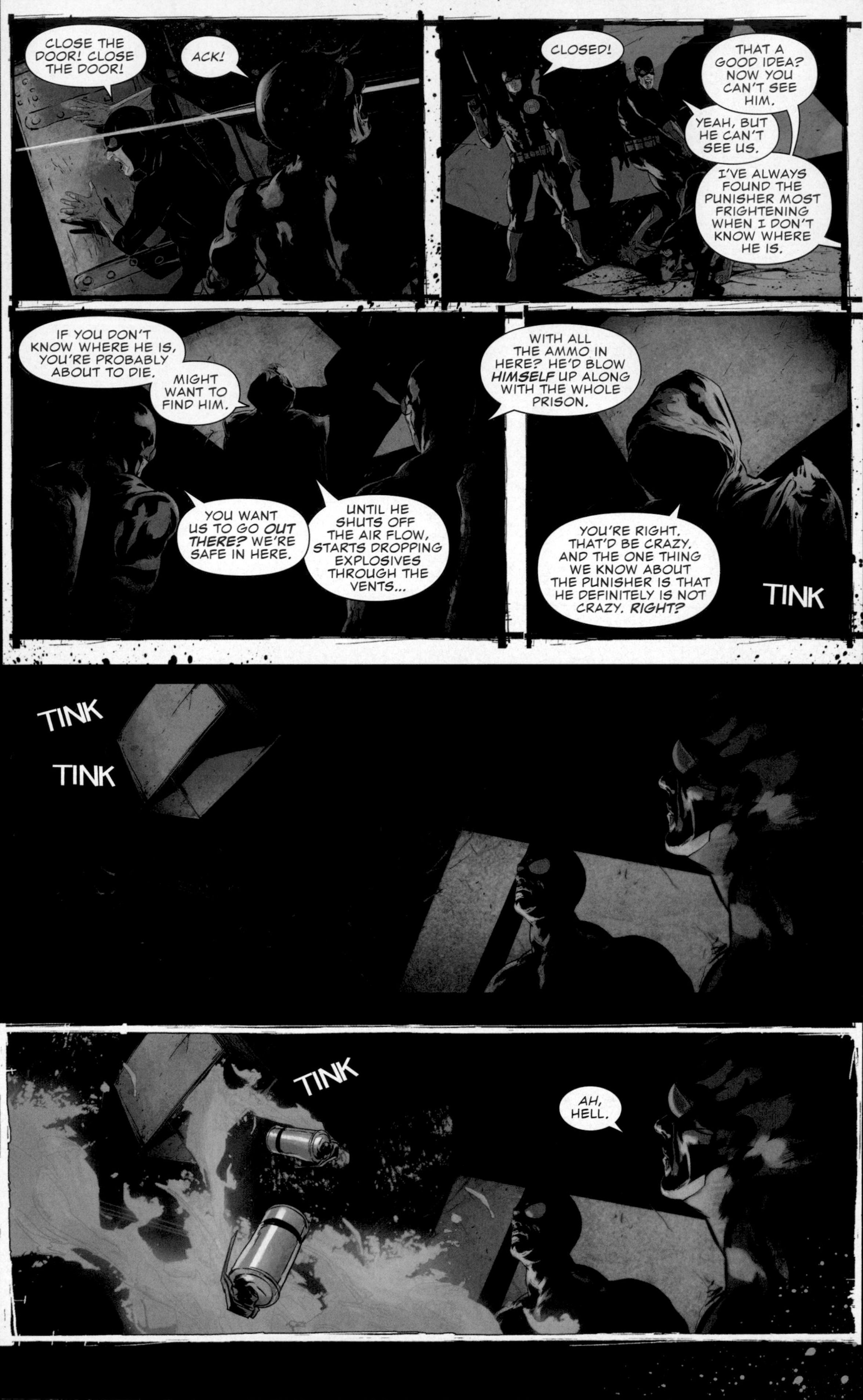
CLOSE THE DOOR! CLOSE THE DOOR!
ACK!
CLOSED!
THAT A GOOD IDEA? NOW YOU CAN'T SEE HIM.
YEAH, BUT HE CAN'T SEE US.
I'VE ALWAYS FOUND THE PUNISHER MOST FRIGHTENING WHEN I DON'T KNOW WHERE HE IS.
IF YOU DON'T KNOW WHERE HE IS, YOU'RE PROBABLY ABOUT TO DIE.
MIGHT WANT TO FIND HIM.
YOU WANT US TO GO OUT THERE? WE'RE SAFE IN HERE.
UNTIL HE SHUTS OFF THE AIR FLOW, STARTS DROPPING EXPLOSIVES THROUGH THE VENTS...
WITH ALL THE AMMO IN HERE? HE'D BLOW HIMSELF UP ALONG WITH THE WHOLE PRISON.
YOU'RE RIGHT. THAT'D BE CRAZY. AND THE ONE THING WE KNOW ABOUT THE PUNISHER IS THAT HE DEFINITELY IS NOT CRAZY. RIGHT?
TINK
TINK
TINK
TINK
AH, HELL.

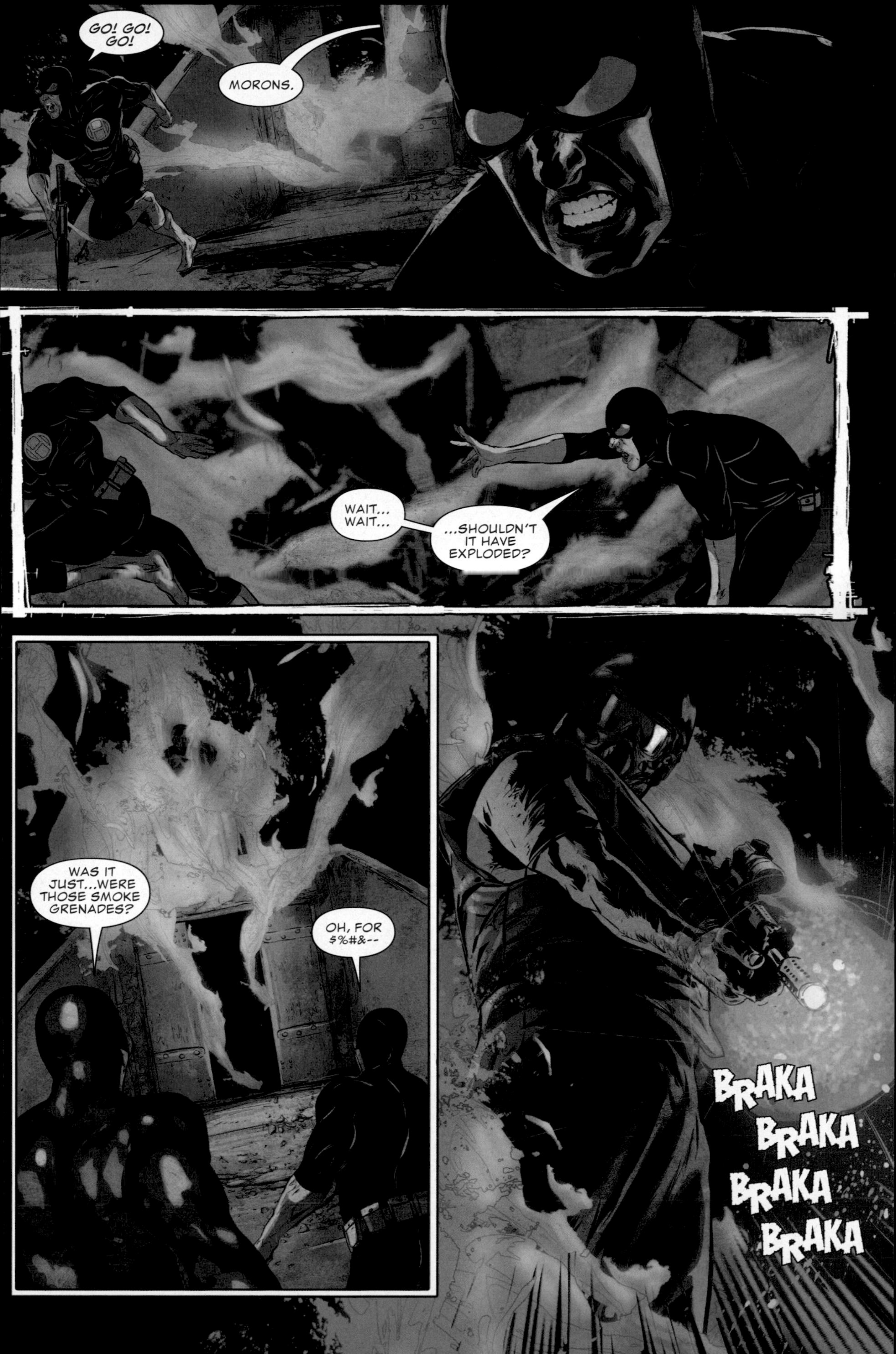
GO! GO! GO!
MORONS.
WAIT... WAIT...
...SHOULDN'T IT HAVE EXPLODED?
WAS IT JUST...WERE THOSE SMOKE GRENADES?
OH, FOR $%#&--
BRAKA BRAKA BRAKA BRAKA

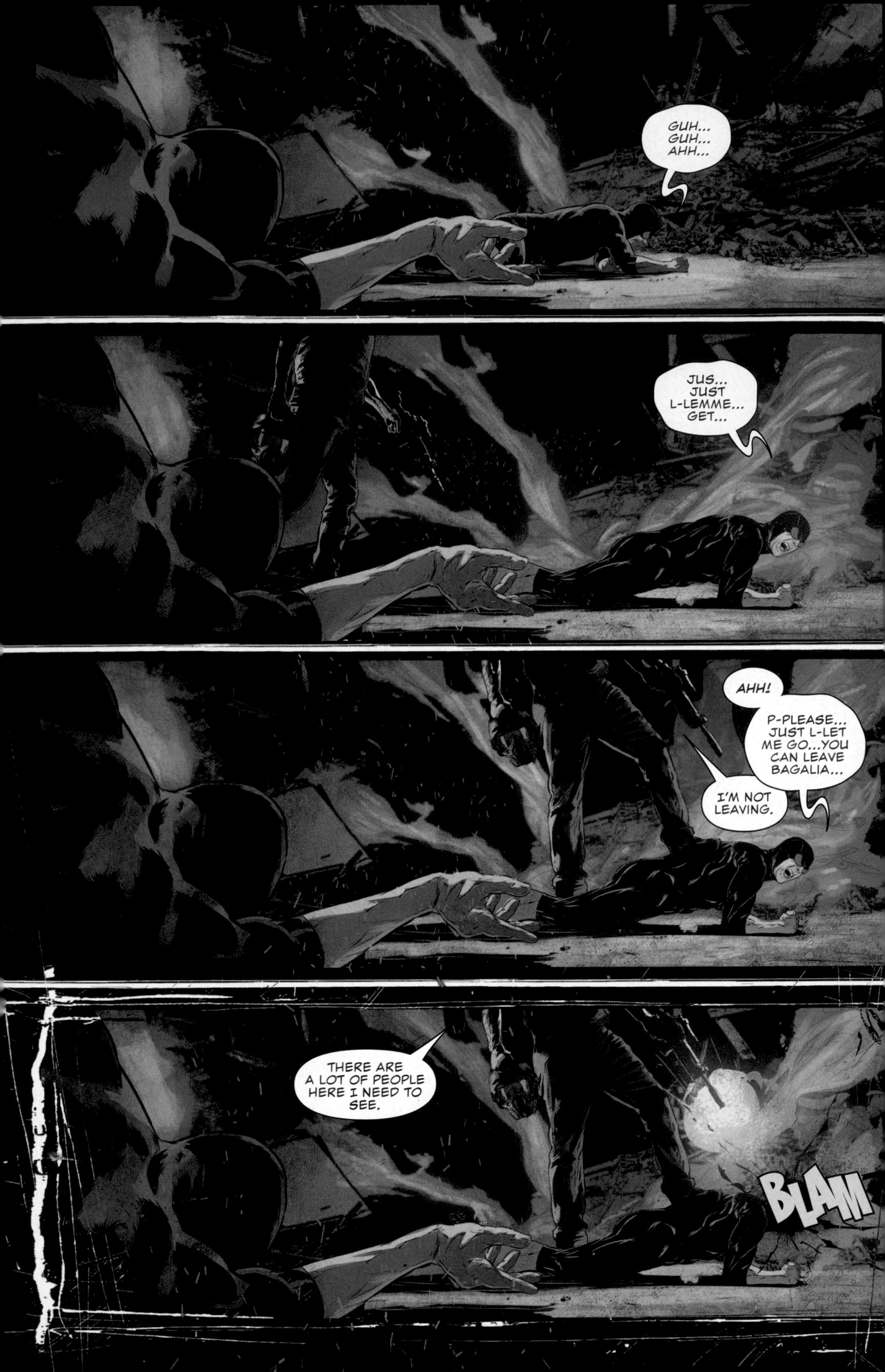
GUH... GUH... AHH...
JUS... JUST L-LEMME... GET...
AHH!
P-PLEASE... JUST L-LET ME GO...YOU CAN LEAVE BAGALIA...
I'M NOT LEAVING.
THERE ARE A LOT OF PEOPLE HERE I NEED TO SEE.
BLAM

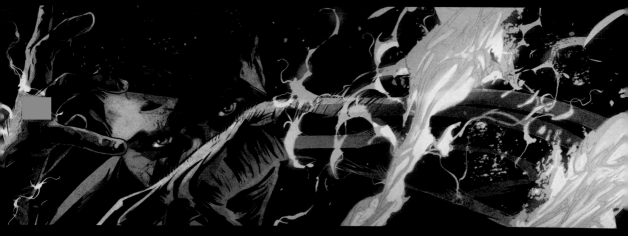

OH, FRANK. DID YOU REALLY THINK YOU COULD LEAVE THIS PLACE WITHOUT SAYING GOODBYE TO ME?

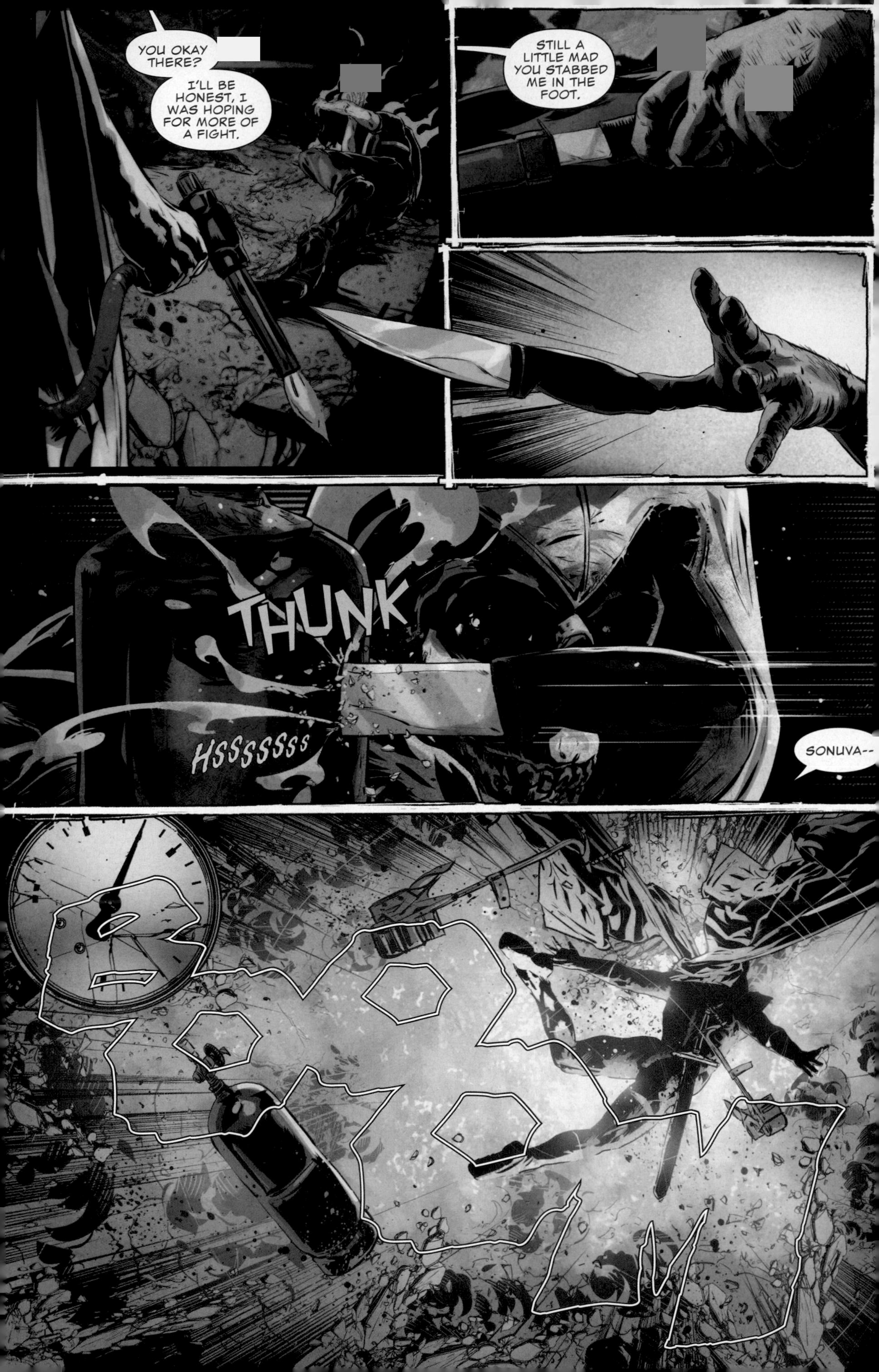

YOU OKAY THERE?
I'LL BE HONEST, I WAS HOPING FOR MORE OF A FIGHT.
STILL A LITTLE MAD YOU STABBED ME IN THE FOOT.
THUNK
HSSSSSSS
SONUVA--
BOOM

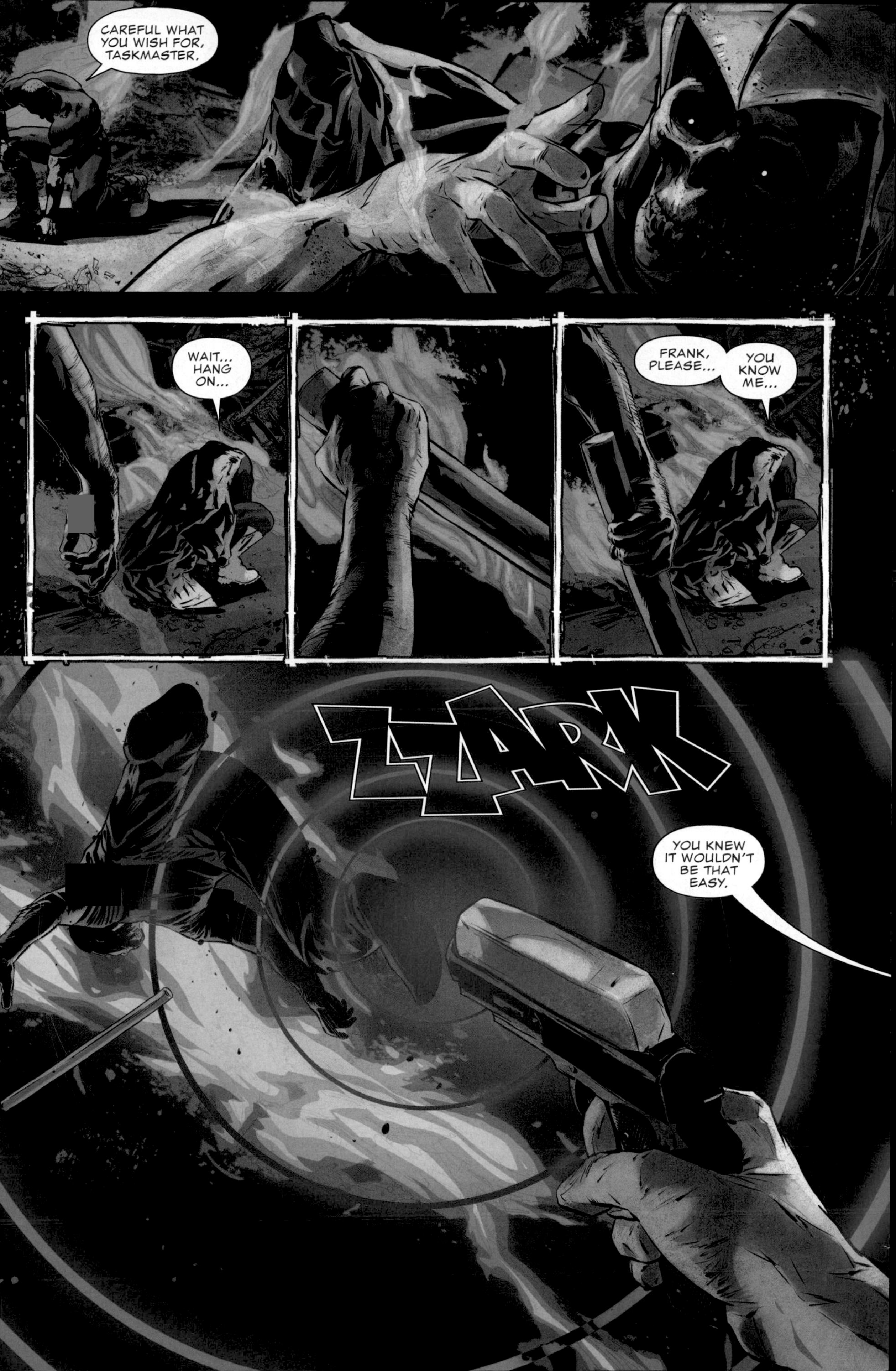
CAREFUL WHAT YOU WISH FOR, TASKMASTER.
WAIT... HANG ON...
FRANK, PLEASE...
YOU KNOW ME...
ZZARK
YOU KNEW IT WOULDN'T BE THAT EASY.

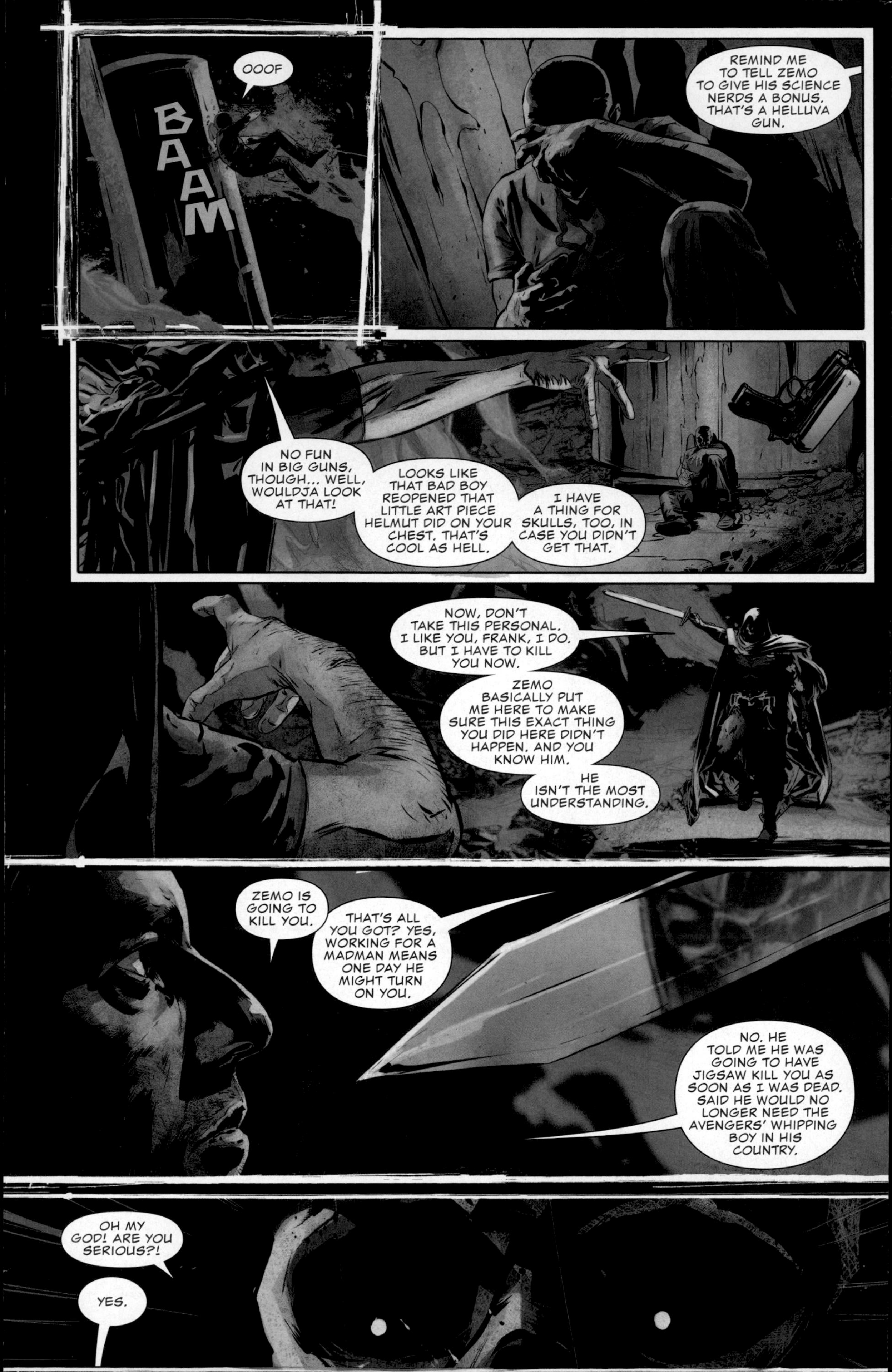

OOOF
BAAAM
REMIND ME TO TELL ZEMO TO GIVE HIS SCIENCE NERDS A BONUS. THAT'S A HELLUVA GUN.
NO FUN IN BIG GUNS, THOUGH... WELL, WOULDJA LOOK AT THAT!
LOOKS LIKE THAT BAD BOY REOPENED THAT LITTLE ART PIECE HELMUT DID ON YOUR CHEST. THAT'S COOL AS HELL.
I HAVE A THING FOR SKULLS, TOO, IN CASE YOU DIDN'T GET THAT.
NOW, DON'T TAKE THIS PERSONAL. I LIKE YOU, FRANK, I DO. BUT I HAVE TO KILL YOU NOW.
ZEMO BASICALLY PUT ME HERE TO MAKE SURE THIS EXACT THING YOU DID HERE DIDN'T HAPPEN, AND YOU KNOW HIM.
HE ISN'T THE MOST UNDERSTANDING.
ZEMO IS GOING TO KILL YOU.
THAT'S ALL YOU GOT? YES, WORKING FOR A MADMAN MEANS ONE DAY HE MIGHT TURN ON YOU.
NO. HE TOLD ME HE WAS GOING TO HAVE JIGSAW KILL YOU AS SOON AS I WAS DEAD. SAID HE WOULD NO LONGER NEED THE AVENGERS' WHIPPING BOY IN HIS COUNTRY.
OH MY GOD! ARE YOU SERIOUS?!
YES.

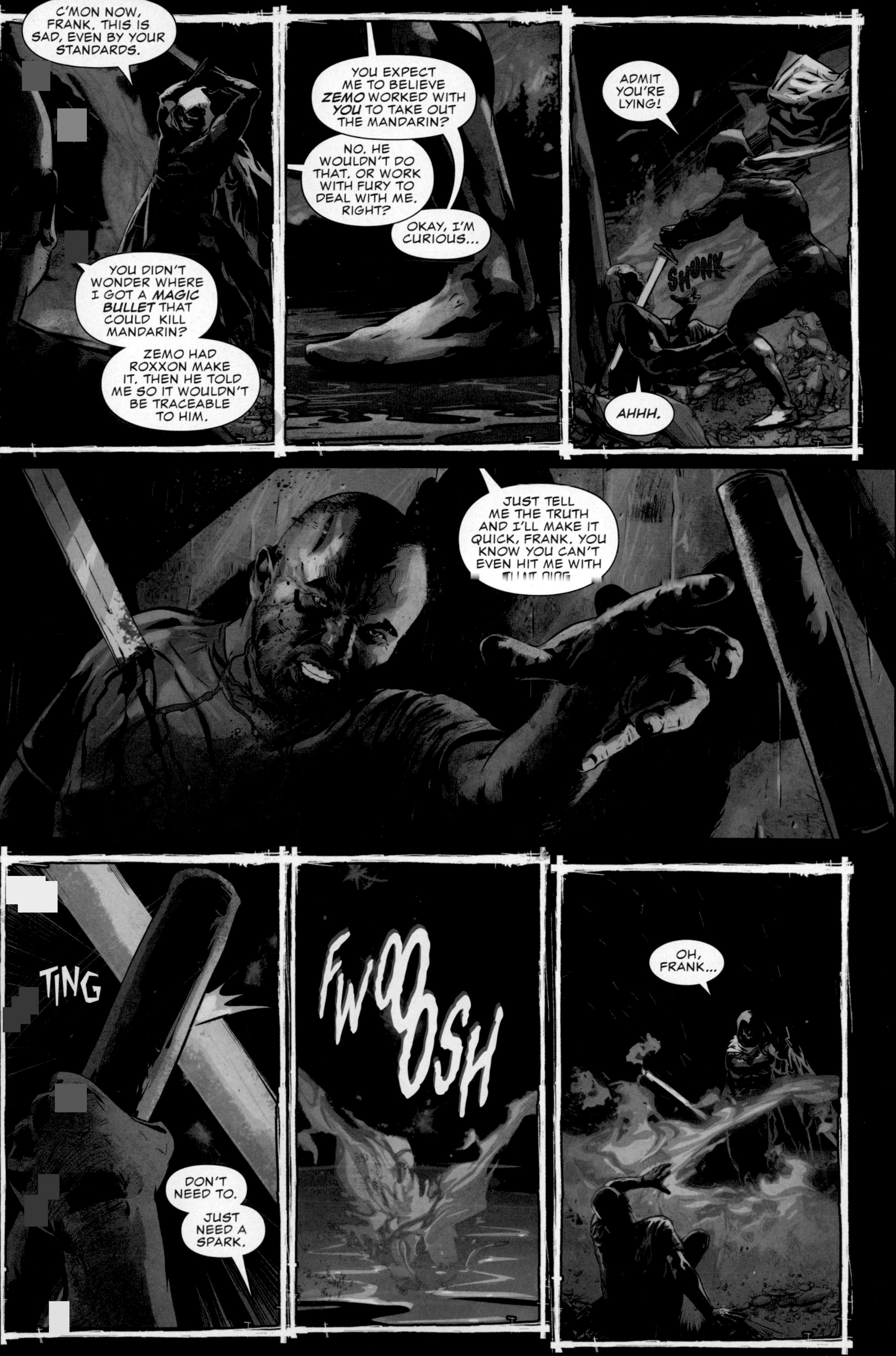
C'MON NOW, FRANK. THIS IS SAD, EVEN BY YOUR STANDARDS.
YOU DIDN'T WONDER WHERE I GOT A *MAGIC BULLET* THAT COULD KILL MANDARIN?
ZEMO HAD ROXXON MAKE IT. THEN HE TOLD ME SO IT WOULDN'T BE TRACEABLE TO HIM.
YOU EXPECT ME TO BELIEVE *ZEMO* WORKED WITH *YOU* TO TAKE OUT THE MANDARIN?
NO. HE WOULDN'T DO THAT. OR WORK WITH FURY TO DEAL WITH ME. RIGHT?
OKAY, I'M CURIOUS...
ADMIT YOU'RE LYING!
SHUNK
AHHH.
JUST TELL ME THE TRUTH AND I'LL MAKE IT QUICK, FRANK. YOU KNOW YOU CAN'T EVEN HIT ME WITH
TING
DON'T NEED TO.
JUST NEED A SPARK.
FWOOOSH
OH, FRANK...

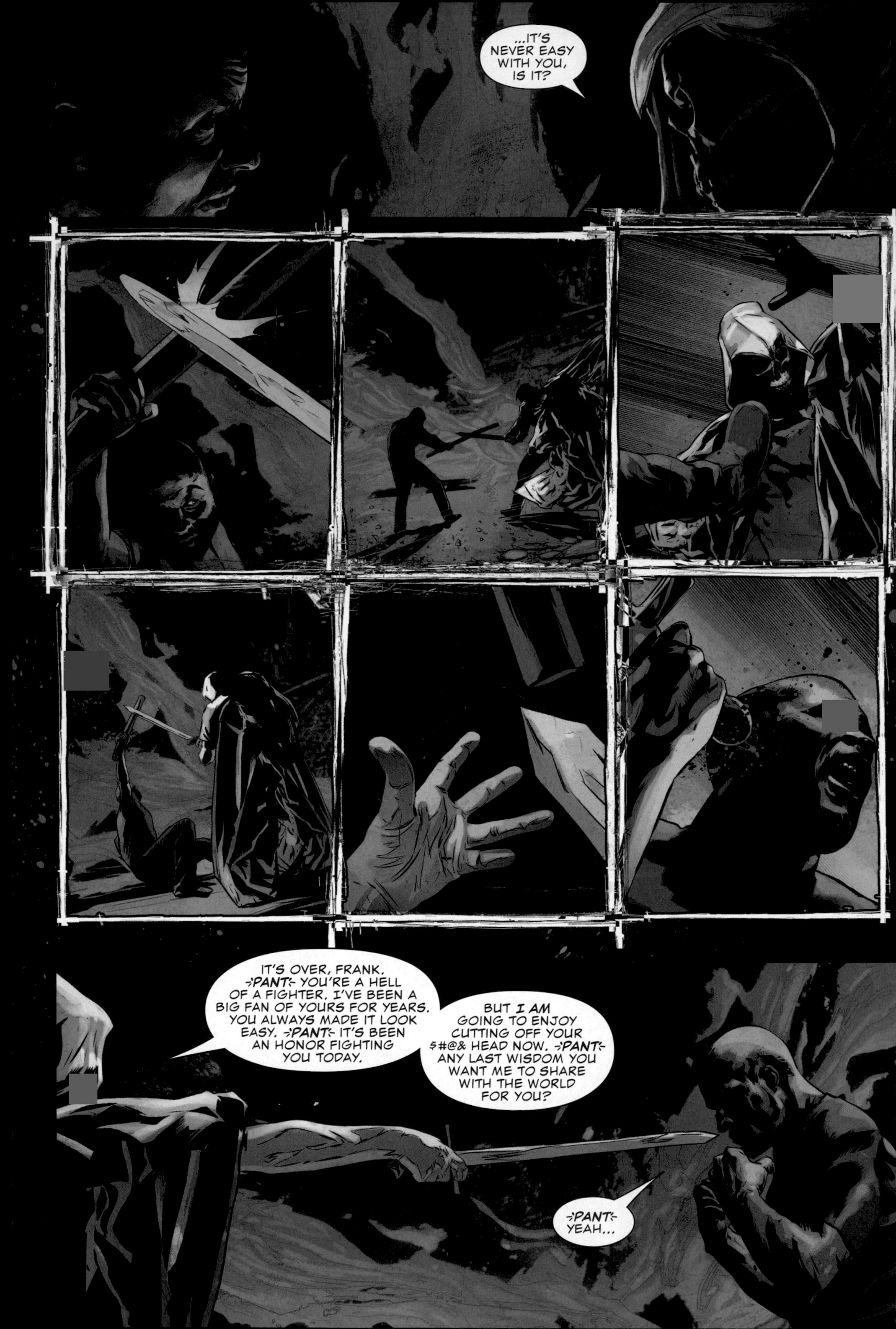
...IT'S NEVER EASY WITH YOU, IS IT?
IT'S OVER, FRANK. -PANT- YOU'RE A HELL OF A FIGHTER. I'VE BEEN A BIG FAN OF YOURS FOR YEARS. YOU ALWAYS MADE IT LOOK EASY. -PANT- IT'S BEEN AN HONOR FIGHTING YOU TODAY.
BUT I AM GOING TO ENJOY CUTTING OFF YOUR $#@& HEAD NOW. -PANT- ANY LAST WISDOM YOU WANT ME TO SHARE WITH THE WORLD FOR YOU?
-PANT- YEAH...

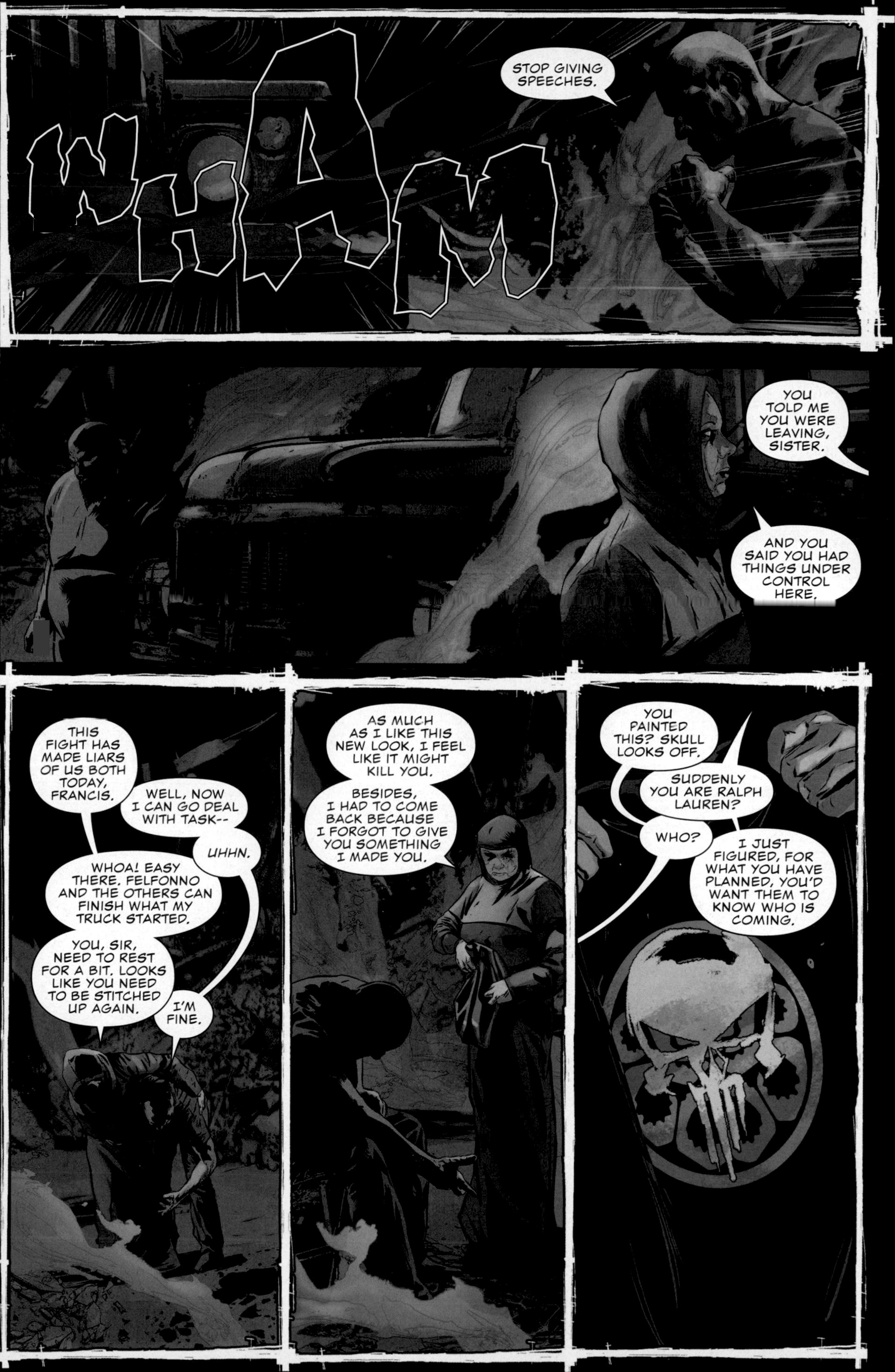
WHAM
STOP GIVING SPEECHES.
YOU TOLD ME YOU WERE LEAVING, SISTER.
AND YOU SAID YOU HAD THINGS UNDER CONTROL HERE.
THIS FIGHT HAS MADE LIARS OF US BOTH TODAY, FRANCIS.
WELL, NOW I CAN GO DEAL WITH TASK--
UHHN.
WHOA! EASY THERE. FELFONNO AND THE OTHERS CAN FINISH WHAT MY TRUCK STARTED.
YOU, SIR, NEED TO REST FOR A BIT. LOOKS LIKE YOU NEED TO BE STITCHED UP AGAIN.
I'M FINE.
AS MUCH AS I LIKE THIS NEW LOOK, I FEEL LIKE IT MIGHT KILL YOU.
BESIDES, I HAD TO COME BACK BECAUSE I FORGOT TO GIVE YOU SOMETHING I MADE YOU.
YOU PAINTED THIS? SKULL LOOKS OFF.
SUDDENLY YOU ARE RALPH LAUREN?
WHO?
I JUST FIGURED, FOR WHAT YOU HAVE PLANNED, YOU'D WANT THEM TO KNOW WHO IS COMING.

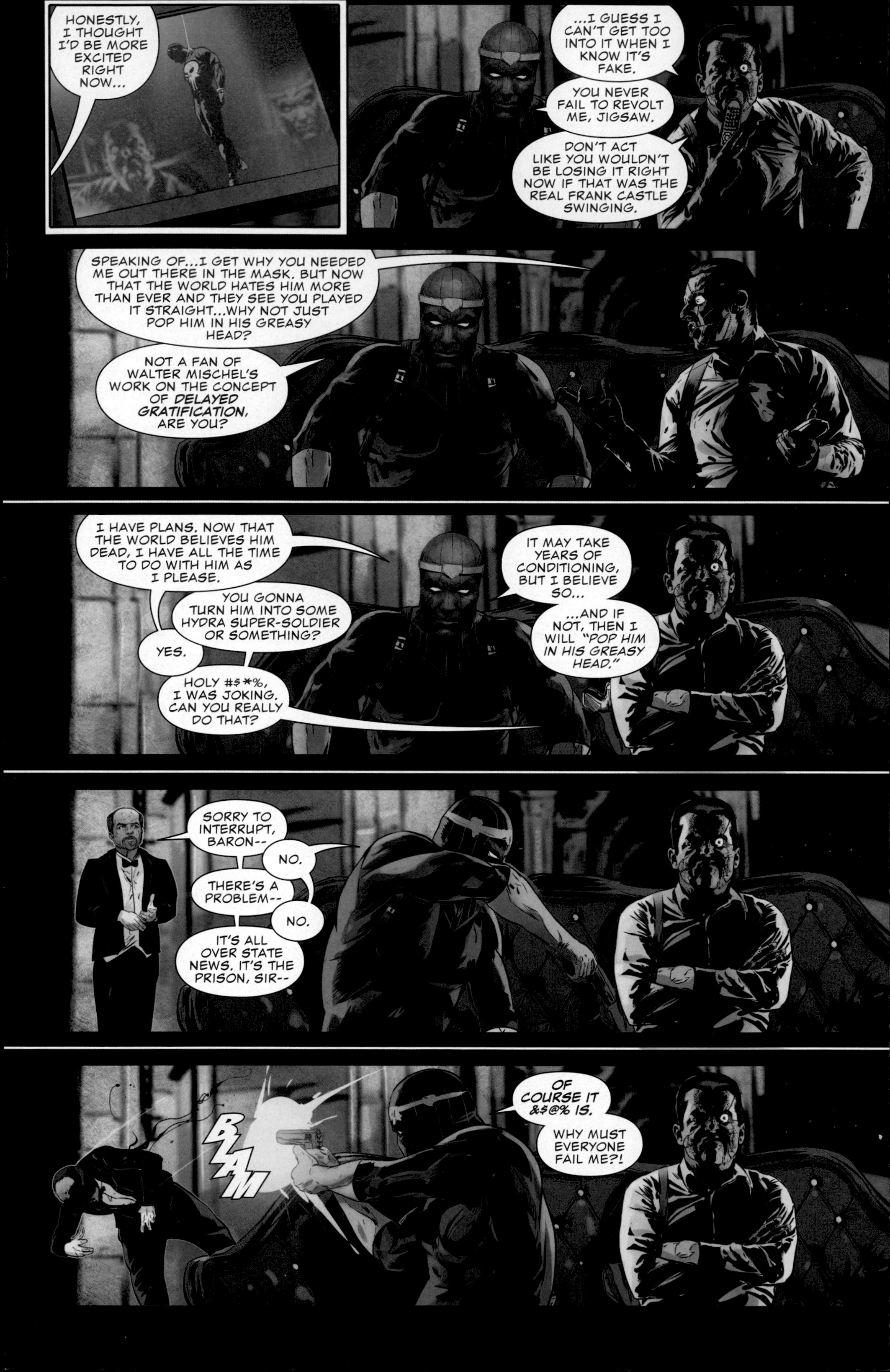
HONESTLY, I THOUGHT I'D BE MORE EXCITED RIGHT NOW...
...I GUESS I CAN'T GET TOO INTO IT WHEN I KNOW IT'S FAKE.
YOU NEVER FAIL TO REVOLT ME, JIGSAW.
DON'T ACT LIKE YOU WOULDN'T BE LOSING IT RIGHT NOW IF THAT WAS THE REAL FRANK CASTLE SWINGING.
SPEAKING OF...I GET WHY YOU NEEDED ME OUT THERE IN THE MASK. BUT NOW THAT THE WORLD HATES HIM MORE THAN EVER AND THEY SEE YOU PLAYED IT STRAIGHT...WHY NOT JUST POP HIM IN HIS GREASY HEAD?
NOT A FAN OF WALTER MISCHEL'S WORK ON THE CONCEPT OF ***DELAYED GRATIFICATION,*** ARE YOU?
I HAVE PLANS. NOW THAT THE WORLD BELIEVES HIM DEAD, I HAVE ALL THE TIME TO DO WITH HIM AS I PLEASE.
YOU GONNA TURN HIM INTO SOME HYDRA SUPER-SOLDIER OR SOMETHING?
YES.
HOLY #$*%, I WAS JOKING. CAN YOU REALLY DO THAT?
IT MAY TAKE YEARS OF CONDITIONING, BUT I BELIEVE SO...
...AND IF NOT, THEN I WILL *"POP HIM IN HIS GREASY HEAD."*
SORRY TO INTERRUPT, BARON--
NO.
THERE'S A PROBLEM--
NO.
IT'S ALL OVER STATE NEWS. IT'S THE PRISON, SIR--
BLAM
OF COURSE IT &$@% IS.
WHY MUST EVERYONE FAIL ME?!

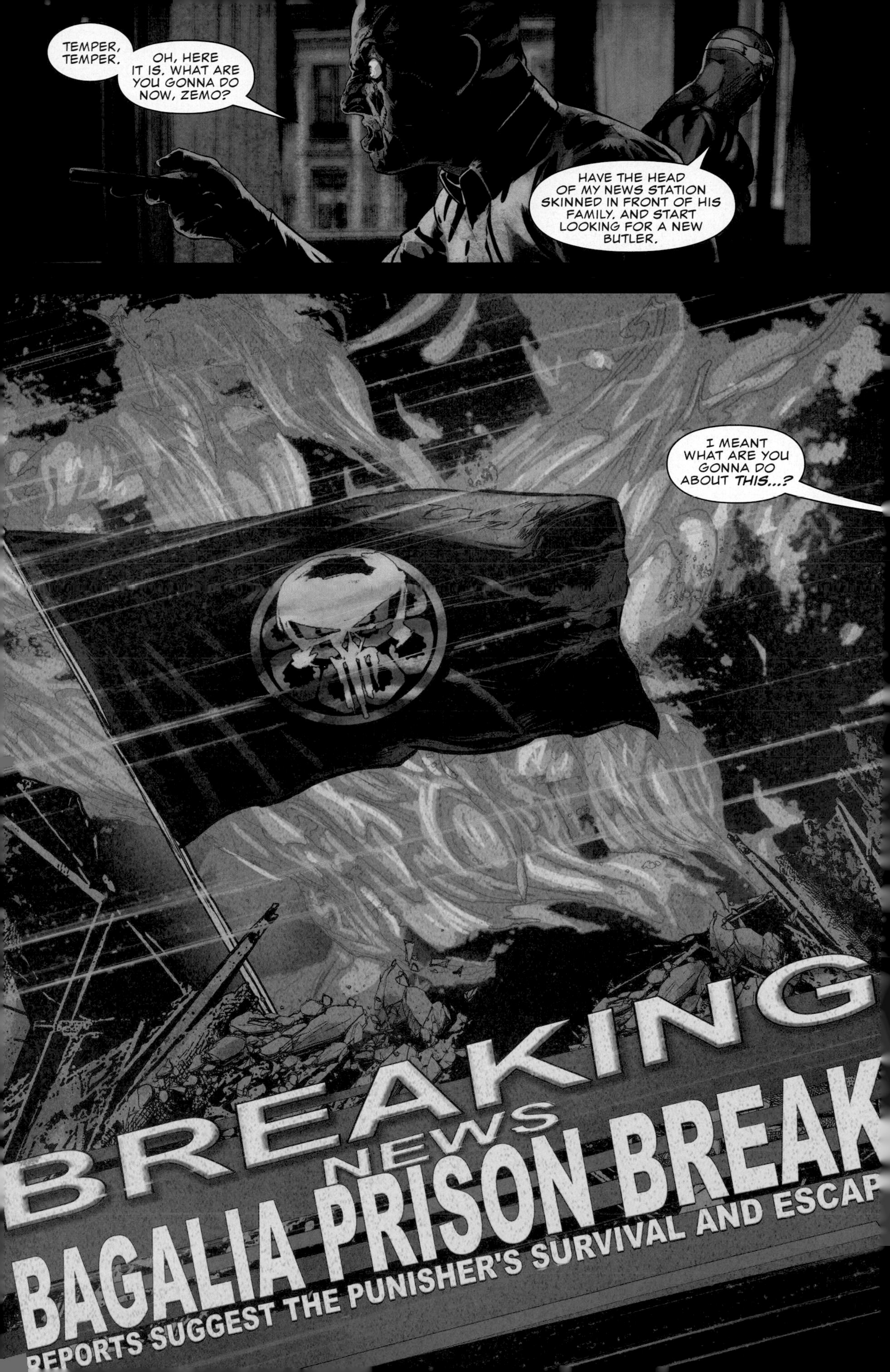
TEMPER, TEMPER.
OH, HERE IT IS. WHAT ARE YOU GONNA DO NOW, ZEMO?
HAVE THE HEAD OF MY NEWS STATION SKINNED IN FRONT OF HIS FAMILY, AND START LOOKING FOR A NEW BUTLER.
I MEANT WHAT ARE YOU GONNA DO ABOUT *THIS...?*
BREAKING NEWS
BAGALIA PRISON BREAK
REPORTS SUGGEST THE PUNISHER'S SURVIVAL AND ESCAP

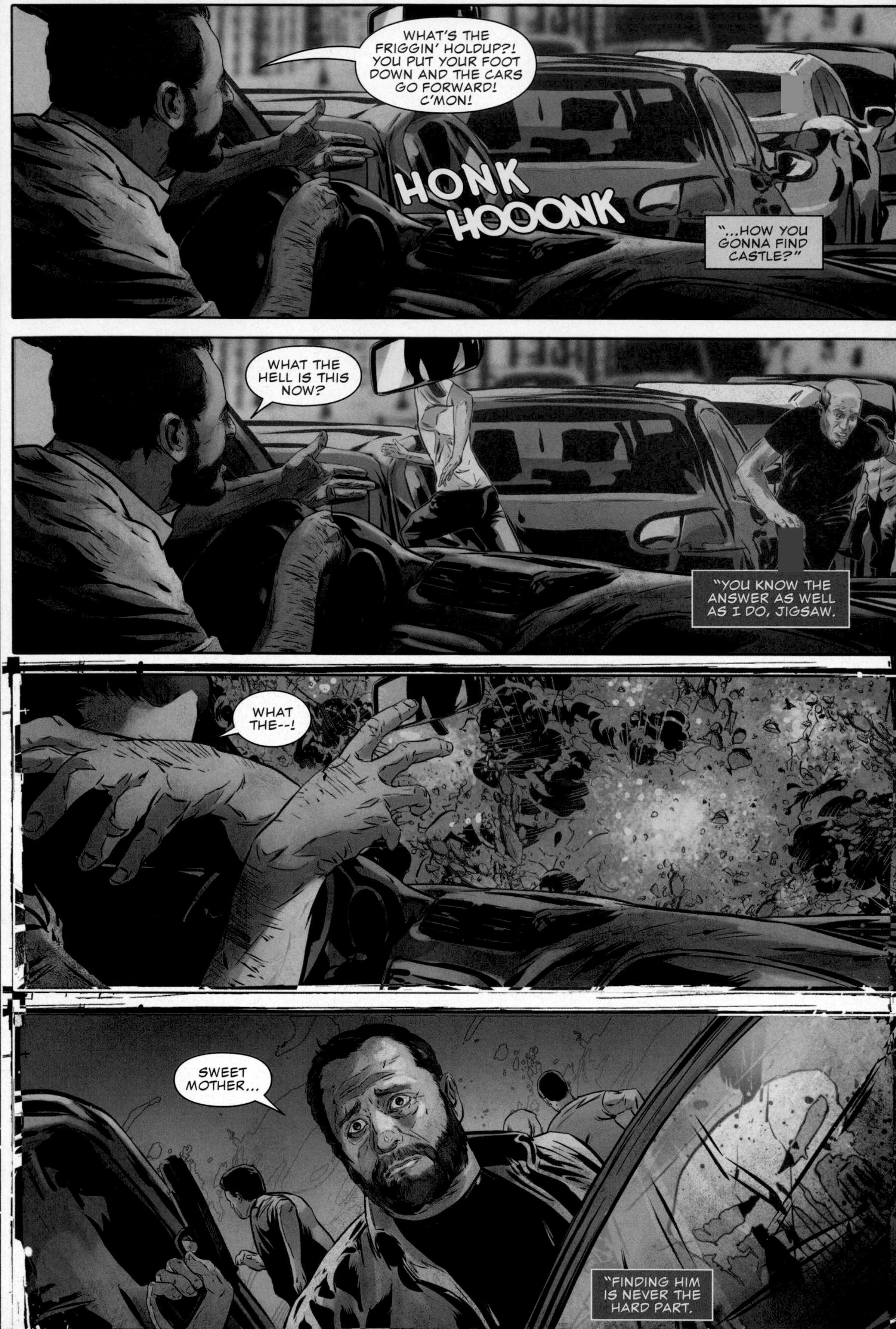
WHAT'S THE FRIGGIN' HOLDUP?! YOU PUT YOUR FOOT DOWN AND THE CARS GO FORWARD! C'MON!
HONK
HOOONK
"...HOW YOU GONNA FIND CASTLE?"
WHAT THE HELL IS THIS NOW?
"YOU KNOW THE ANSWER AS WELL AS I DO, JIGSAW.
WHAT THE--!
SWEET MOTHER...
"FINDING HIM IS NEVER THE HARD PART.

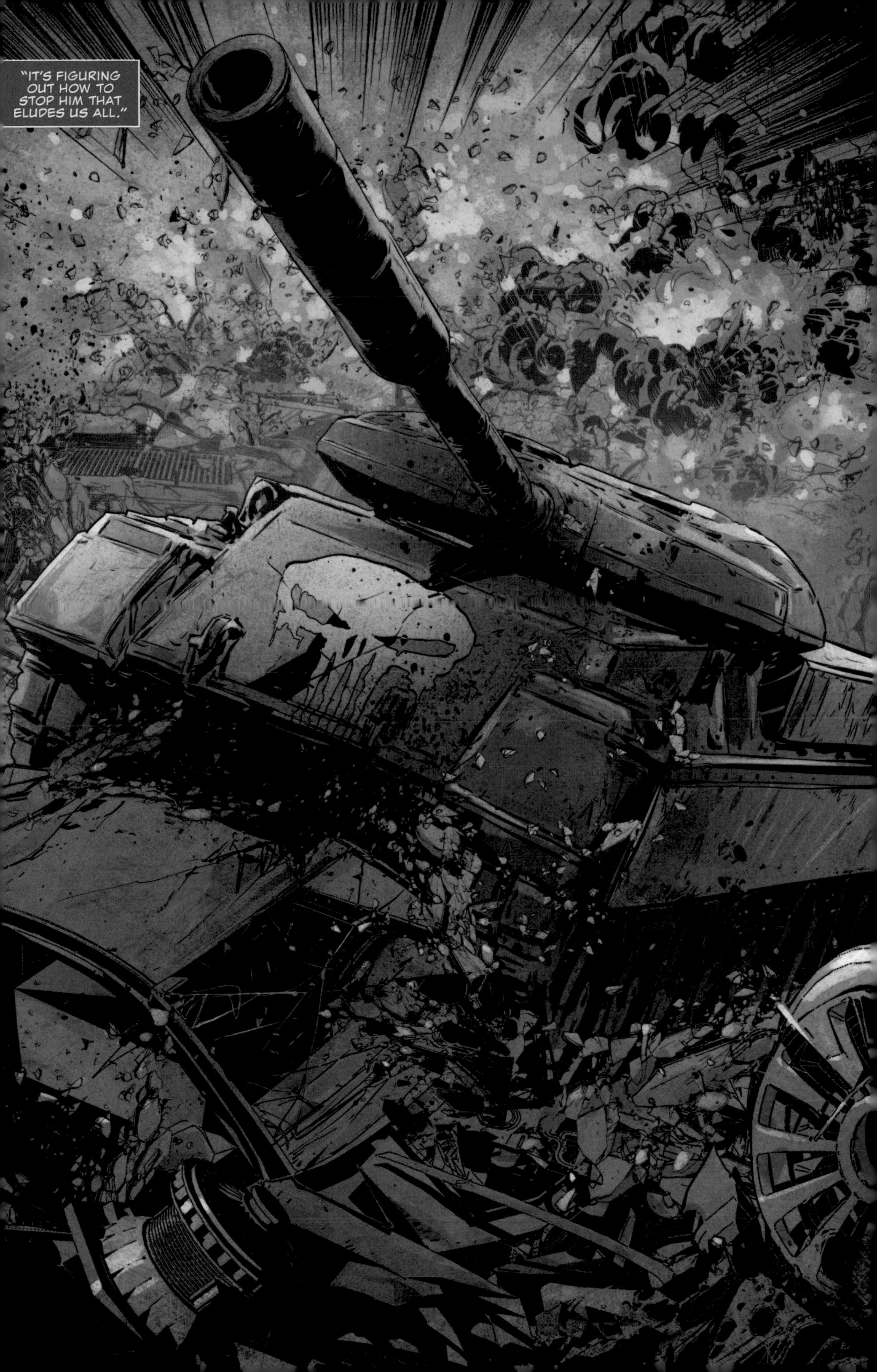
"IT'S FIGURING OUT HOW TO STOP HIM THAT ELUDES US ALL."

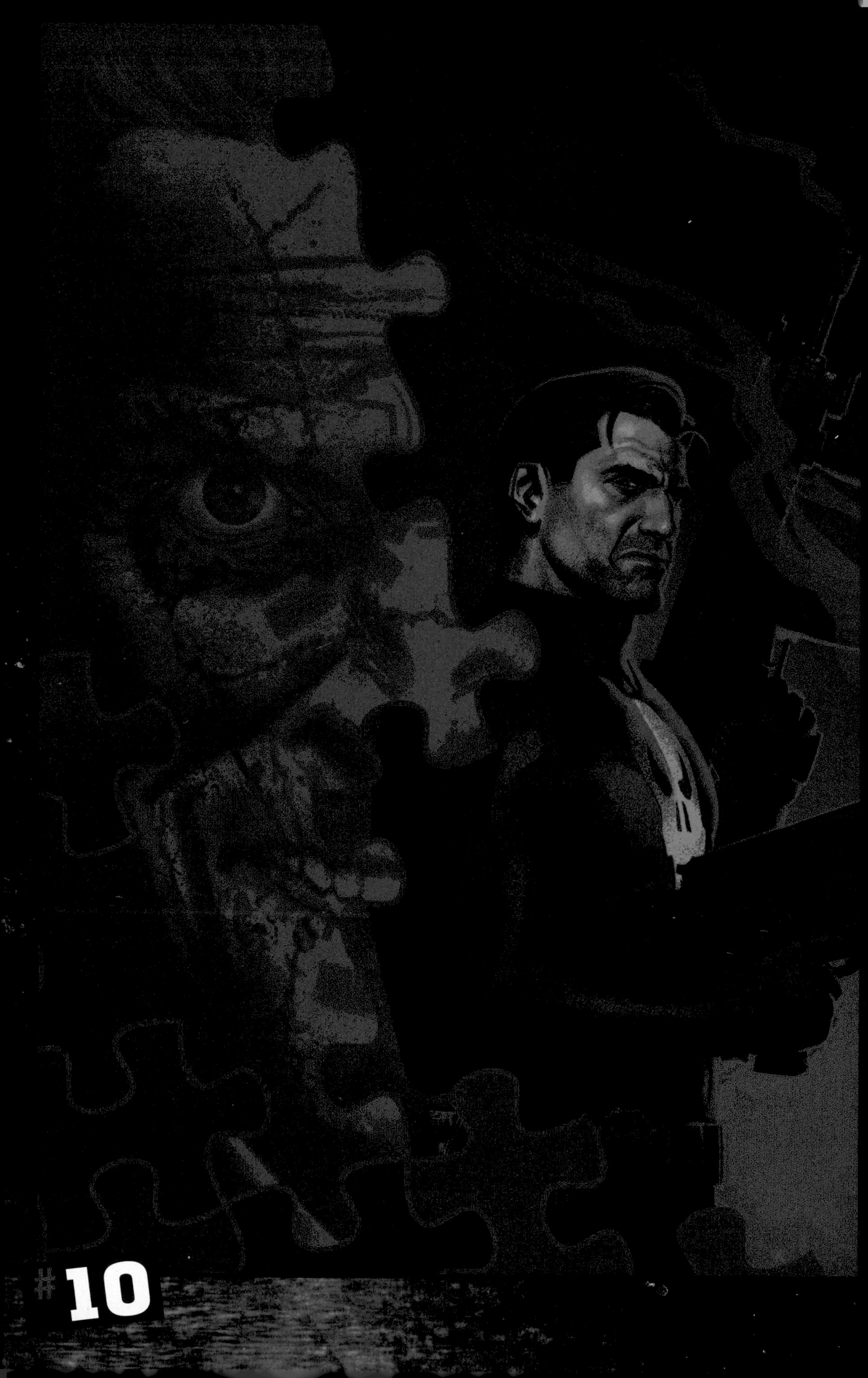
#10

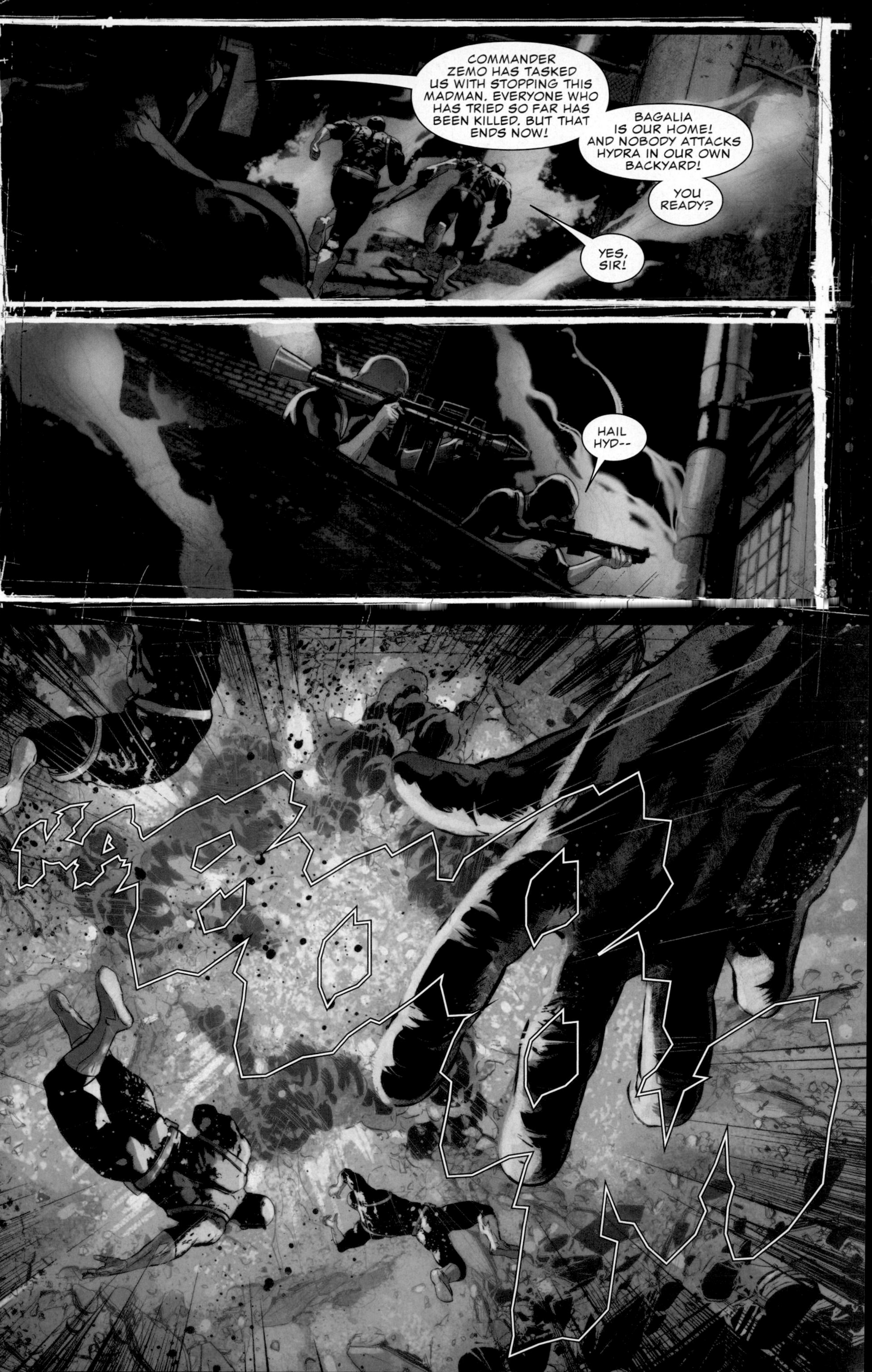
COMMANDER ZEMO HAS TASKED US WITH STOPPING THIS MADMAN. EVERYONE WHO HAS TRIED SO FAR HAS BEEN KILLED. BUT THAT ENDS NOW!
BAGALIA IS OUR HOME! AND NOBODY ATTACKS HYDRA IN OUR OWN BACKYARD!
YOU READY?
YES, SIR!
HAIL HYD--

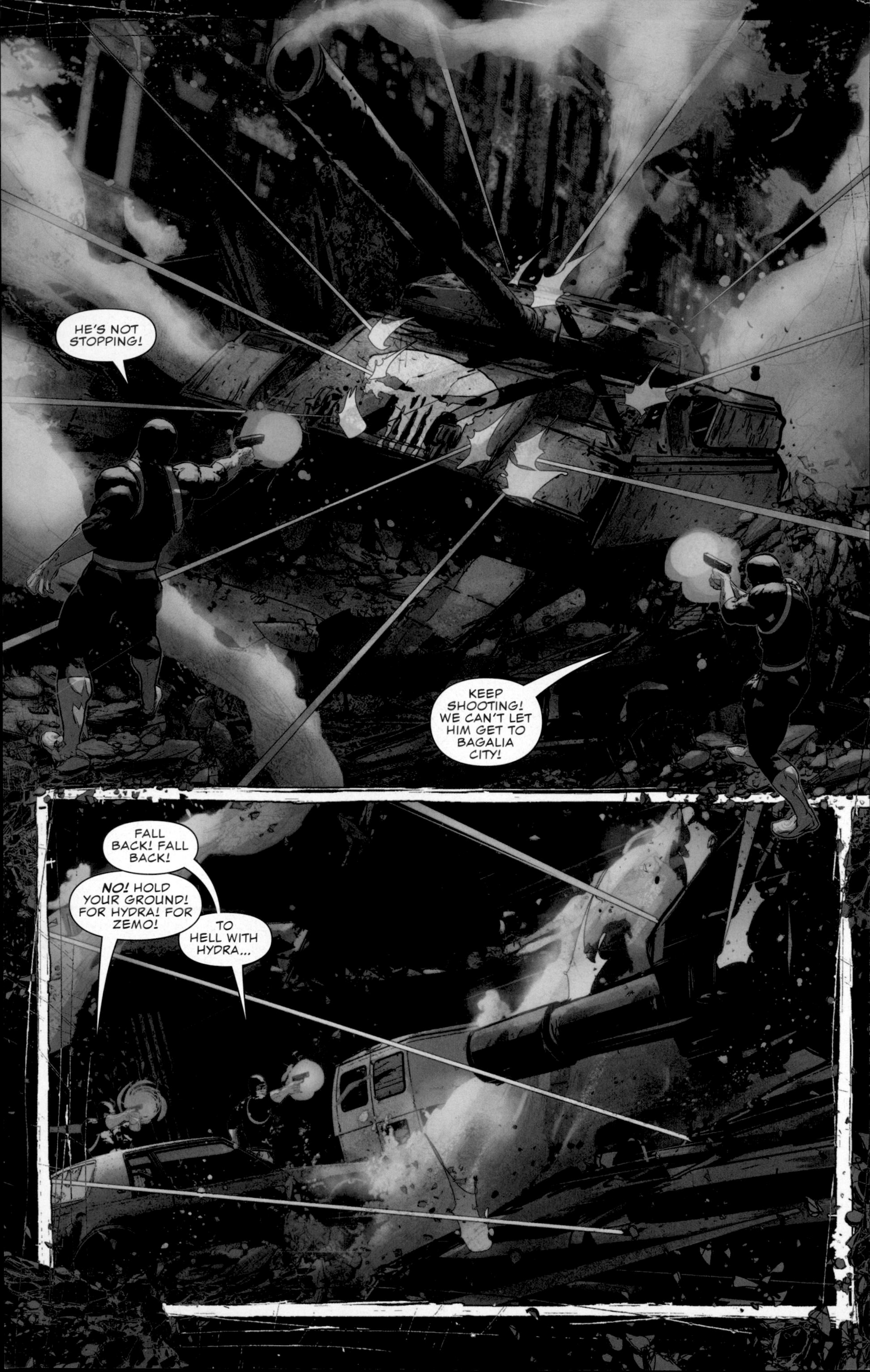
HE'S NOT STOPPING!
KEEP SHOOTING! WE CAN'T LET HIM GET TO BAGALIA CITY!
FALL BACK! FALL BACK!
NO! HOLD YOUR GROUND! FOR HYDRA! FOR ZEMO!
TO HELL WITH HYDRA...

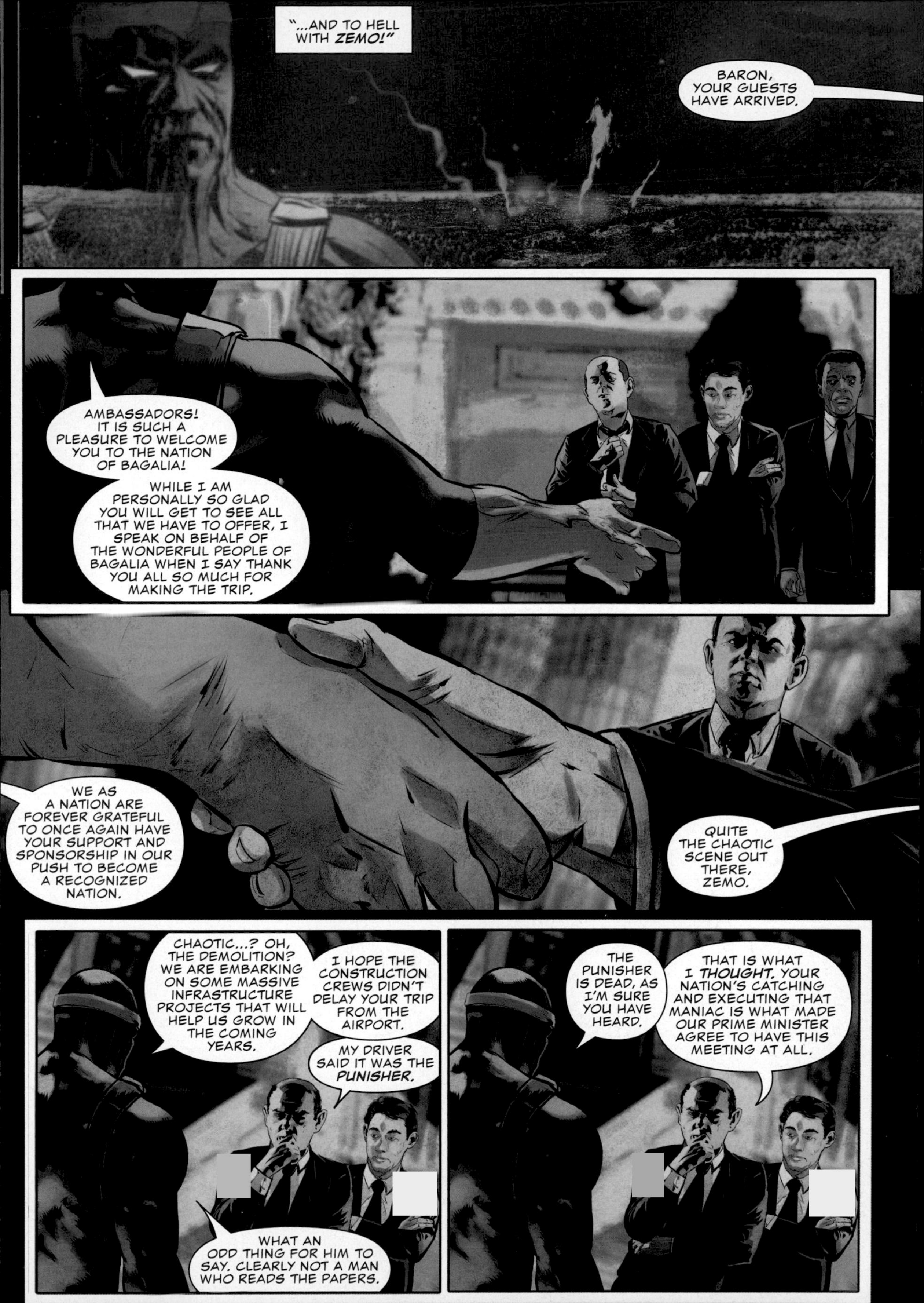

"...AND TO HELL WITH ZEMO!"
BARON, YOUR GUESTS HAVE ARRIVED.
AMBASSADORS! IT IS SUCH A PLEASURE TO WELCOME YOU TO THE NATION OF BAGALIA!
WHILE I AM PERSONALLY SO GLAD YOU WILL GET TO SEE ALL THAT WE HAVE TO OFFER, I SPEAK ON BEHALF OF THE WONDERFUL PEOPLE OF BAGALIA WHEN I SAY THANK YOU ALL SO MUCH FOR MAKING THE TRIP.
WE AS A NATION ARE FOREVER GRATEFUL TO ONCE AGAIN HAVE YOUR SUPPORT AND SPONSORSHIP IN OUR PUSH TO BECOME A RECOGNIZED NATION.
QUITE THE CHAOTIC SCENE OUT THERE, ZEMO.
CHAOTIC...? OH, THE DEMOLITION? WE ARE EMBARKING ON SOME MASSIVE INFRASTRUCTURE PROJECTS THAT WILL HELP US GROW IN THE COMING YEARS.
I HOPE THE CONSTRUCTION CREWS DIDN'T DELAY YOUR TRIP FROM THE AIRPORT.
MY DRIVER SAID IT WAS THE PUNISHER.
WHAT AN ODD THING FOR HIM TO SAY. CLEARLY NOT A MAN WHO READS THE PAPERS.
THE PUNISHER IS DEAD, AS I'M SURE YOU HAVE HEARD.
THAT IS WHAT I THOUGHT. YOUR NATION'S CATCHING AND EXECUTING THAT MANIAC IS WHAT MADE OUR PRIME MINISTER AGREE TO HAVE THIS MEETING AT ALL.

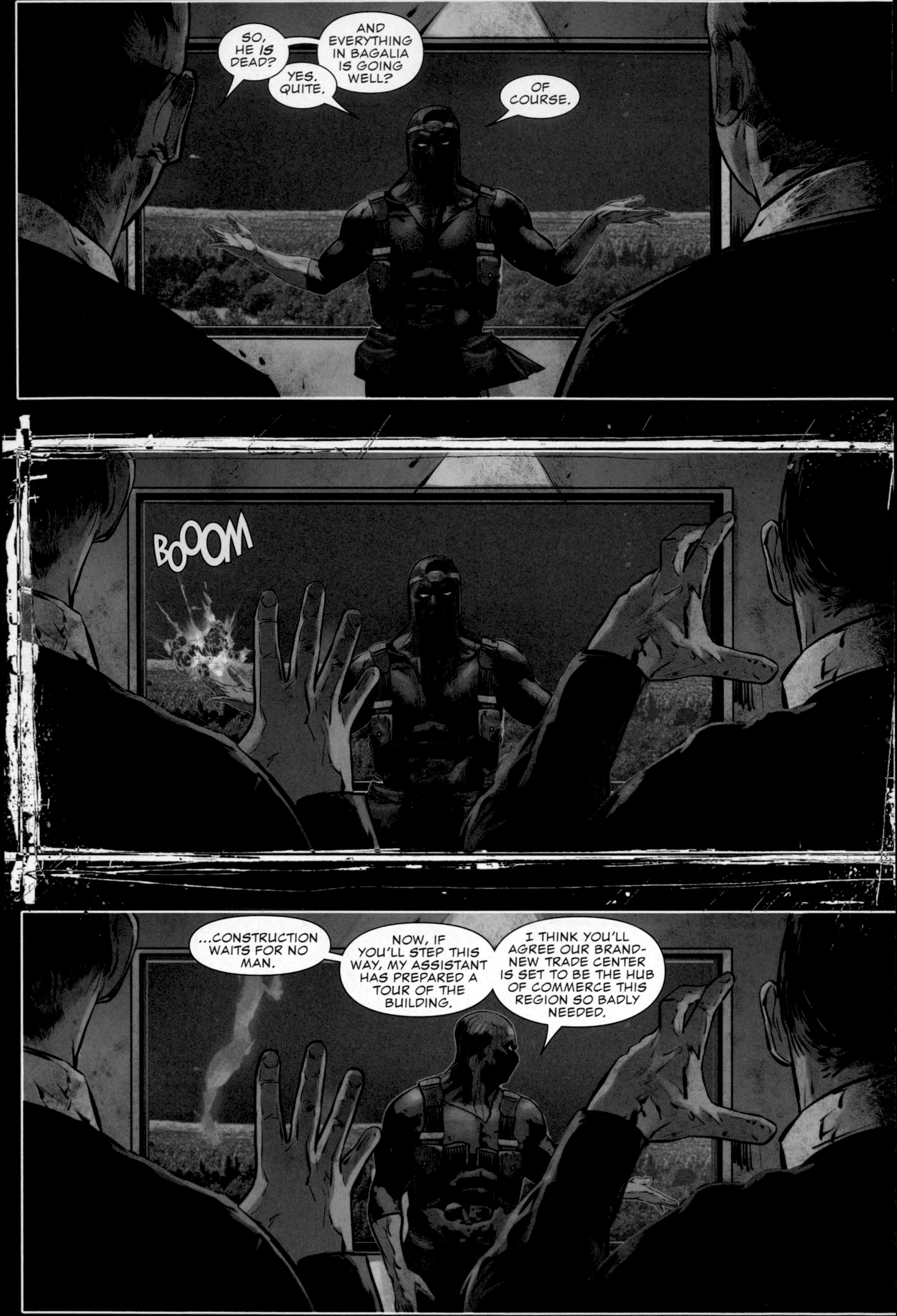

SO, HE IS DEAD?
YES. QUITE.
AND EVERYTHING IN BAGALIA IS GOING WELL?
OF COURSE.
BOOOM
...CONSTRUCTION WAITS FOR NO MAN.
NOW, IF YOU'LL STEP THIS WAY, MY ASSISTANT HAS PREPARED A TOUR OF THE BUILDING.
I THINK YOU'LL AGREE OUR BRAND-NEW TRADE CENTER IS SET TO BE THE HUB OF COMMERCE THIS REGION SO BADLY NEEDED.

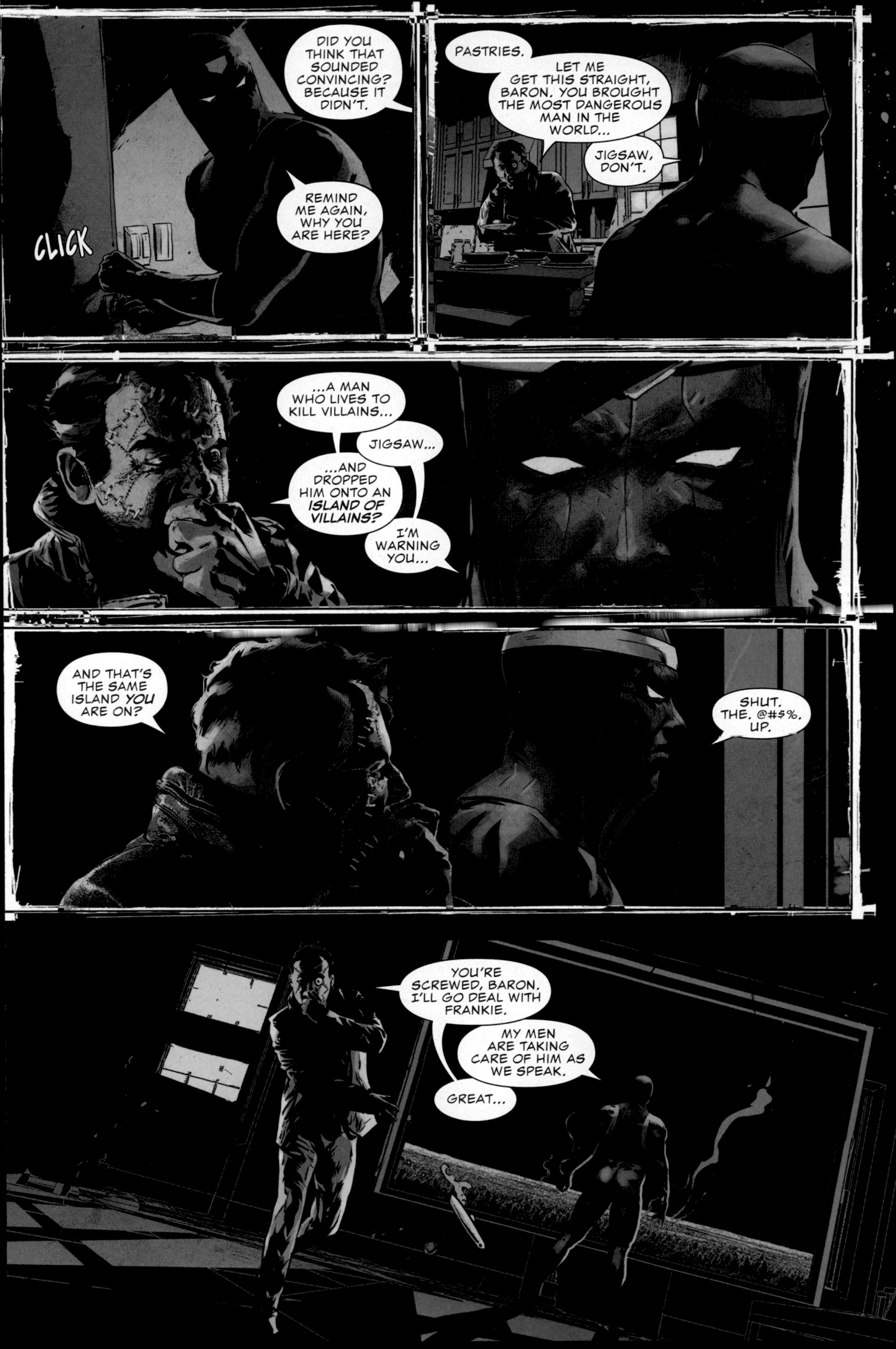
DID YOU THINK THAT SOUNDED CONVINCING? BECAUSE IT DIDN'T.
REMIND ME AGAIN, WHY YOU ARE HERE?
CLICK
PASTRIES.
LET ME GET THIS STRAIGHT, BARON. YOU BROUGHT THE MOST DANGEROUS MAN IN THE WORLD...
JIGSAW, DON'T.
...A MAN WHO LIVES TO KILL VILLAINS...
JIGSAW...
...AND DROPPED HIM ONTO AN ISLAND OF VILLAINS?
I'M WARNING YOU...
AND THAT'S THE SAME ISLAND YOU ARE ON?
SHUT. THE. @#$%. UP.
YOU'RE SCREWED, BARON. I'LL GO DEAL WITH FRANKIE.
MY MEN ARE TAKING CARE OF HIM AS WE SPEAK.
GREAT...

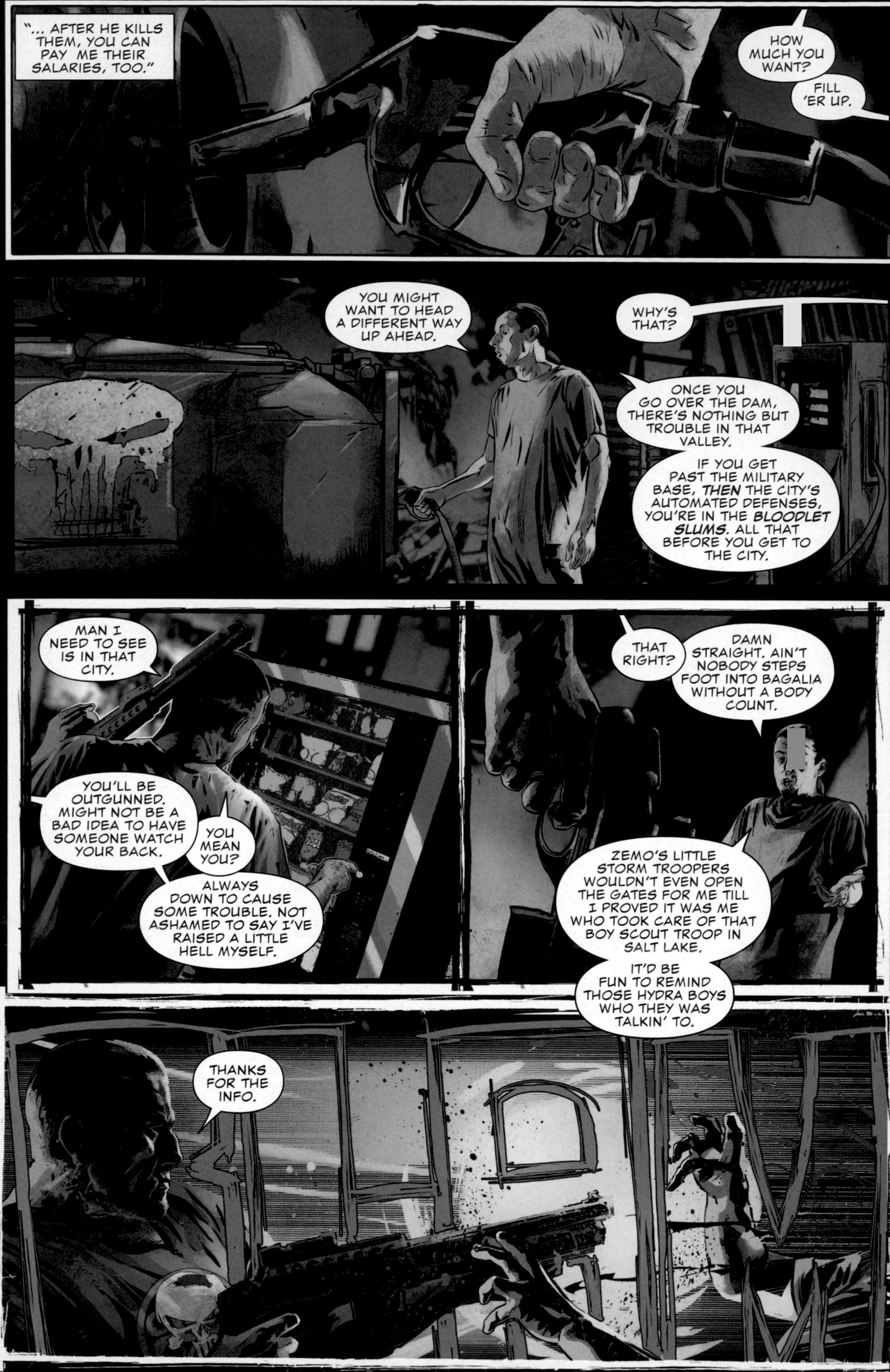
"... AFTER HE KILLS THEM, YOU CAN PAY ME THEIR SALARIES, TOO."
HOW MUCH YOU WANT?
FILL 'ER UP.
YOU MIGHT WANT TO HEAD A DIFFERENT WAY UP AHEAD.
WHY'S THAT?
ONCE YOU GO OVER THE DAM, THERE'S NOTHING BUT TROUBLE IN THAT VALLEY.
IF YOU GET PAST THE MILITARY BASE, THEN THE CITY'S AUTOMATED DEFENSES, YOU'RE IN THE BLOODLET SLUMS. ALL THAT BEFORE YOU GET TO THE CITY.
MAN I NEED TO SEE IS IN THAT CITY.
YOU'LL BE OUTGUNNED. MIGHT NOT BE A BAD IDEA TO HAVE SOMEONE WATCH YOUR BACK.
YOU MEAN YOU?
ALWAYS DOWN TO CAUSE SOME TROUBLE. NOT ASHAMED TO SAY I'VE RAISED A LITTLE HELL MYSELF.
THAT RIGHT?
DAMN STRAIGHT. AIN'T NOBODY STEPS FOOT INTO BAGALIA WITHOUT A BODY COUNT.
ZEMO'S LITTLE STORM TROOPERS WOULDN'T EVEN OPEN THE GATES FOR ME TILL I PROVED IT WAS ME WHO TOOK CARE OF THAT BOY SCOUT TROOP IN SALT LAKE.
IT'D BE FUN TO REMIND THOSE HYDRA BOYS WHO THEY WAS TALKIN' TO.
THANKS FOR THE INFO.

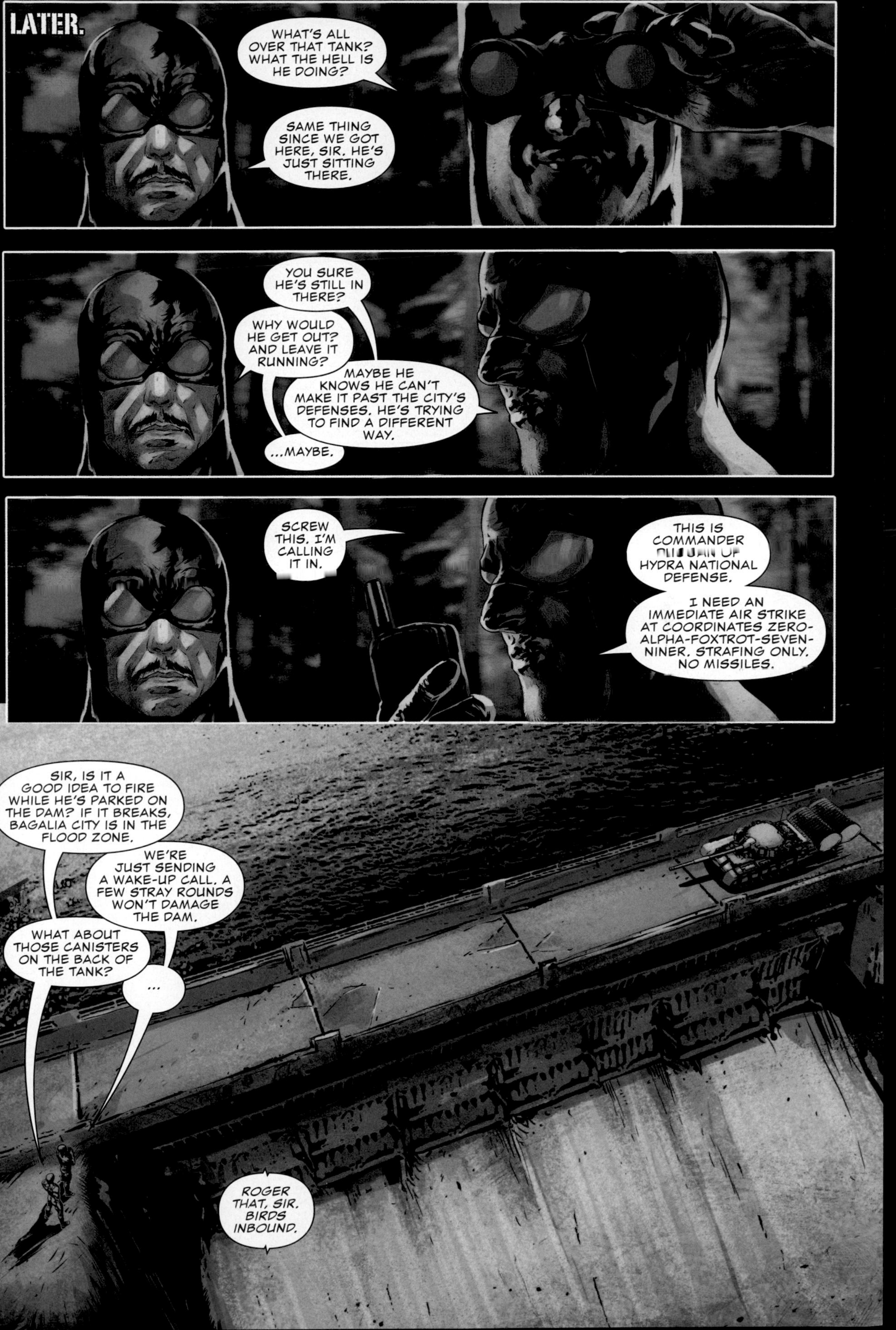

LATER.
WHAT'S ALL OVER THAT TANK? WHAT THE HELL IS HE DOING?
SAME THING SINCE WE GOT HERE, SIR. HE'S JUST SITTING THERE.
YOU SURE HE'S STILL IN THERE?
WHY WOULD HE GET OUT? AND LEAVE IT RUNNING?
MAYBE HE KNOWS HE CAN'T MAKE IT PAST THE CITY'S DEFENSES. HE'S TRYING TO FIND A DIFFERENT WAY.
...MAYBE.
SCREW THIS. I'M CALLING IT IN.
THIS IS COMMANDER
HYDRA NATIONAL DEFENSE.
I NEED AN IMMEDIATE AIR STRIKE AT COORDINATES ZERO-ALPHA-FOXTROT-SEVEN-NINER. STRAFING ONLY. NO MISSILES.
SIR, IS IT A GOOD IDEA TO FIRE WHILE HE'S PARKED ON THE DAM? IF IT BREAKS, BAGALIA CITY IS IN THE FLOOD ZONE.
WE'RE JUST SENDING A WAKE-UP CALL. A FEW STRAY ROUNDS WON'T DAMAGE THE DAM.
WHAT ABOUT THOSE CANISTERS ON THE BACK OF THE TANK?
...
ROGER THAT, SIR. BIRDS INBOUND.

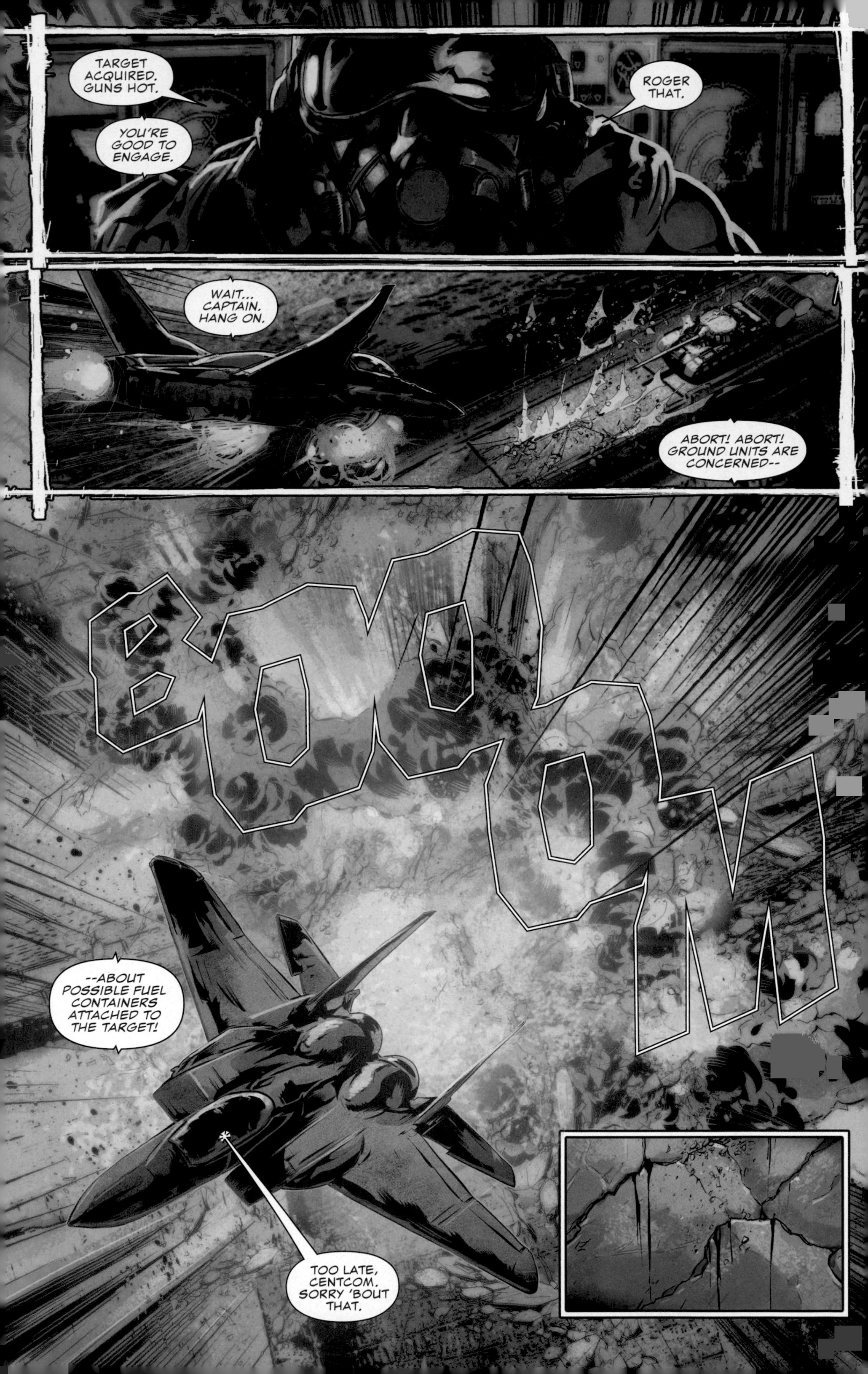
TARGET ACQUIRED. GUNS HOT.
YOU'RE GOOD TO ENGAGE.
ROGER THAT.
WAIT... CAPTAIN. HANG ON.
ABORT! ABORT! GROUND UNITS ARE CONCERNED--
BOOOOM
--ABOUT POSSIBLE FUEL CONTAINERS ATTACHED TO THE TARGET!
TOO LATE, CENTCOM. SORRY 'BOUT THAT.

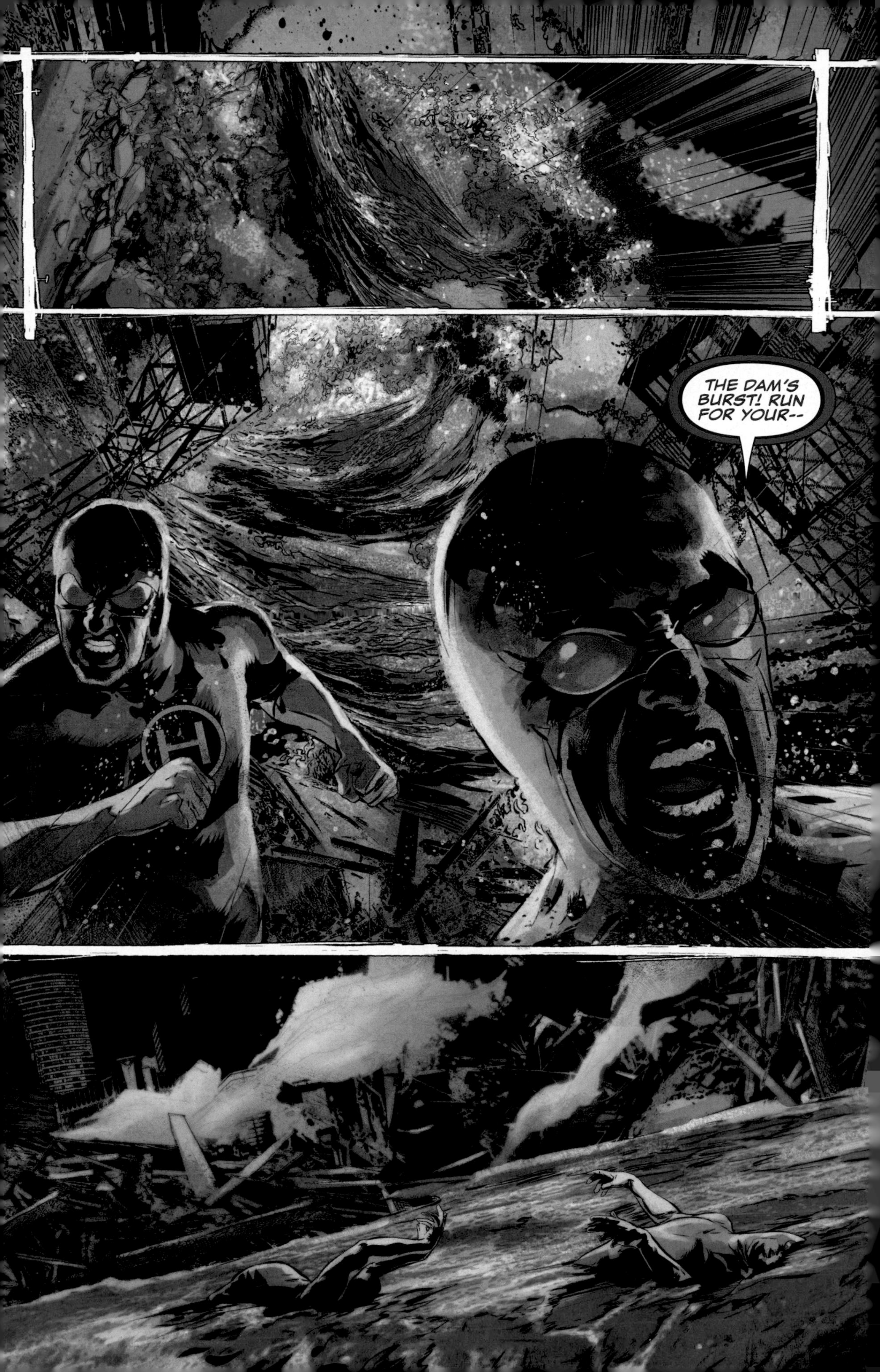
THE DAM'S BURST! RUN FOR YOUR--

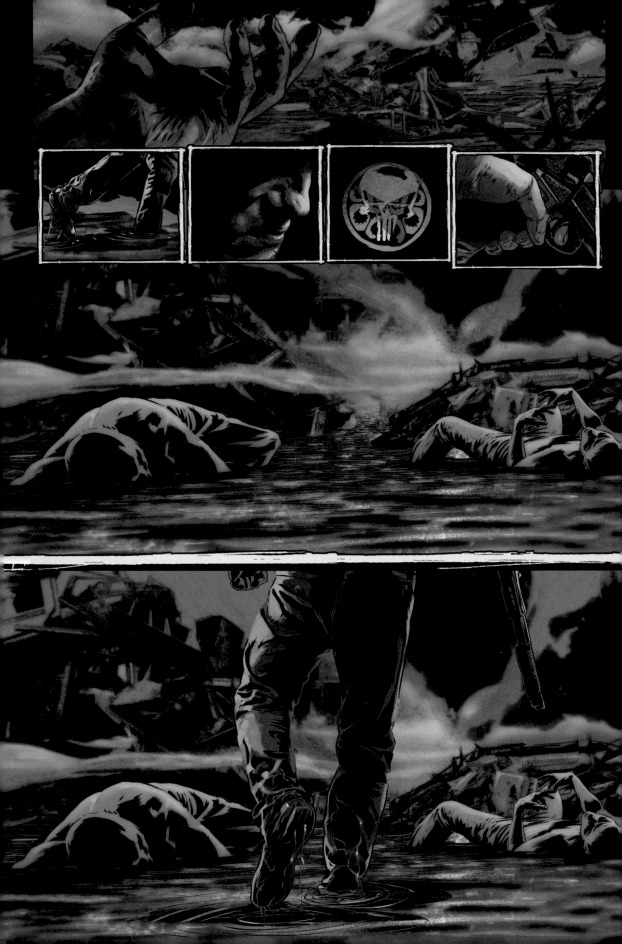

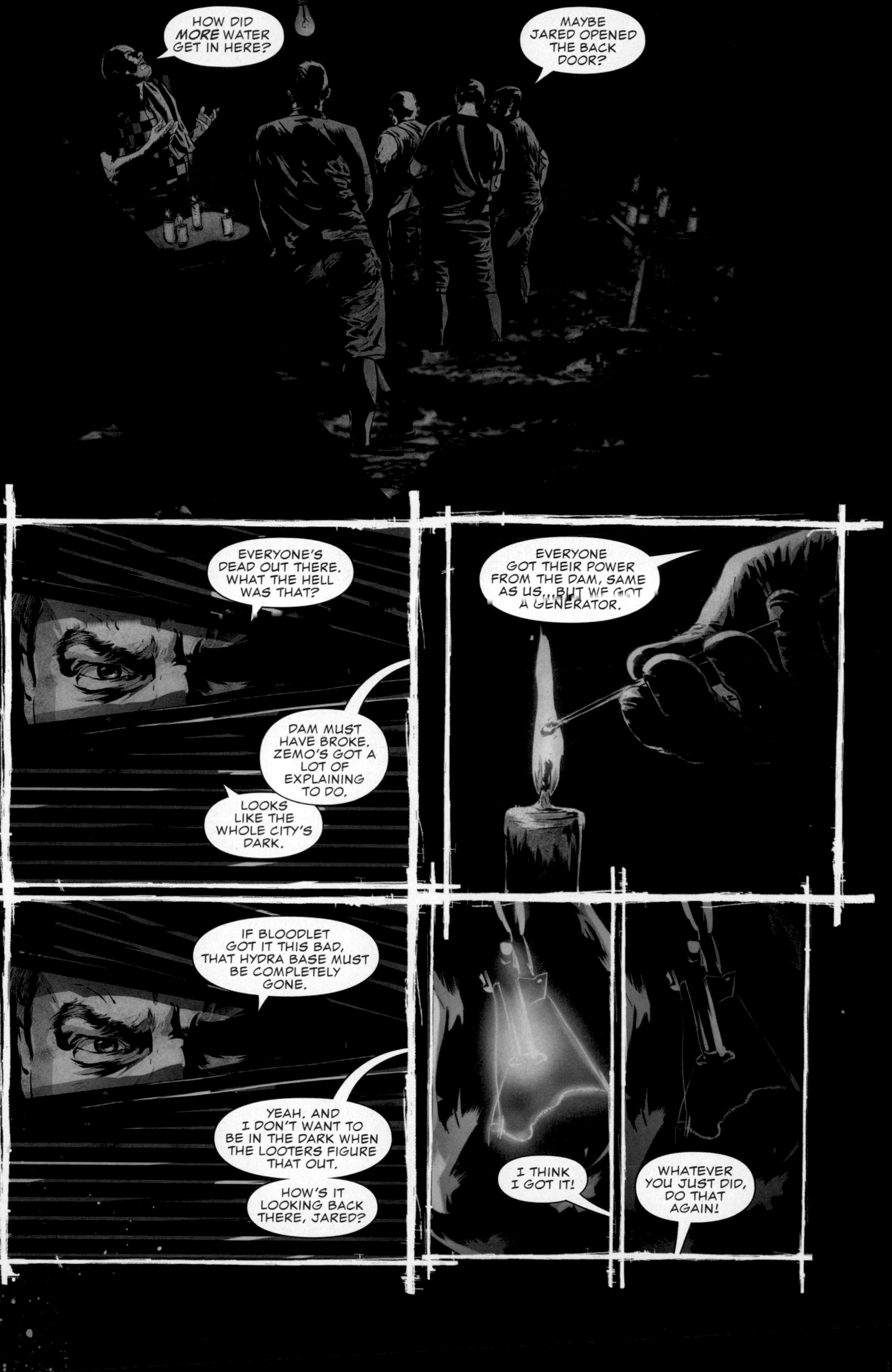
HOW DID MORE WATER GET IN HERE?
MAYBE JARED OPENED THE BACK DOOR?
EVERYONE'S DEAD OUT THERE. WHAT THE HELL WAS THAT?
DAM MUST HAVE BROKE. ZEMO'S GOT A LOT OF EXPLAINING TO DO.
LOOKS LIKE THE WHOLE CITY'S DARK.
EVERYONE GOT THEIR POWER FROM THE DAM, SAME AS US...BUT WE GOT A GENERATOR.
IF BLOODLET GOT IT THIS BAD, THAT HYDRA BASE MUST BE COMPLETELY GONE.
YEAH. AND I DON'T WANT TO BE IN THE DARK WHEN THE LOOTERS FIGURE THAT OUT.
HOW'S IT LOOKING BACK THERE, JARED?
I THINK I GOT IT!
WHATEVER YOU JUST DID, DO THAT AGAIN!

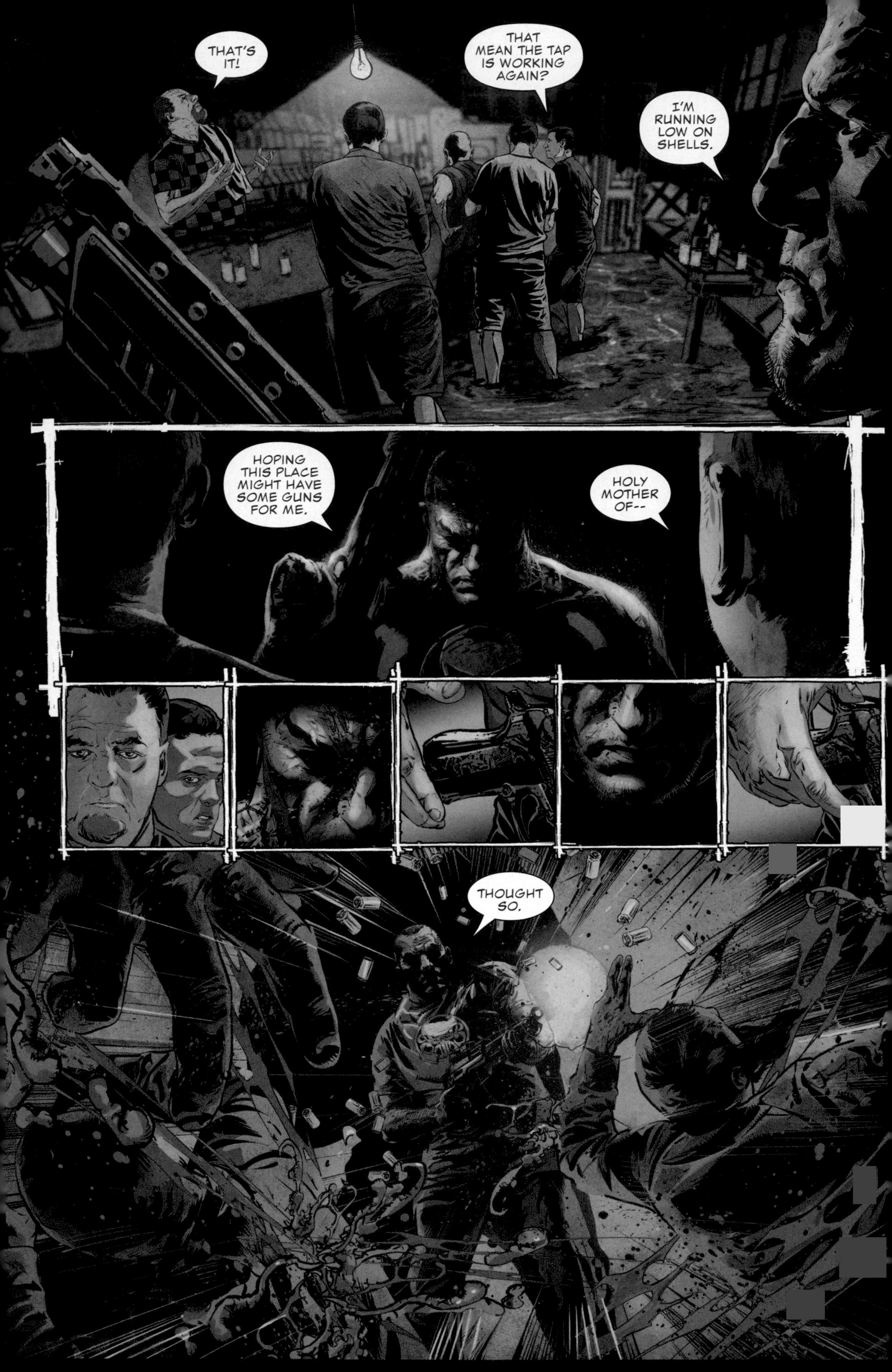
THAT'S IT!
THAT MEAN THE TAP IS WORKING AGAIN?
I'M RUNNING LOW ON SHELLS.
HOPING THIS PLACE MIGHT HAVE SOME GUNS FOR ME.
HOLY MOTHER OF--
THOUGHT SO.

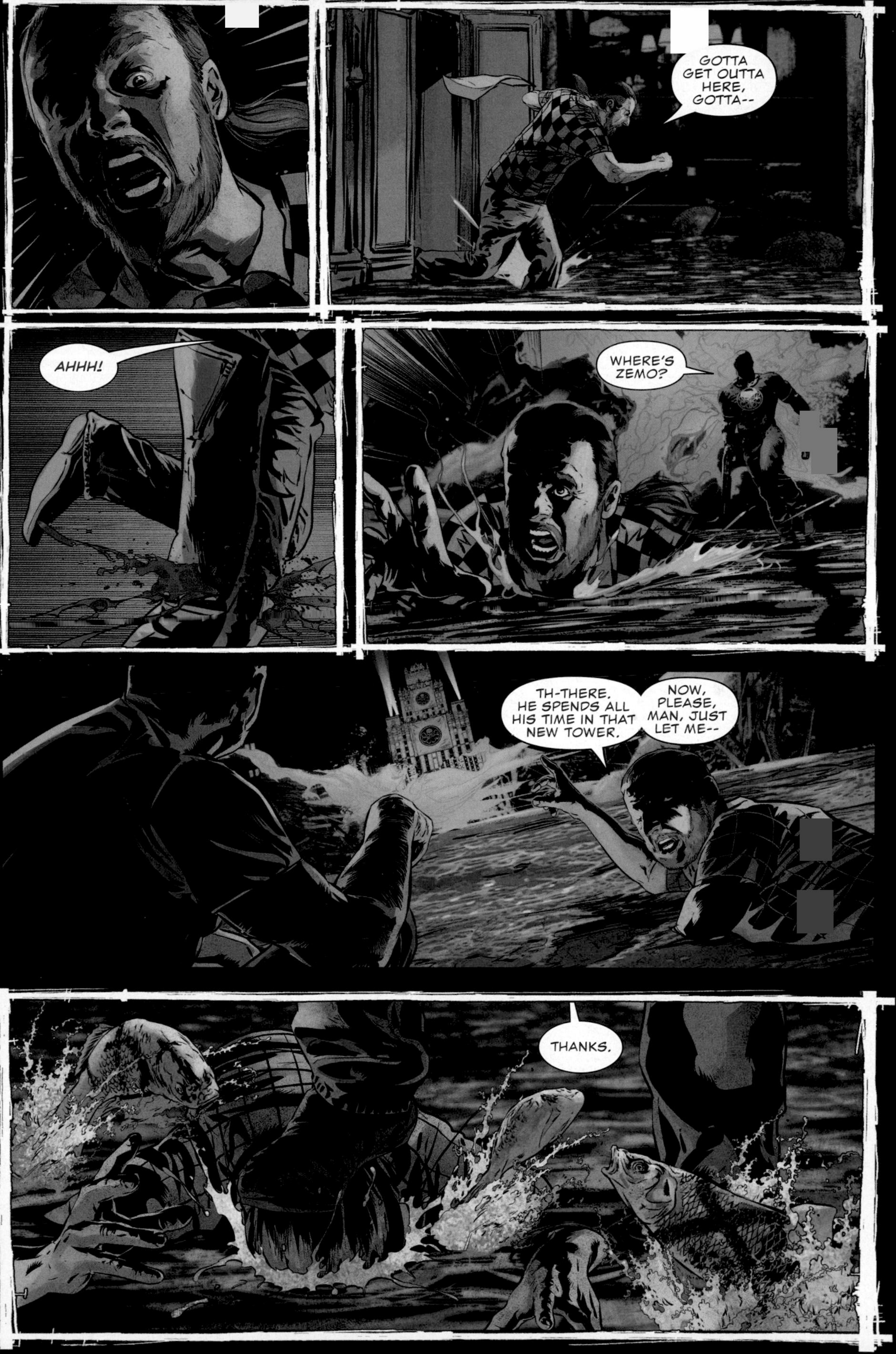
GOTTA GET OUTTA HERE, GOTTA--
AHHH!
WHERE'S ZEMO?
TH-THERE. HE SPENDS ALL HIS TIME IN THAT NEW TOWER.
NOW, PLEASE, MAN, JUST LET ME--
THANKS.

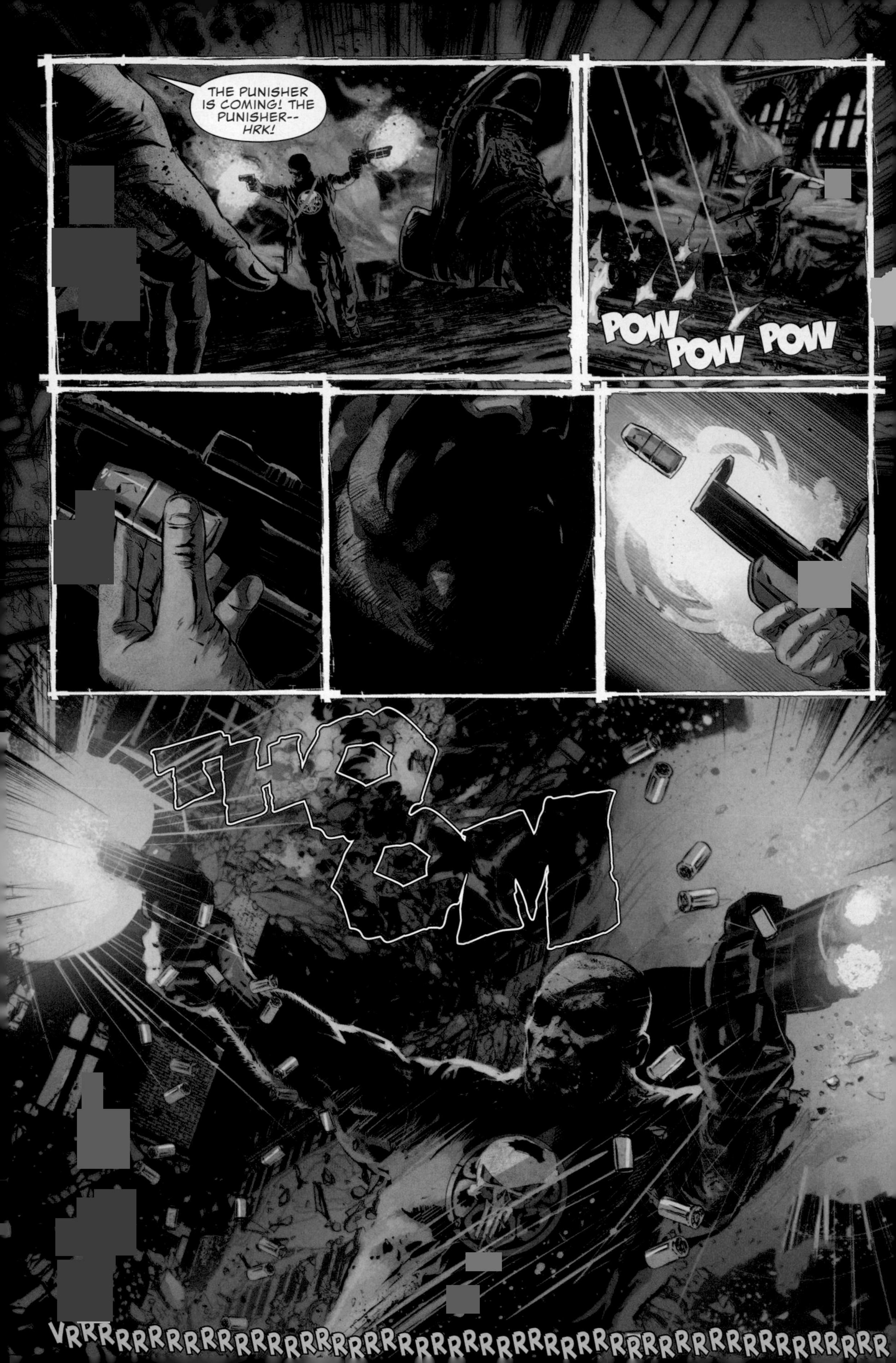
THE PUNISHER IS COMING! THE PUNISHER-- HRK!
POW
POW
POW
THOOM
VRRRRRRRRRRRRRRRRRRRRRRRRRRRRRRRRRRRRRRRRRRRRRRRRR

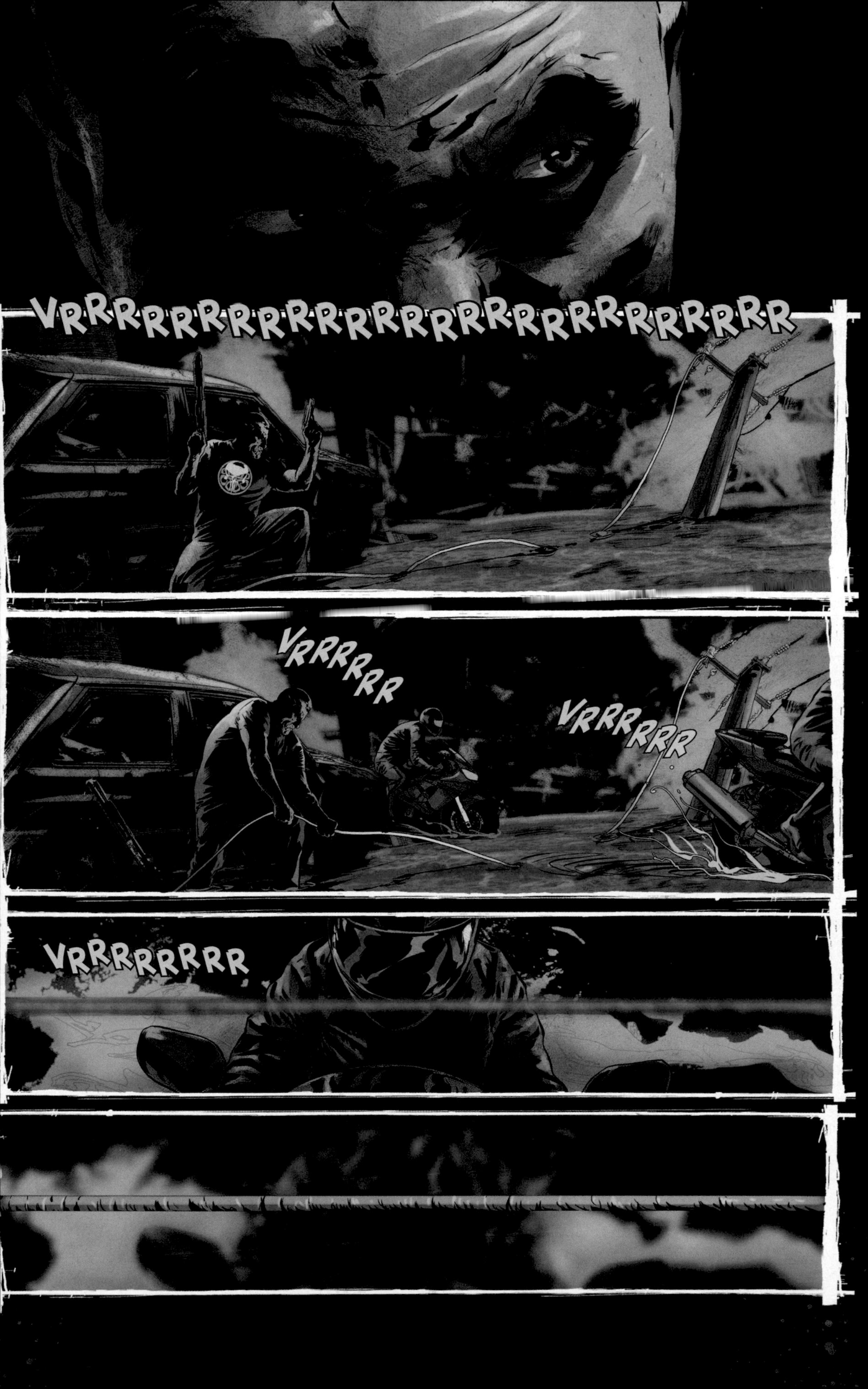

VRRRRRRRRRRRRRRRRRRRRRRRRRR
VRRRRRR
VRRRRRRR
VRRRRRRRR

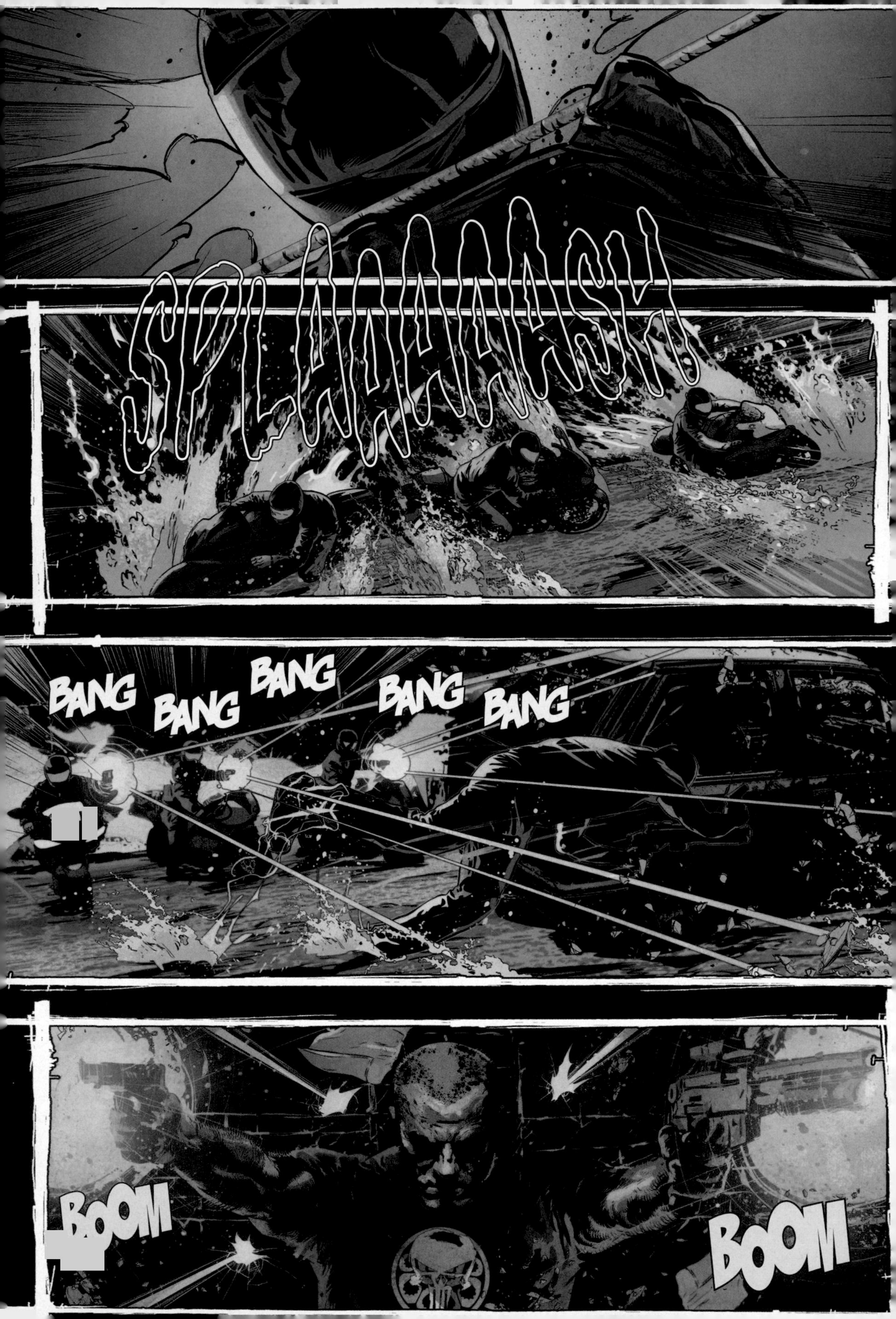
SPLAAAASH
BANG
BANG
BANG
BANG
BANG
BOOM
BOOM

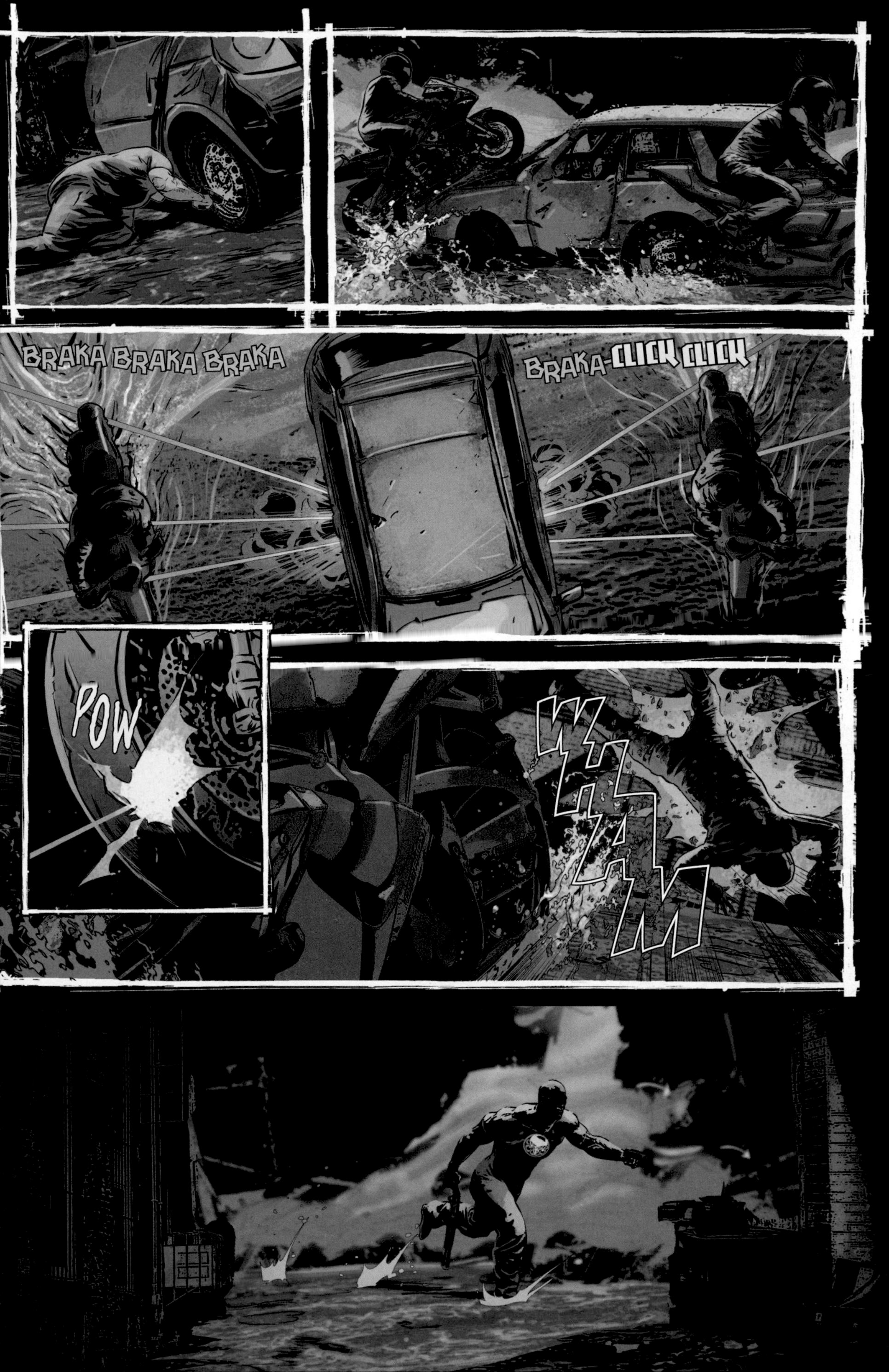
BRAKA BRAKA BRAKA
BRAKA-CLICK CLICK
POW
WHAM

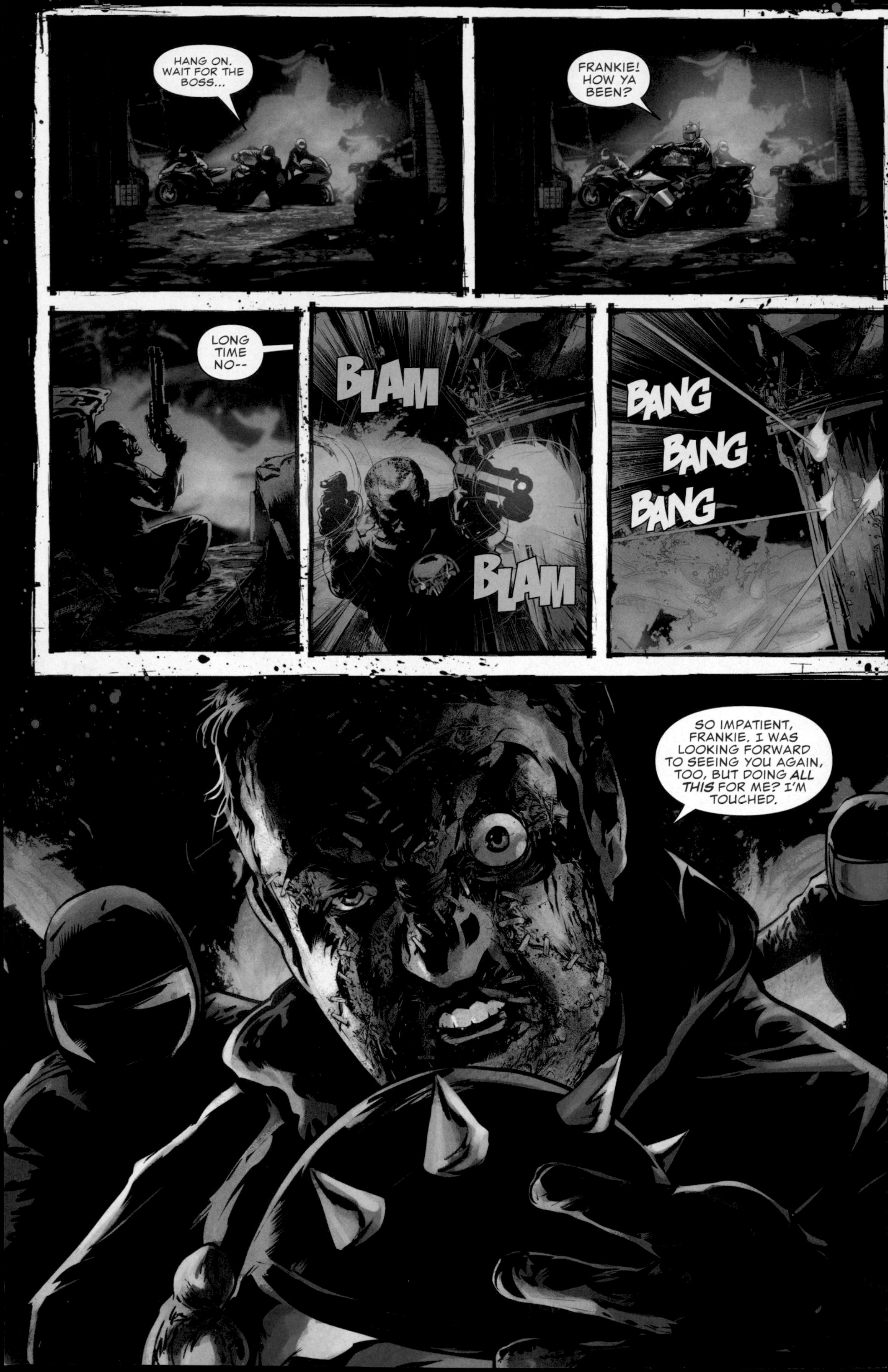
HANG ON. WAIT FOR THE BOSS...
FRANKIE! HOW YA BEEN?
LONG TIME NO--
BLAM
BLAM
BANG
BANG
BANG
SO IMPATIENT, FRANKIE. I WAS LOOKING FORWARD TO SEEING YOU AGAIN, TOO, BUT DOING **ALL THIS** FOR ME? I'M TOUCHED.

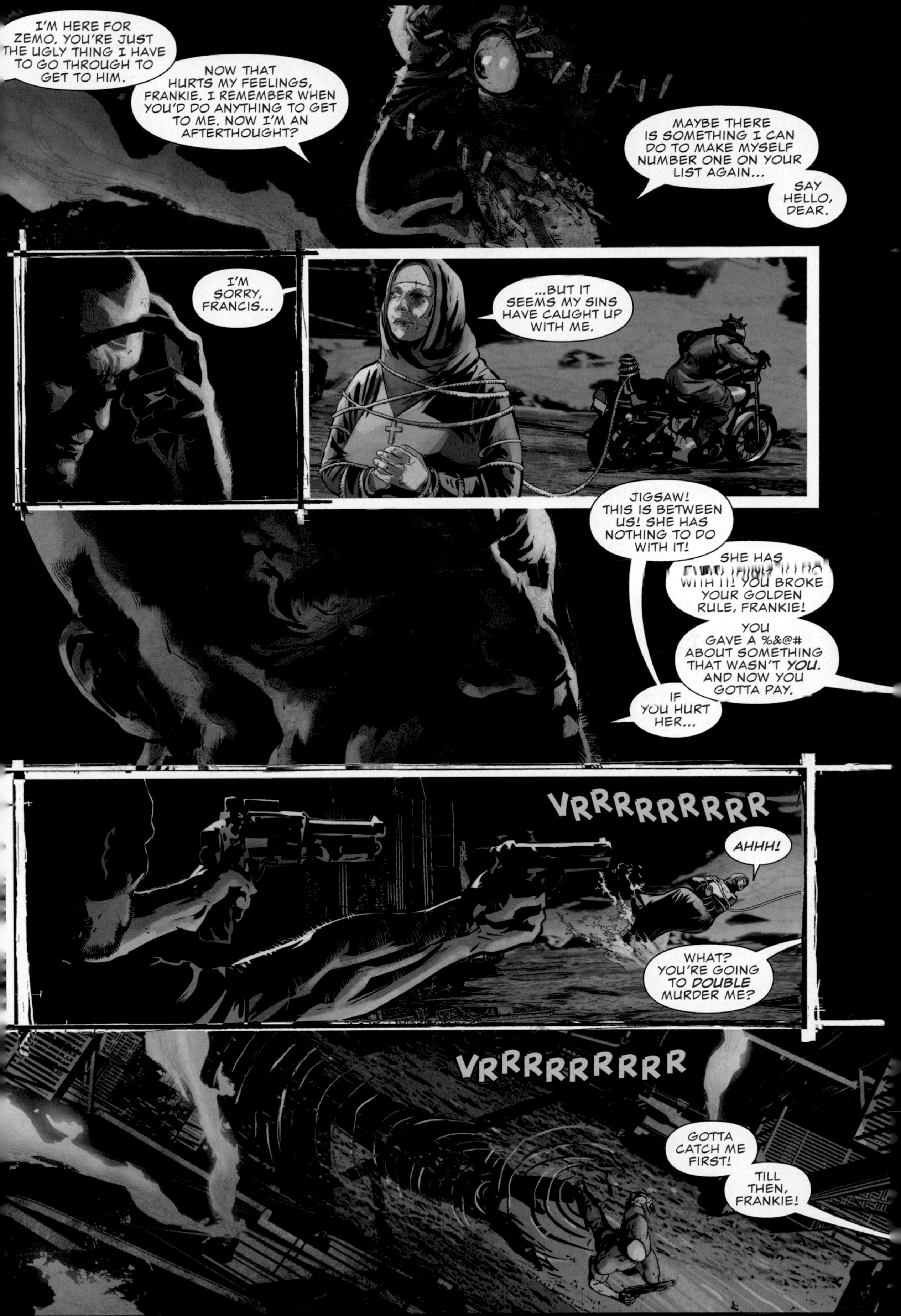
I'M HERE FOR ZEMO. YOU'RE JUST THE UGLY THING I HAVE TO GO THROUGH TO GET TO HIM.
NOW THAT HURTS MY FEELINGS, FRANKIE. I REMEMBER WHEN YOU'D DO ANYTHING TO GET TO ME. NOW I'M AN AFTERTHOUGHT?
MAYBE THERE IS SOMETHING I CAN DO TO MAKE MYSELF NUMBER ONE ON YOUR LIST AGAIN...
SAY HELLO, DEAR.
I'M SORRY, FRANCIS...
...BUT IT SEEMS MY SINS HAVE CAUGHT UP WITH ME.
JIGSAW! THIS IS BETWEEN US! SHE HAS NOTHING TO DO WITH IT!
SHE HAS
WITH IT! YOU BROKE YOUR GOLDEN RULE, FRANKIE!
YOU GAVE A %&@# ABOUT SOMETHING THAT WASN'T *YOU*. AND NOW YOU GOTTA PAY.
IF YOU HURT HER...
VRRRRRRRRRR
AHHH!
WHAT? YOU'RE GOING TO *DOUBLE* MURDER ME?
VRRRRRRRRR
GOTTA CATCH ME FIRST!
TILL THEN, FRANKIE!

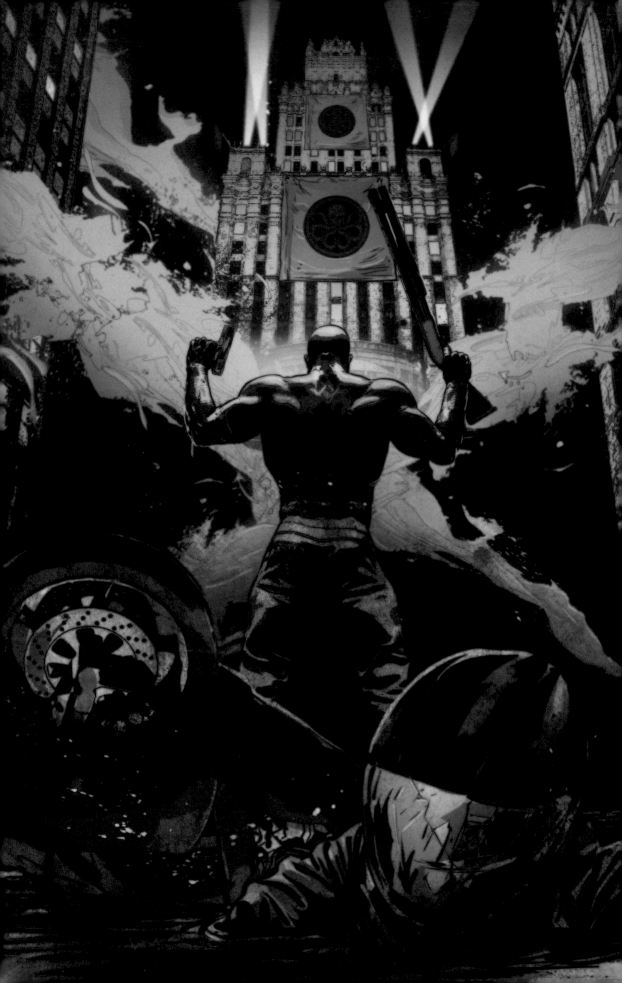

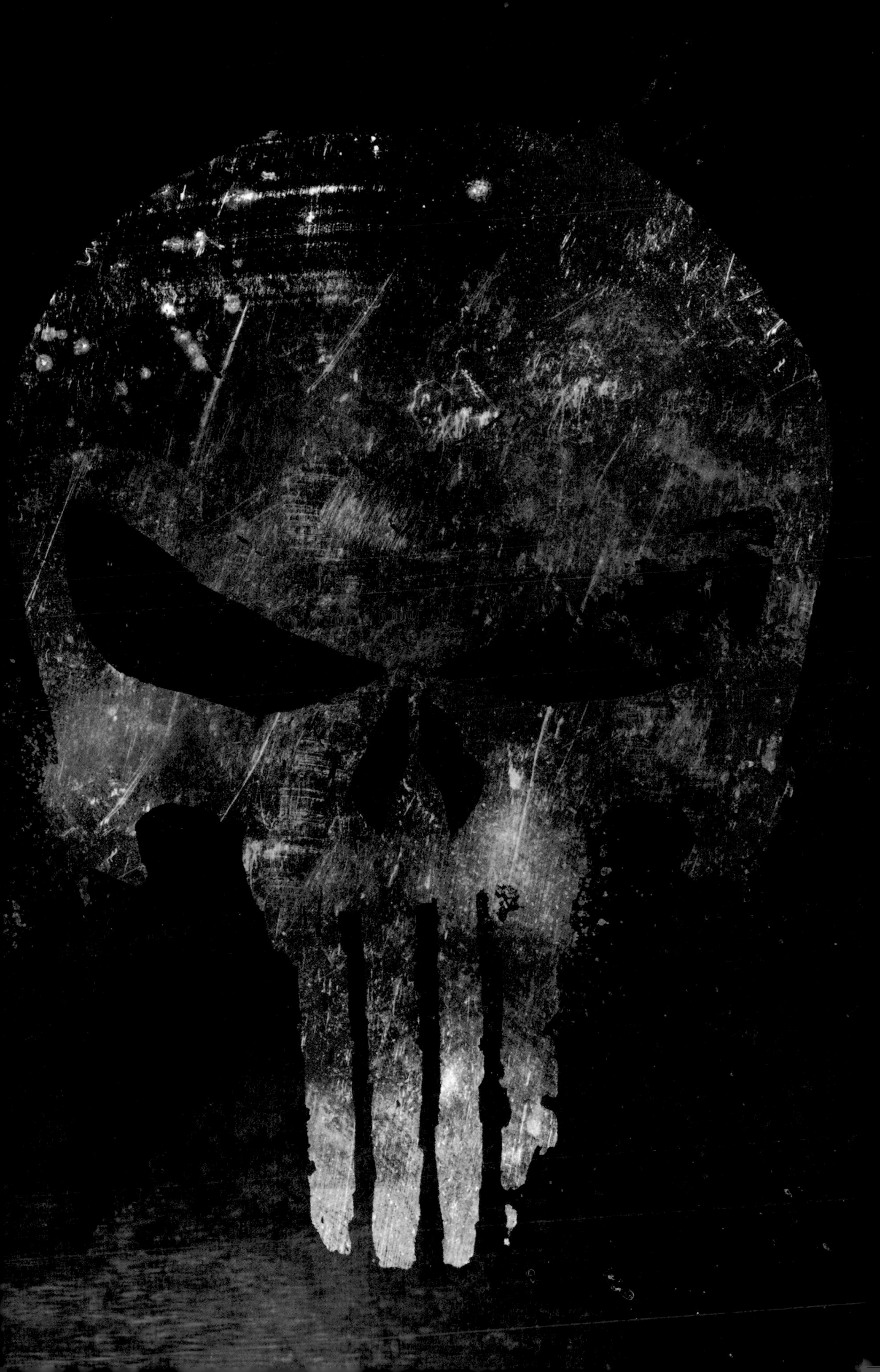

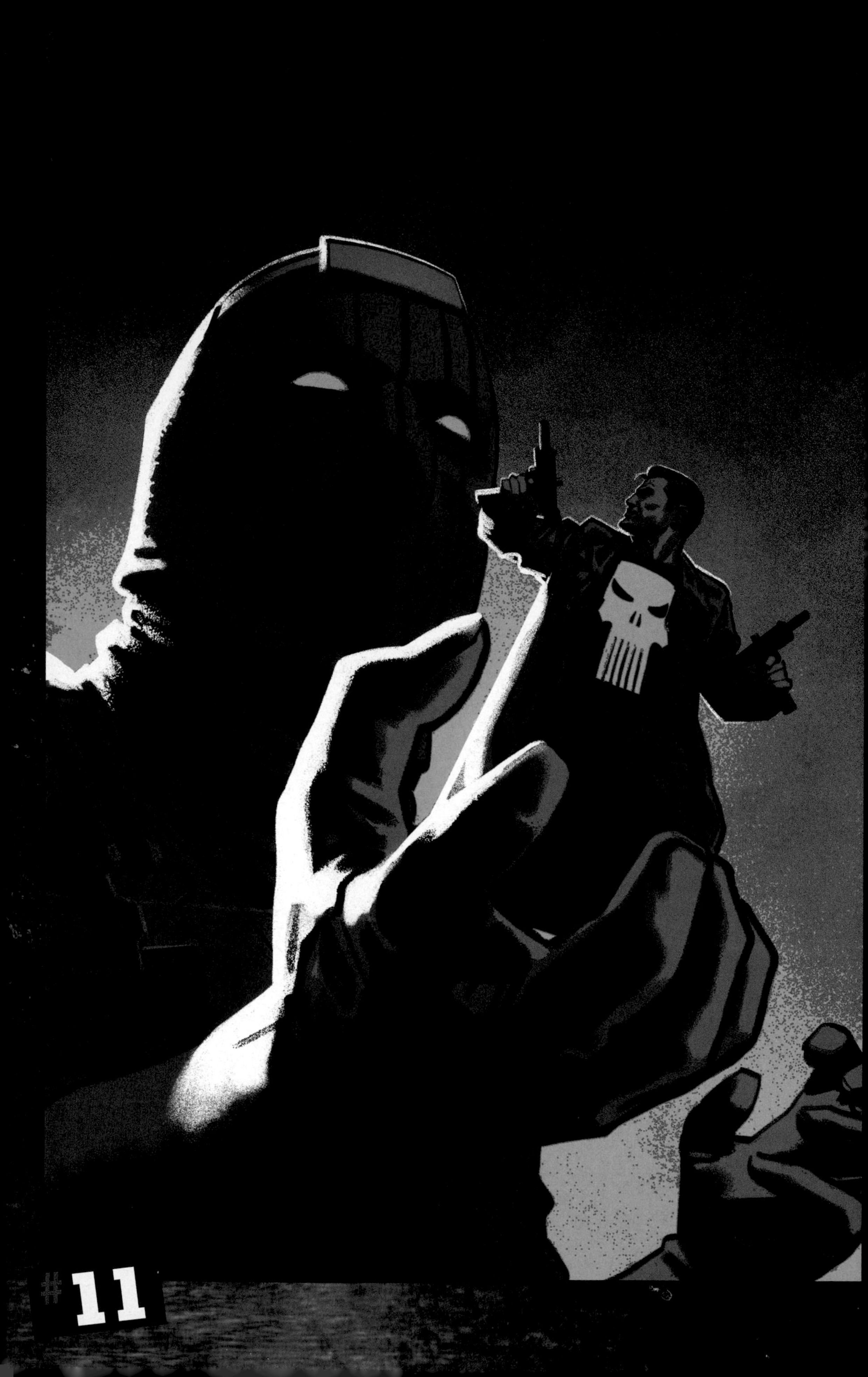
#11

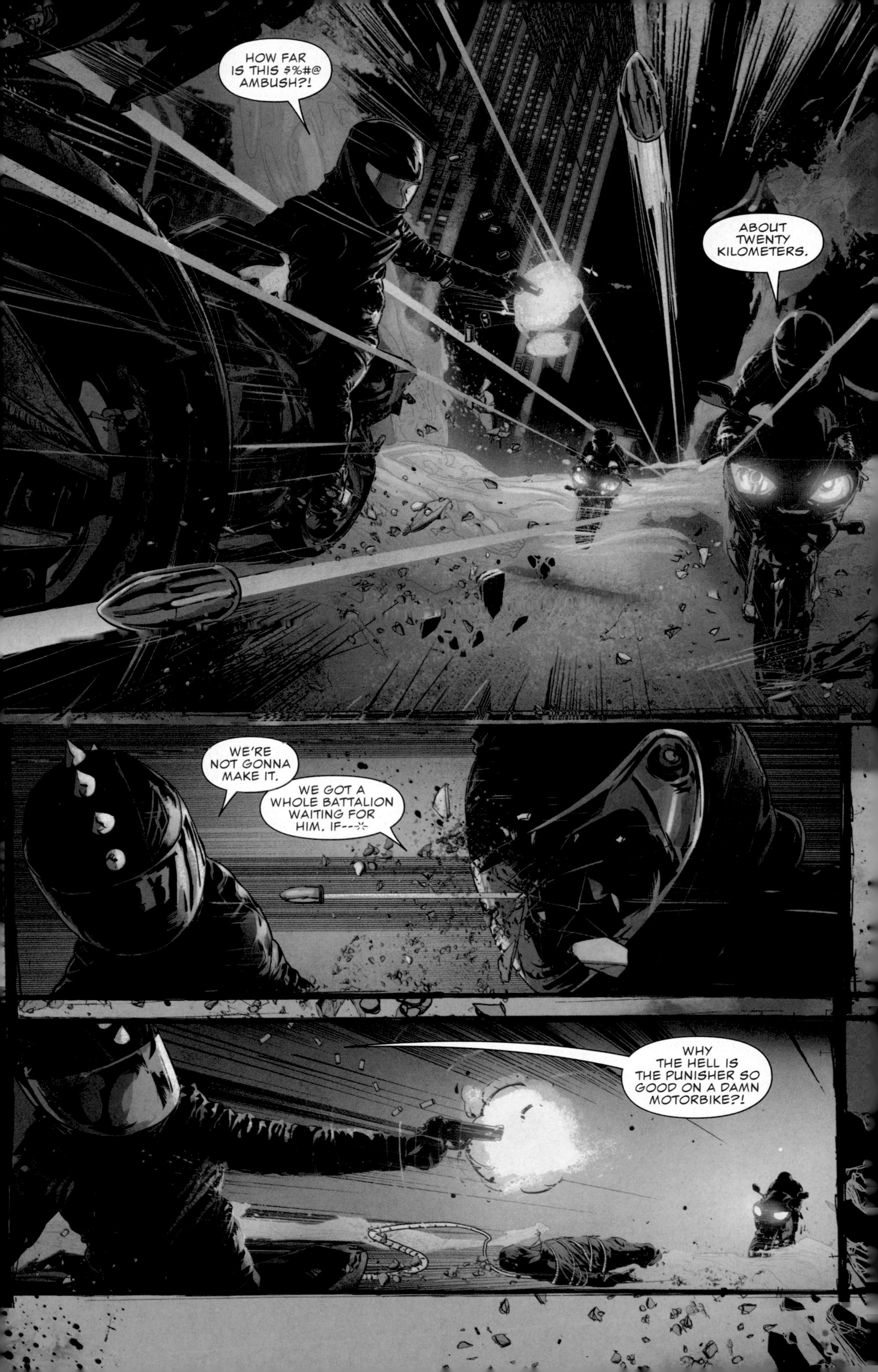
HOW FAR IS THIS $%#@ AMBUSH?!
ABOUT TWENTY KILOMETERS.
WE'RE NOT GONNA MAKE IT.
WE GOT A WHOLE BATTALION WAITING FOR HIM. IF--
WHY THE HELL IS THE PUNISHER SO GOOD ON A DAMN MOTORBIKE?!

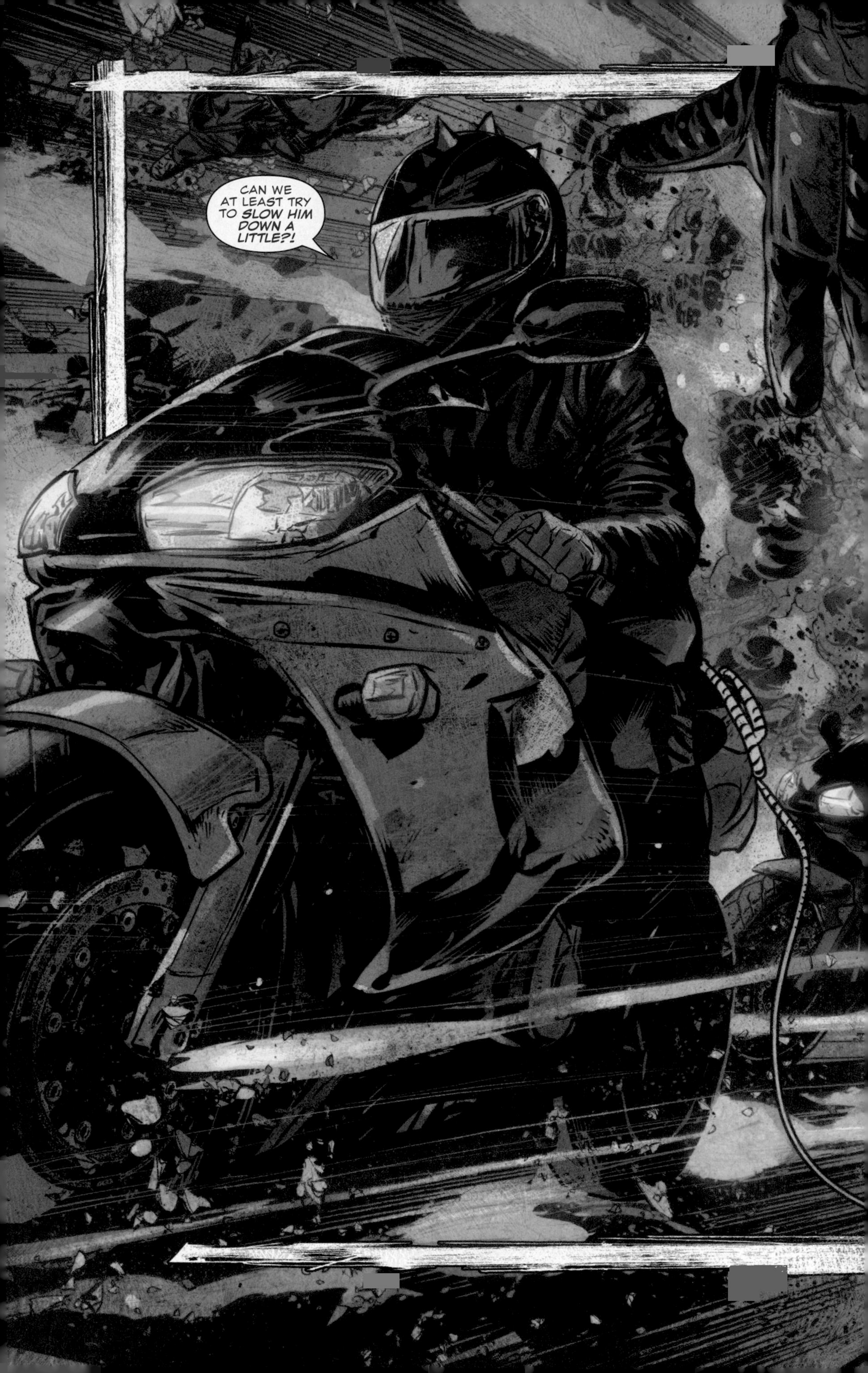
CAN WE AT LEAST TRY TO SLOW HIM DOWN A LITTLE?!

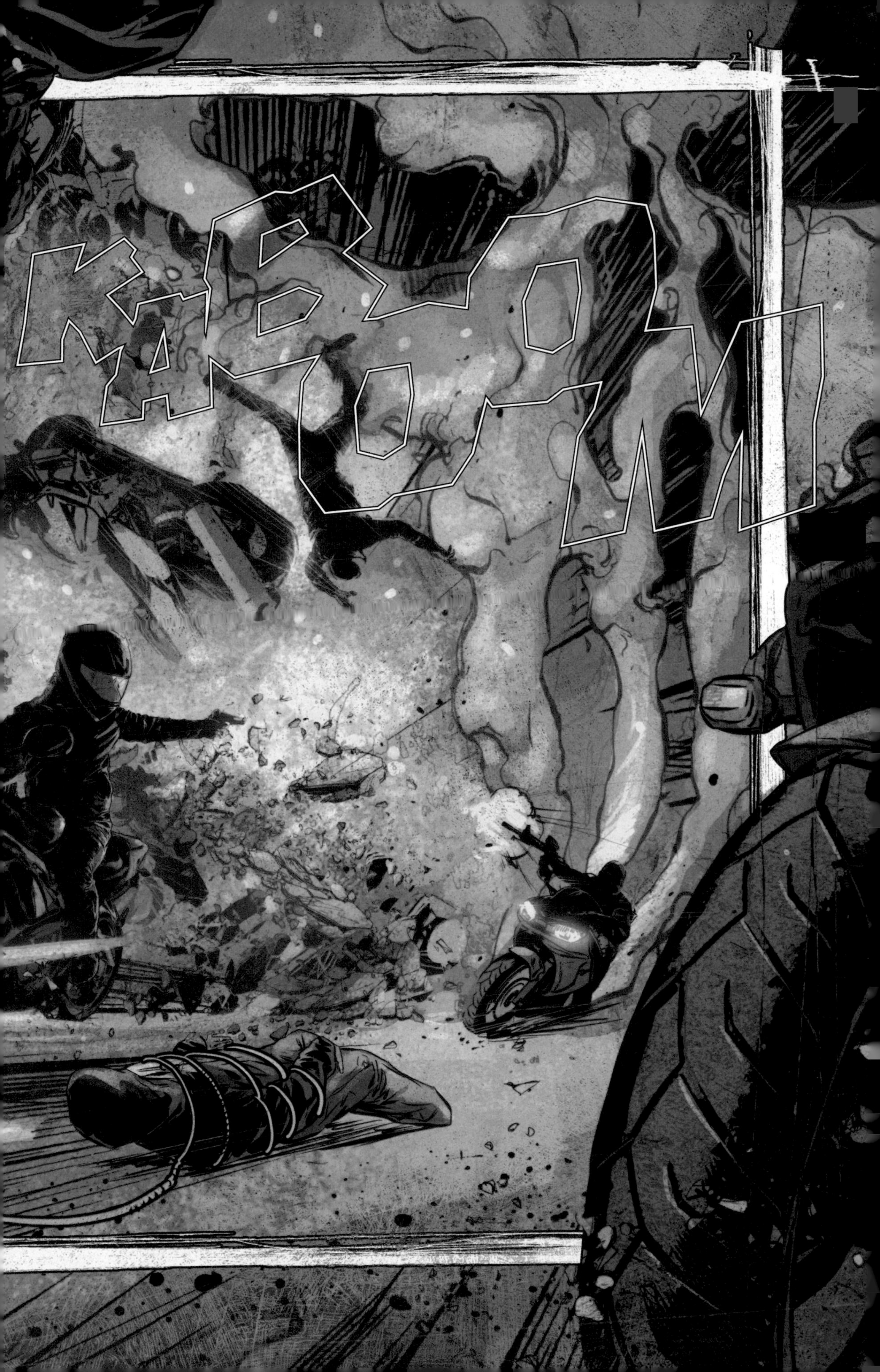
KA-BOOM!

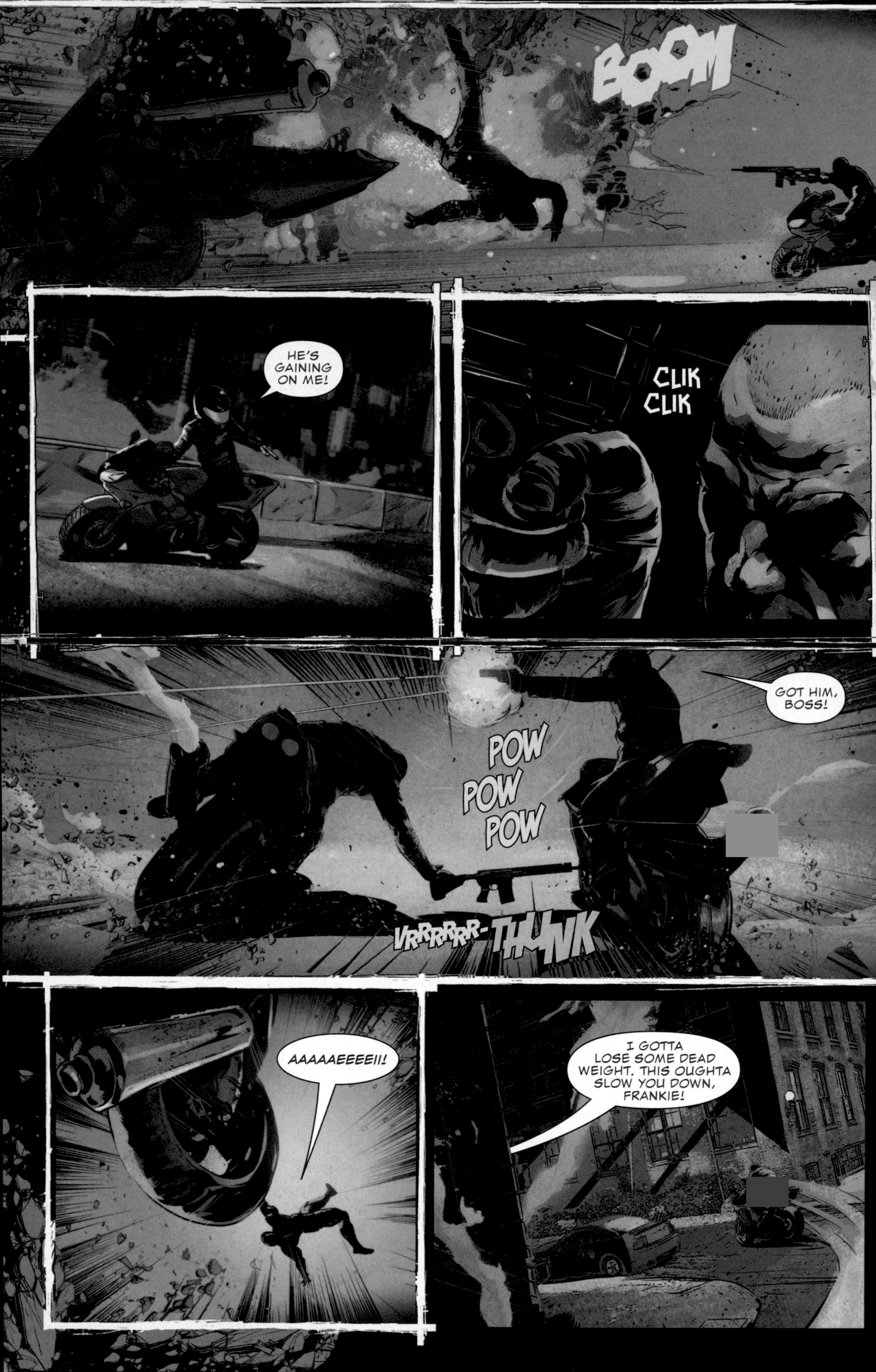
BOOM
HE'S GAINING ON ME!
CLIK CLIK
GOT HIM, BOSS!
POW POW POW
VRRRRRR-THUNK
AAAAAEEEEII!
I GOTTA LOSE SOME DEAD WEIGHT. THIS OUGHTA SLOW YOU DOWN, FRANKIE!

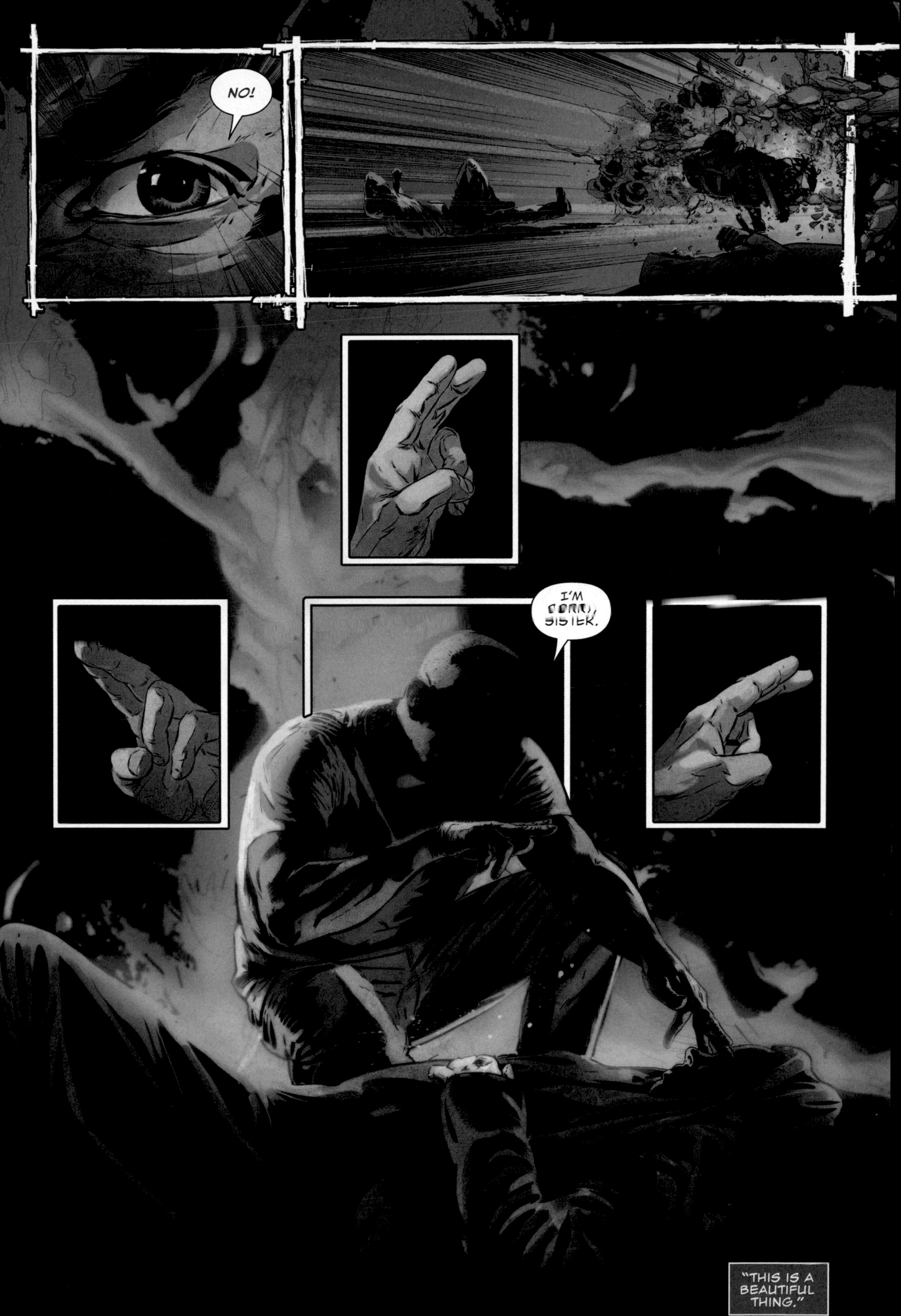
NO!
I'M SISTER.
"THIS IS A BEAUTIFUL THING."

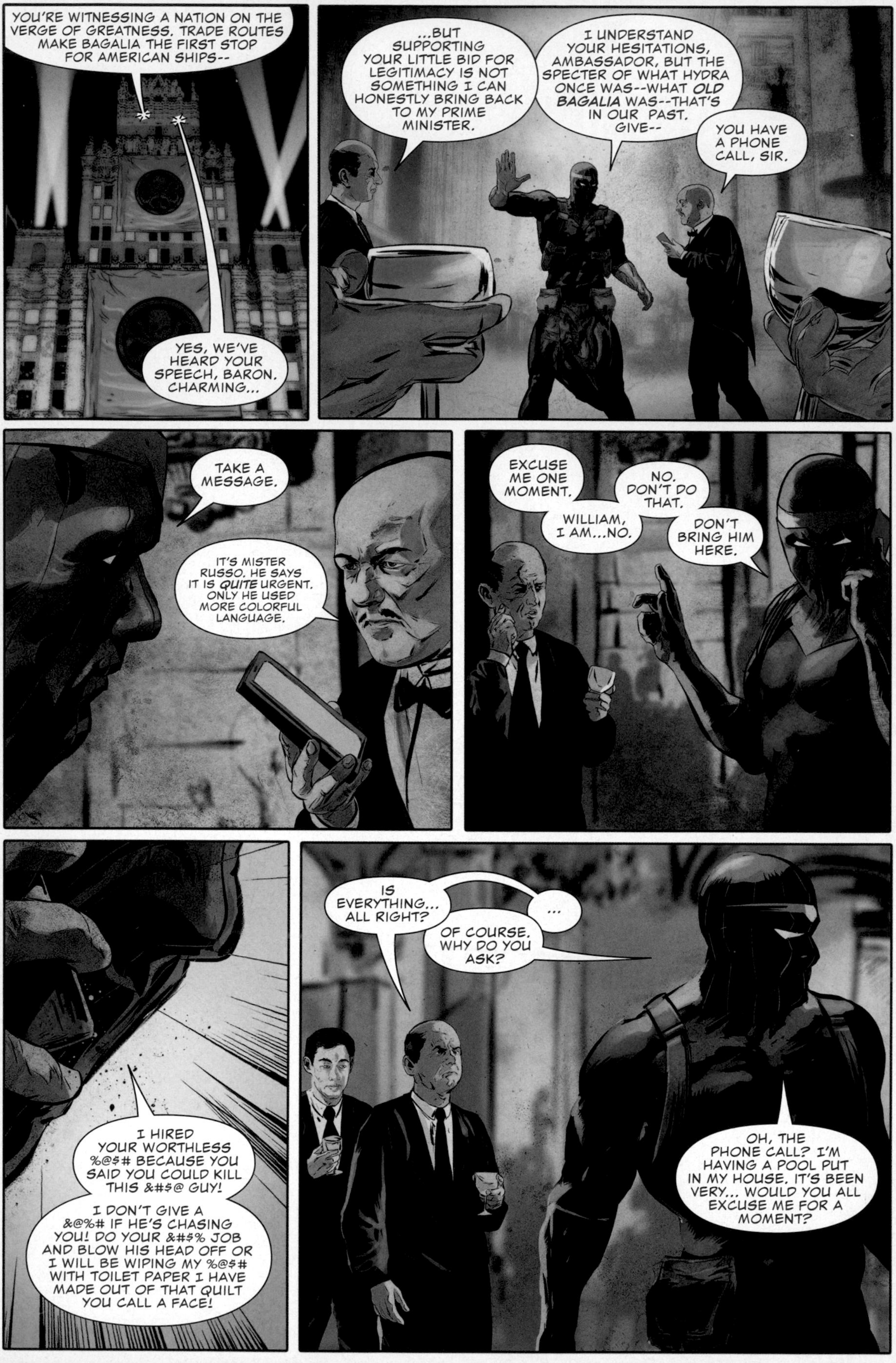
YOU'RE WITNESSING A NATION ON THE VERGE OF GREATNESS. TRADE ROUTES MAKE BAGALIA THE FIRST STOP FOR AMERICAN SHIPS--
YES, WE'VE HEARD YOUR SPEECH, BARON. CHARMING...
...BUT SUPPORTING YOUR LITTLE BID FOR LEGITIMACY IS NOT SOMETHING I CAN HONESTLY BRING BACK TO MY PRIME MINISTER.
I UNDERSTAND YOUR HESITATIONS, AMBASSADOR, BUT THE SPECTER OF WHAT HYDRA ONCE WAS--WHAT OLD BAGALIA WAS--THAT'S IN OUR PAST. GIVE--
YOU HAVE A PHONE CALL, SIR.
TAKE A MESSAGE.
IT'S MISTER RUSSO. HE SAYS IT IS QUITE URGENT. ONLY HE USED MORE COLORFUL LANGUAGE.
EXCUSE ME ONE MOMENT.
WILLIAM, I AM...NO.
NO. DON'T DO THAT.
DON'T BRING HIM HERE.
I HIRED YOUR WORTHLESS %@$# BECAUSE YOU SAID YOU COULD KILL THIS &#$@ GUY!
I DON'T GIVE A &@%# IF HE'S CHASING YOU! DO YOUR &#$% JOB AND BLOW HIS HEAD OFF OR I WILL BE WIPING MY %@$# WITH TOILET PAPER I HAVE MADE OUT OF THAT QUILT YOU CALL A FACE!
IS EVERYTHING... ALL RIGHT?
...
OF COURSE. WHY DO YOU ASK?
OH, THE PHONE CALL? I'M HAVING A POOL PUT IN MY HOUSE. IT'S BEEN VERY... WOULD YOU ALL EXCUSE ME FOR A MOMENT?

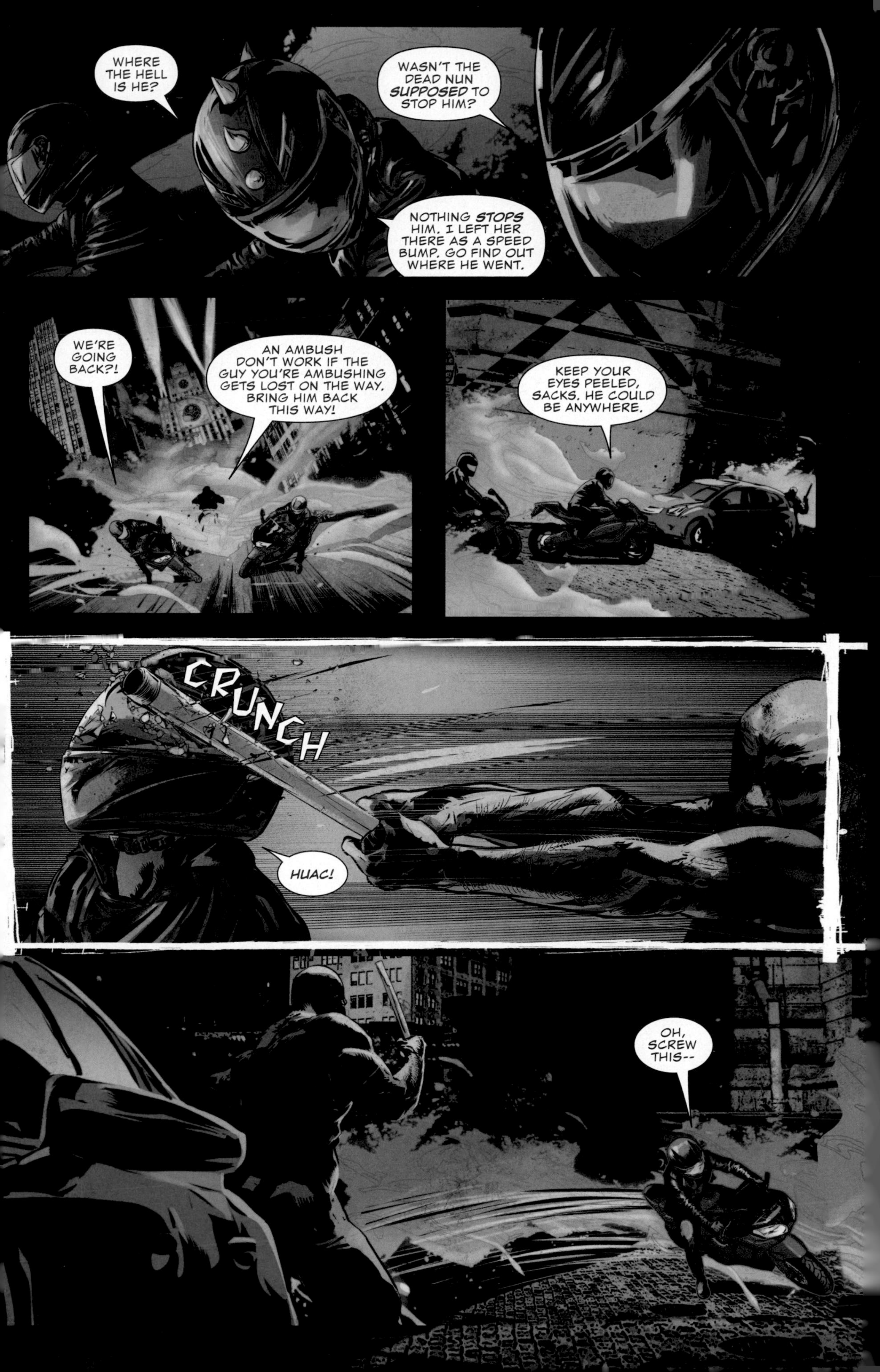
WHERE THE HELL IS HE?
WASN'T THE DEAD NUN *SUPPOSED* TO STOP HIM?
NOTHING *STOPS* HIM. I LEFT HER THERE AS A SPEED BUMP. GO FIND OUT WHERE HE WENT.
WE'RE GOING BACK?!
AN AMBUSH DON'T WORK IF THE GUY YOU'RE AMBUSHING GETS LOST ON THE WAY. BRING HIM BACK THIS WAY!
KEEP YOUR EYES PEELED, SACKS. HE COULD BE ANYWHERE.
CRUNCH
HUAC!
OH, SCREW THIS--

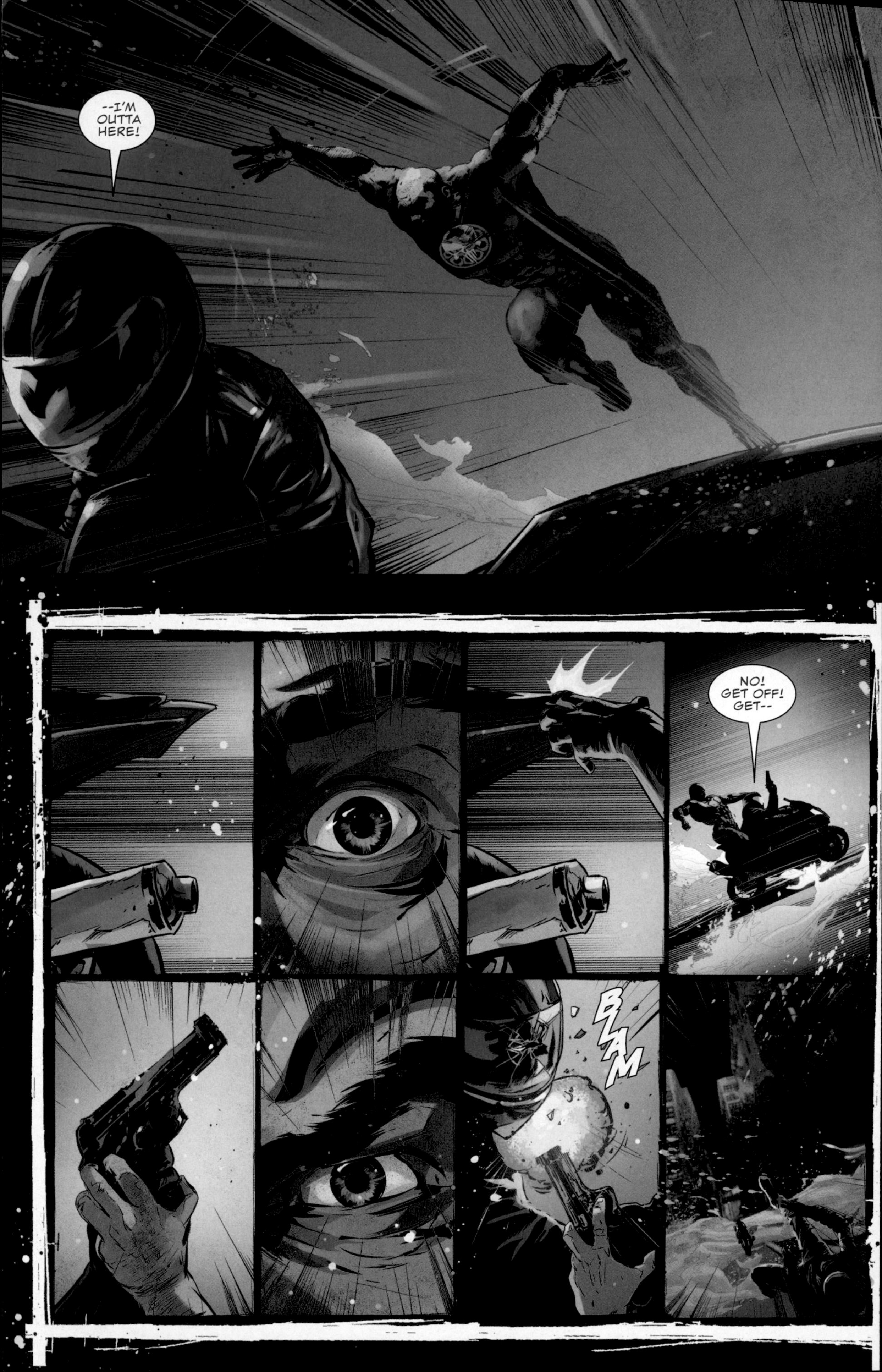
--I'M OUTTA HERE!
NO! GET OFF! GET--
BLAM

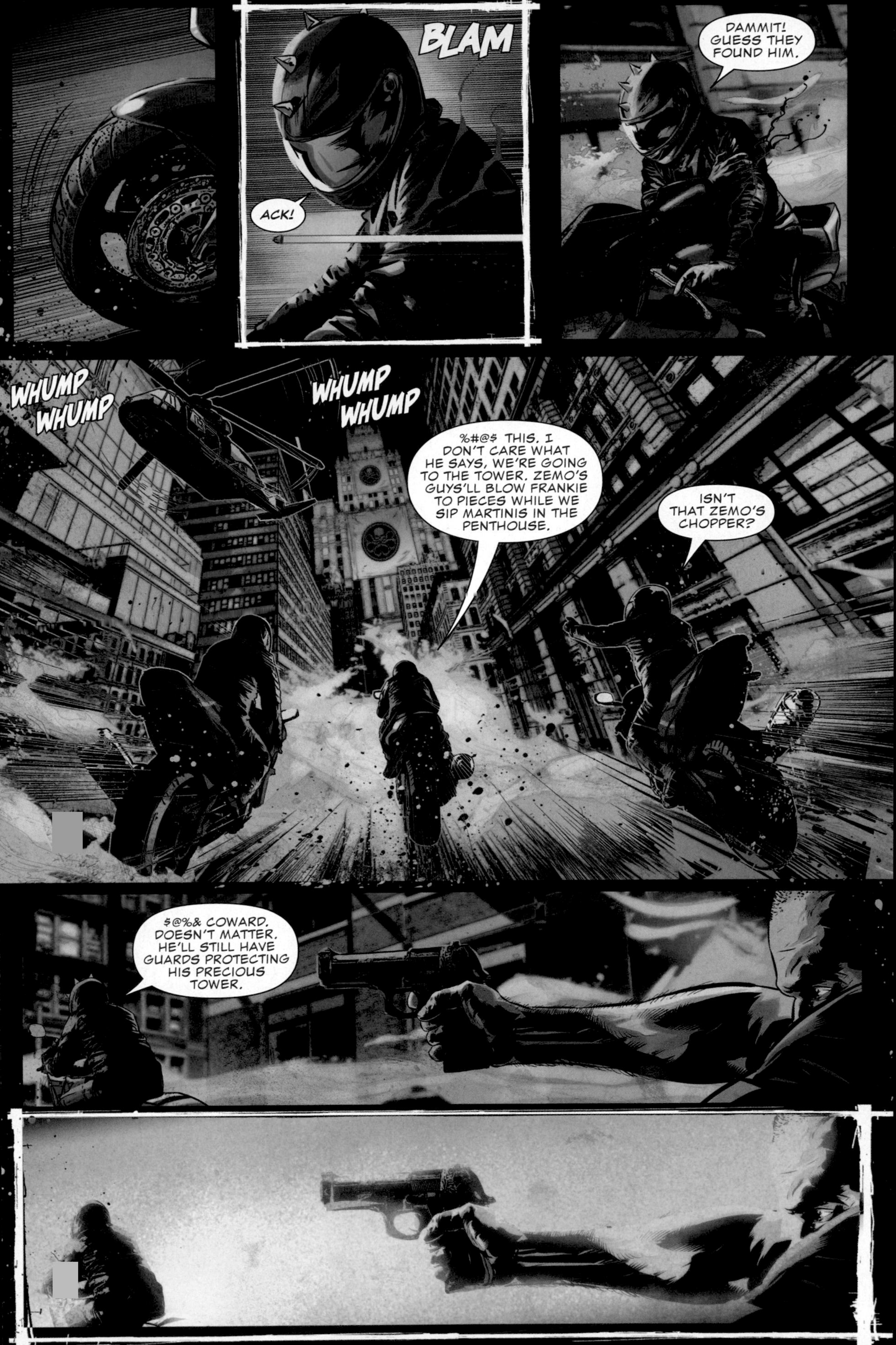
BLAM
ACK!
DAMMIT! GUESS THEY FOUND HIM.
WHUMP WHUMP
WHUMP WHUMP
%#@$ THIS. I DON'T CARE WHAT HE SAYS, WE'RE GOING TO THE TOWER. ZEMO'S GUYS'LL BLOW FRANKIE TO PIECES WHILE WE SIP MARTINIS IN THE PENTHOUSE.
ISN'T THAT ZEMO'S CHOPPER?
$@%& COWARD. DOESN'T MATTER. HE'LL STILL HAVE GUARDS PROTECTING HIS PRECIOUS TOWER.

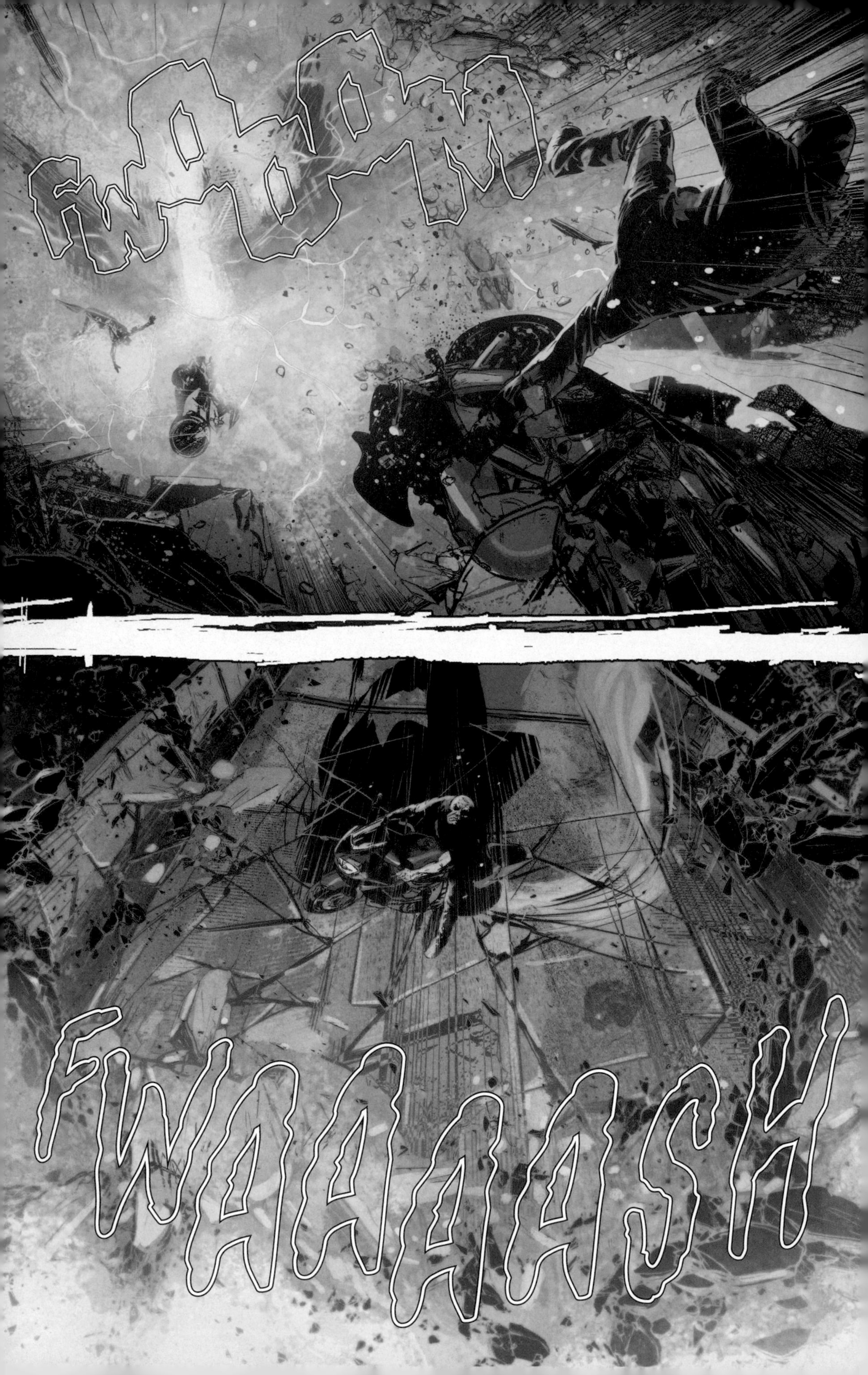
FWOOOM
FWAAAASH

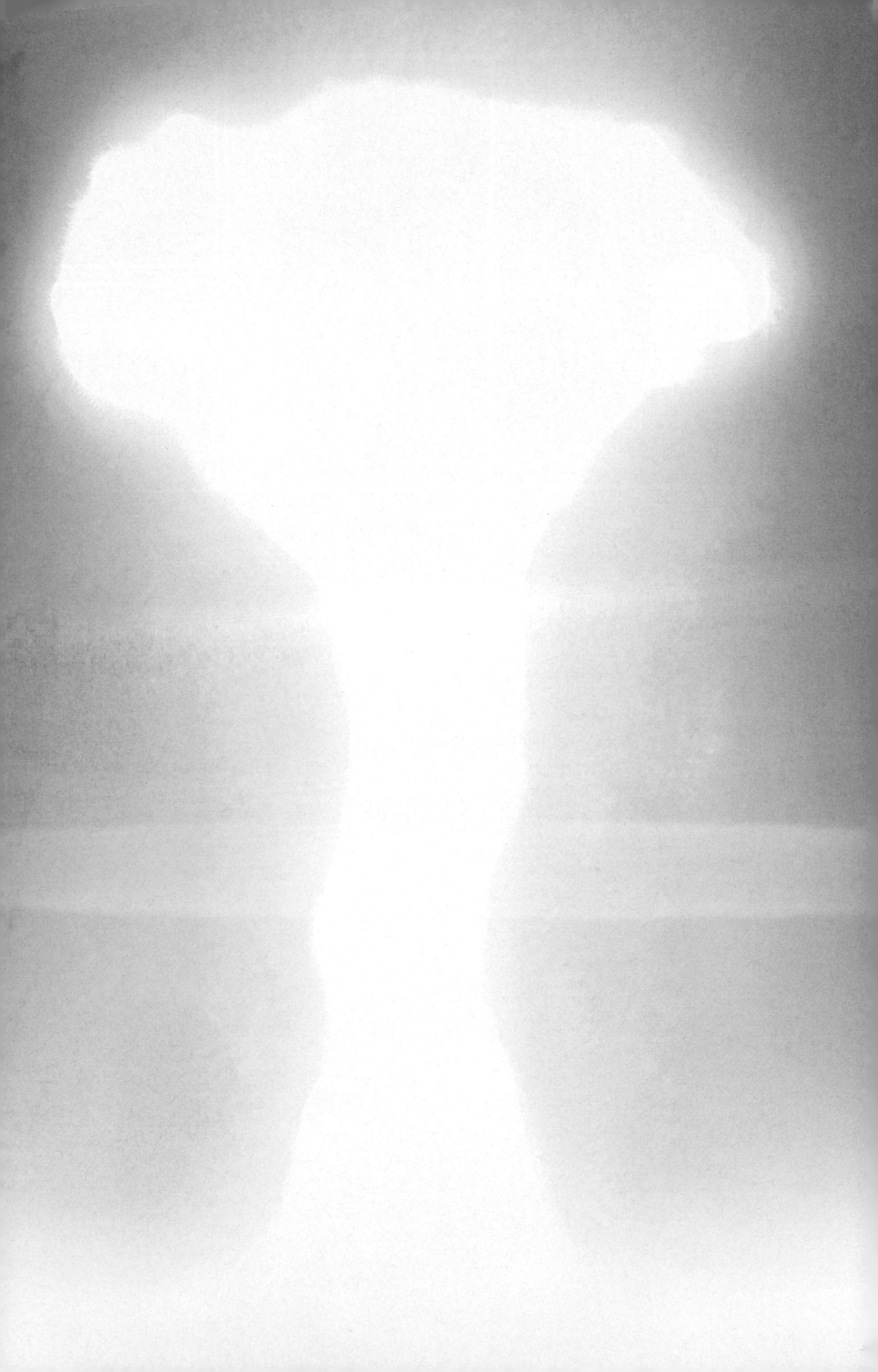

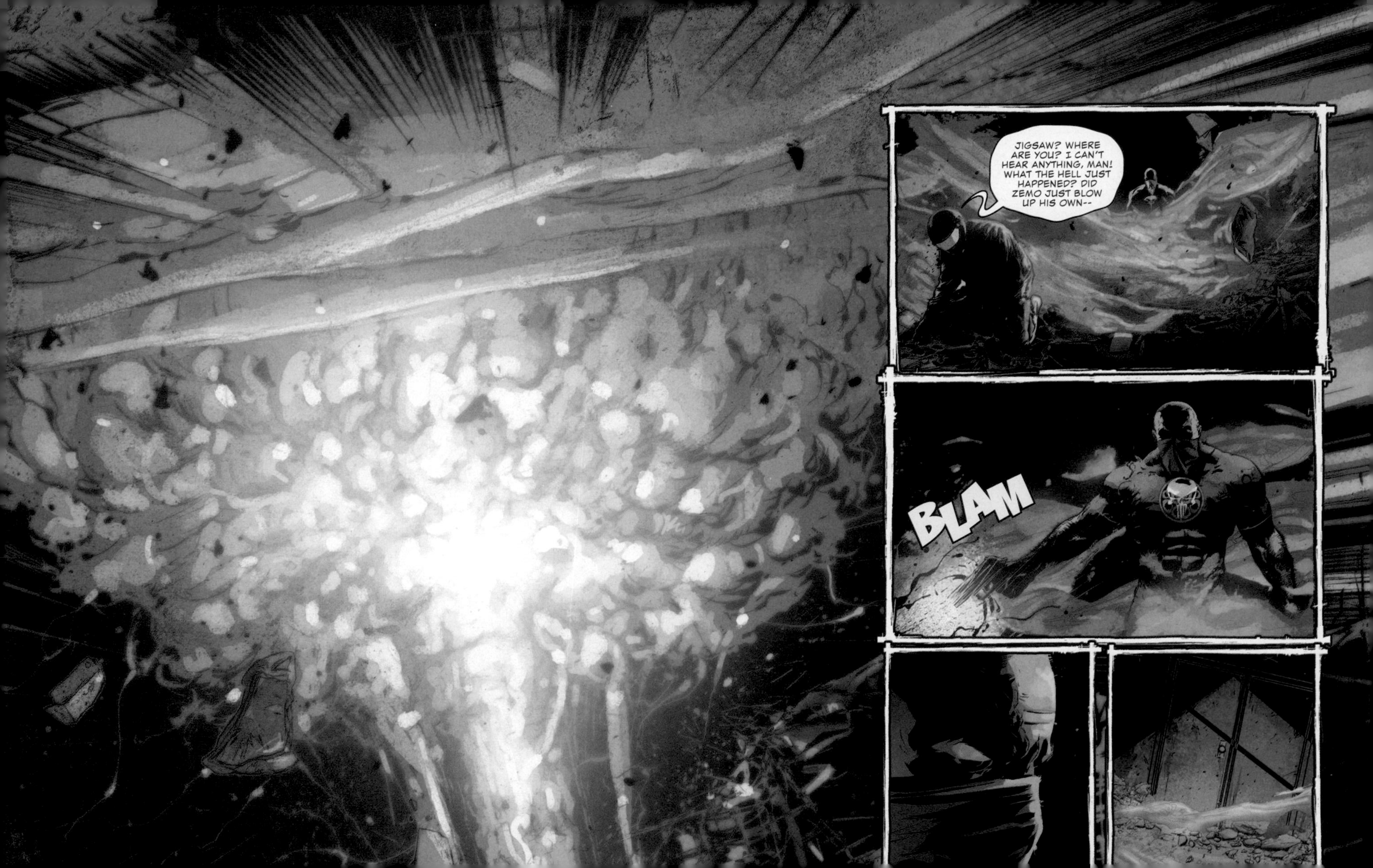
JIGSAW? WHERE ARE YOU? I CAN'T HEAR ANYTHING, MAN! WHAT THE HELL JUST HAPPENED? DID ZEMO JUST BLOW UP HIS OWN--
BLAM

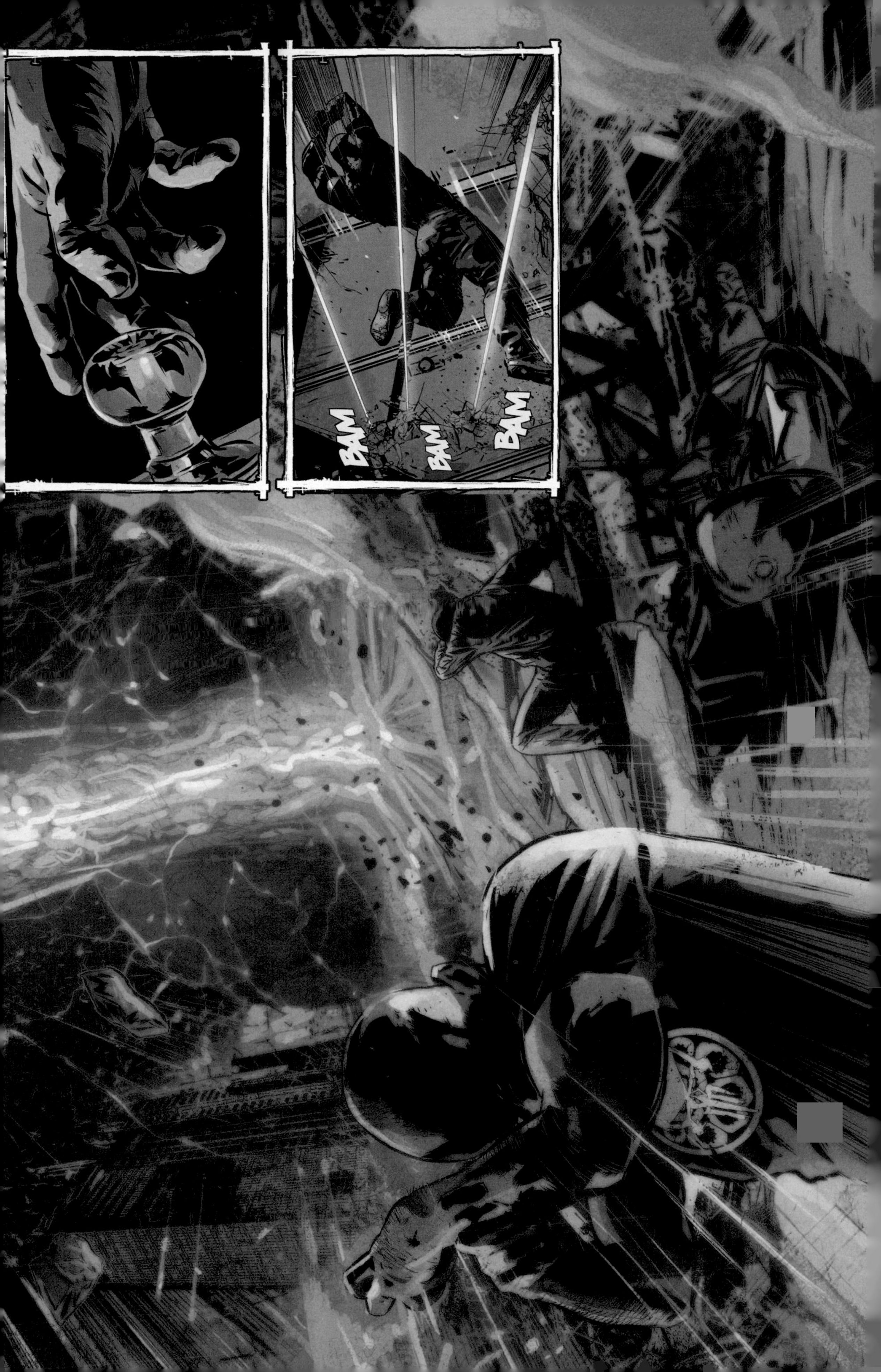
BAM
BAM
BAM

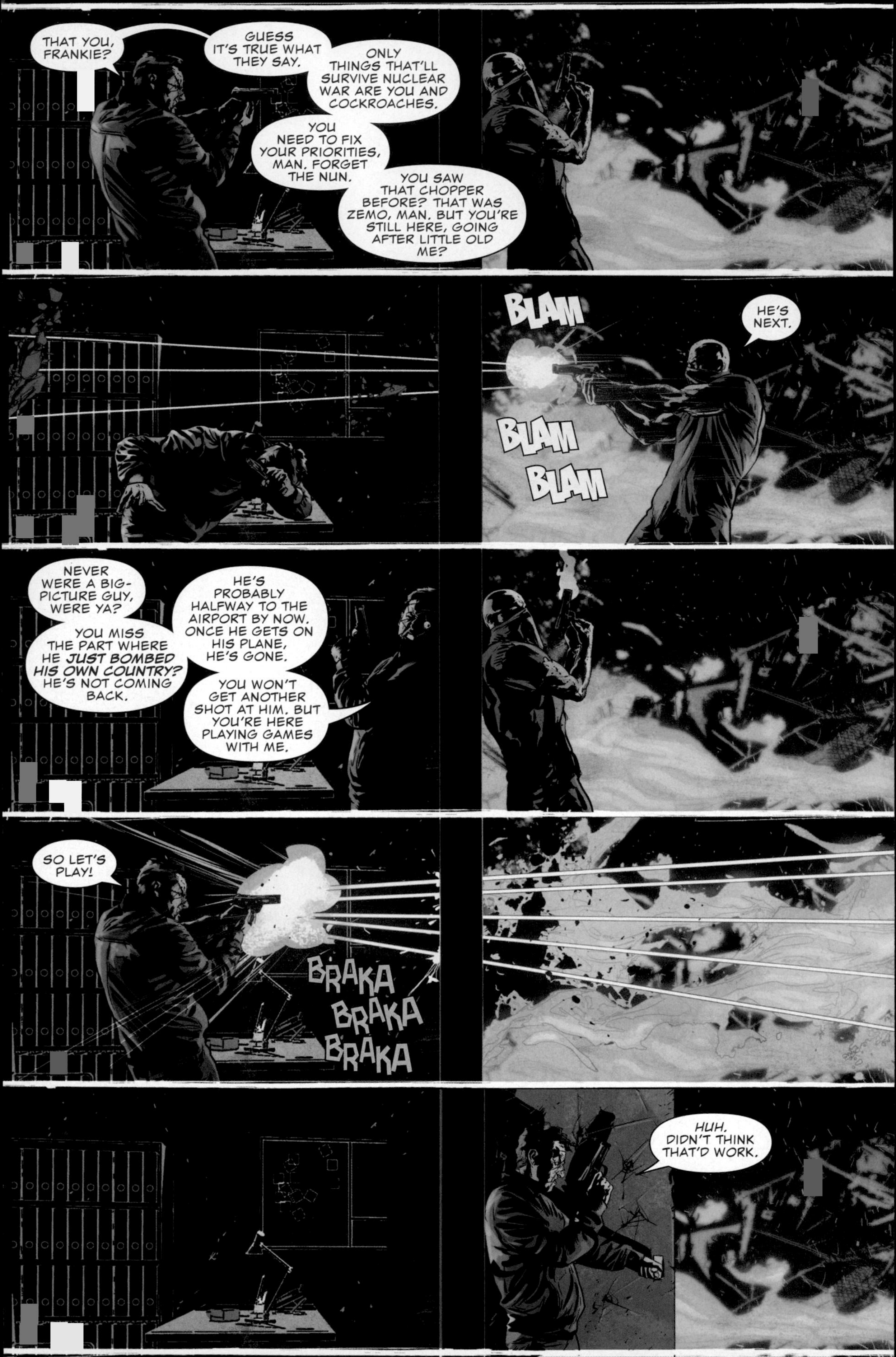
THAT YOU, FRANKIE?
GUESS IT'S TRUE WHAT THEY SAY.
ONLY THINGS THAT'LL SURVIVE NUCLEAR WAR ARE YOU AND COCKROACHES.
YOU NEED TO FIX YOUR PRIORITIES, MAN. FORGET THE NUN.
YOU SAW THAT CHOPPER BEFORE? THAT WAS ZEMO, MAN. BUT YOU'RE STILL HERE, GOING AFTER LITTLE OLD ME?
BLAM
HE'S NEXT.
BLAM
BLAM
NEVER WERE A BIG-PICTURE GUY, WERE YA?
YOU MISS THE PART WHERE HE JUST BOMBED HIS OWN COUNTRY? HE'S NOT COMING BACK.
HE'S PROBABLY HALFWAY TO THE AIRPORT BY NOW. ONCE HE GETS ON HIS PLANE, HE'S GONE.
YOU WON'T GET ANOTHER SHOT AT HIM. BUT YOU'RE HERE PLAYING GAMES WITH ME.
SO LET'S PLAY!
BRAKA
BRAKA
BRAKA
HUH. DIDN'T THINK THAT'D WORK.

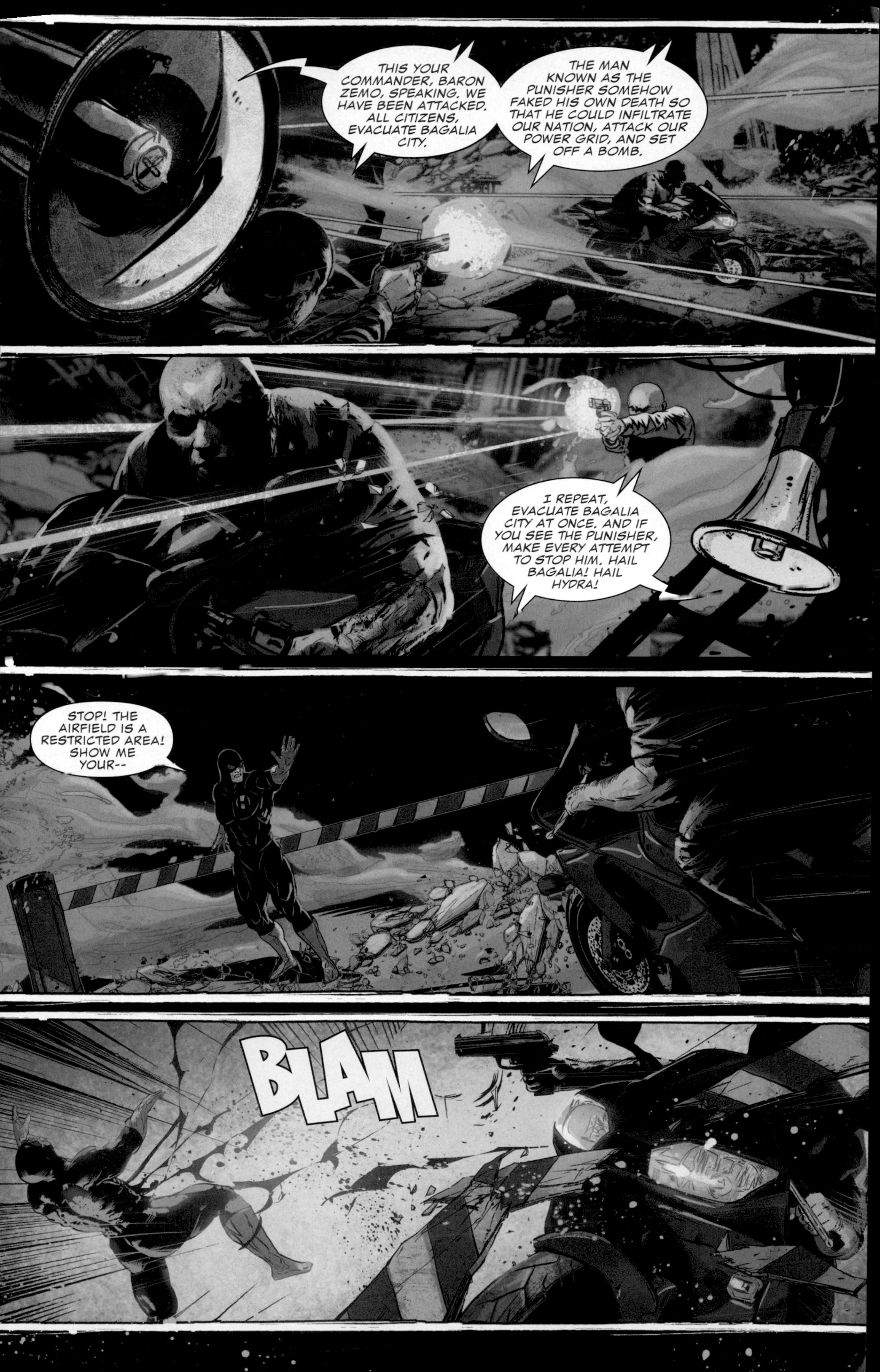
THIS YOUR COMMANDER, BARON ZEMO, SPEAKING. WE HAVE BEEN ATTACKED. ALL CITIZENS, EVACUATE BAGALIA CITY.
THE MAN KNOWN AS THE PUNISHER SOMEHOW FAKED HIS OWN DEATH SO THAT HE COULD INFILTRATE OUR NATION, ATTACK OUR POWER GRID, AND SET OFF A BOMB.
I REPEAT, EVACUATE BAGALIA CITY AT ONCE. AND IF YOU SEE THE PUNISHER, MAKE EVERY ATTEMPT TO STOP HIM. HAIL BAGALIA! HAIL HYDRA!
STOP! THE AIRFIELD IS A RESTRICTED AREA! SHOW ME YOUR--
BLAM

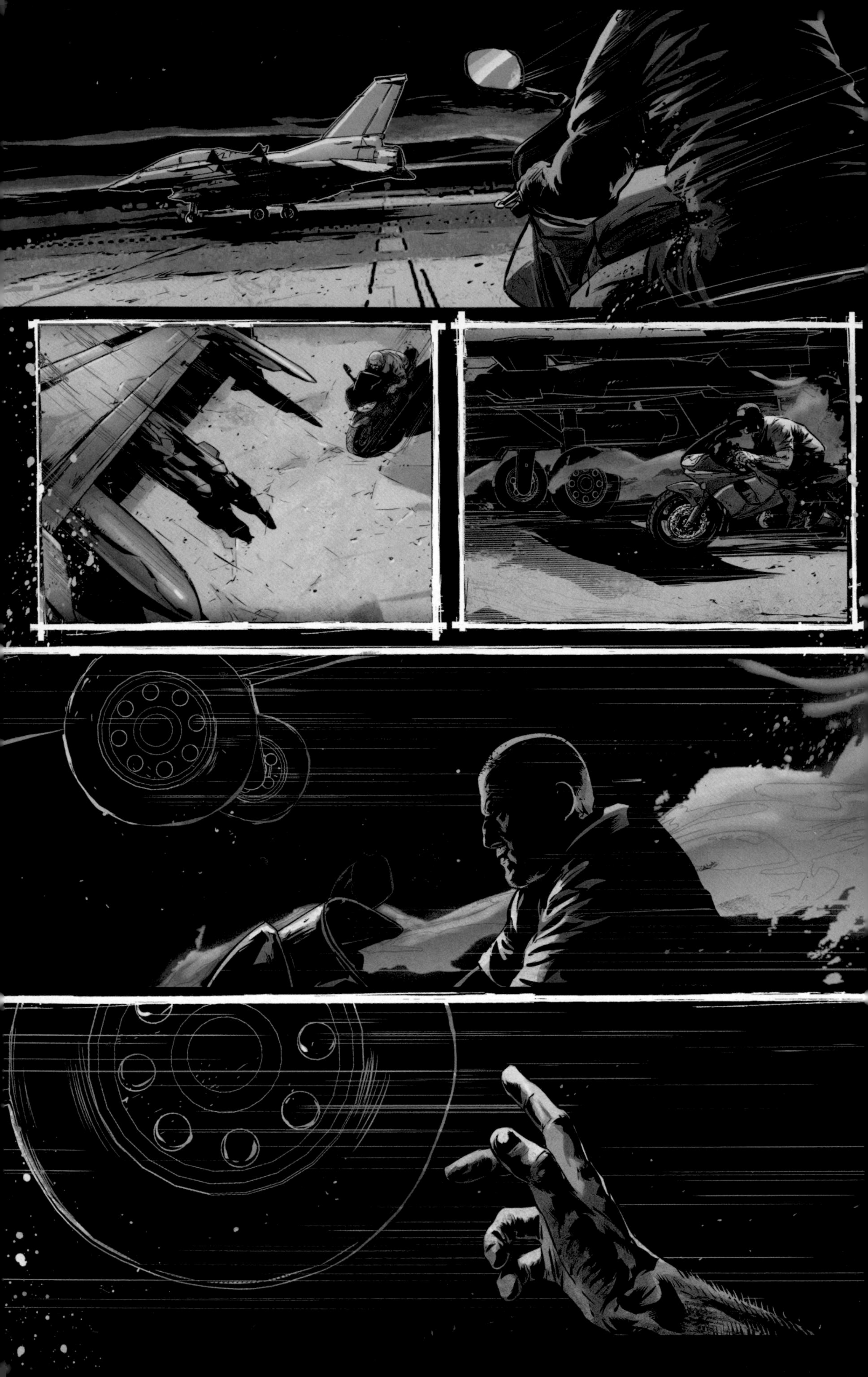

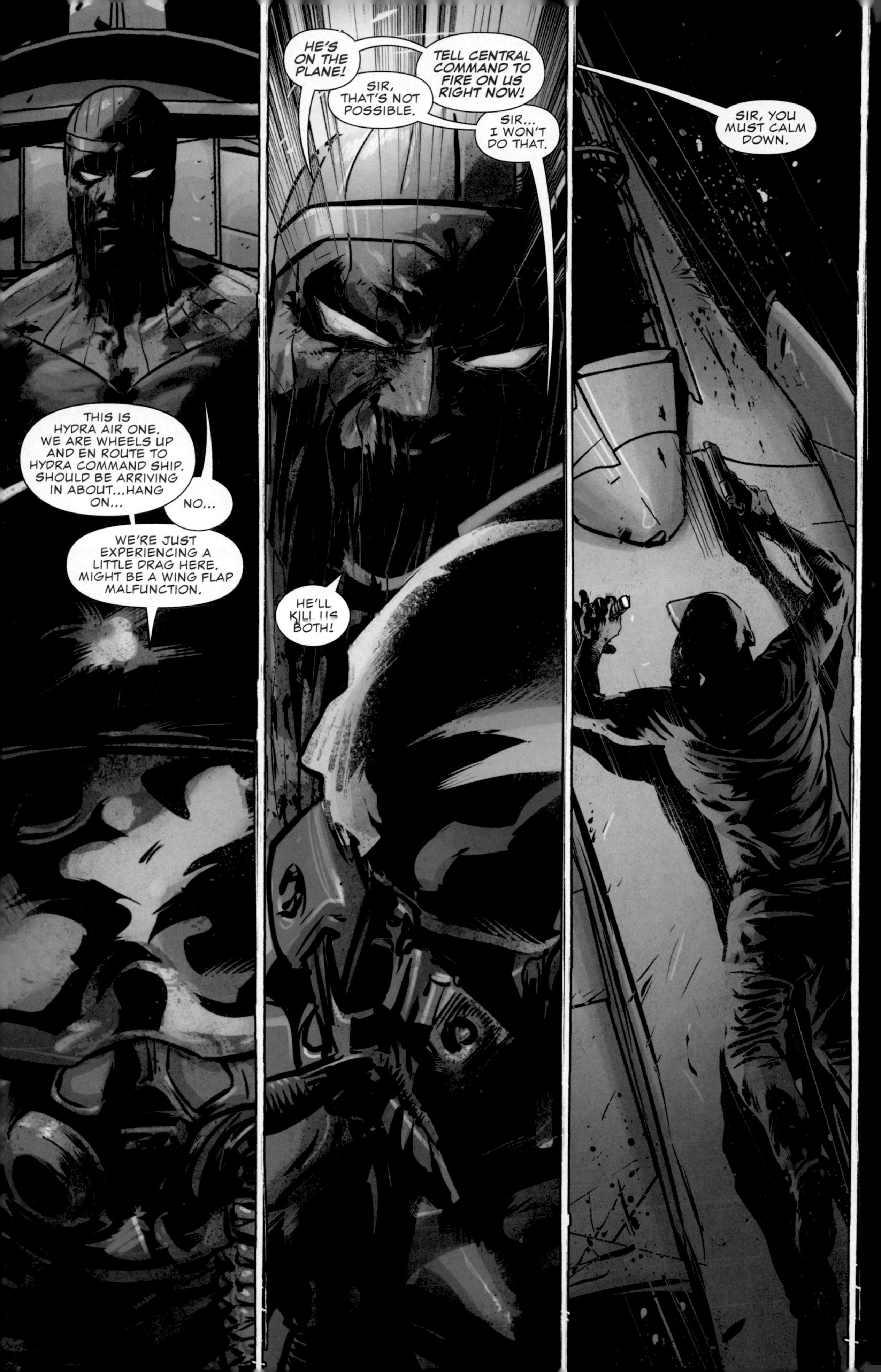
THIS IS HYDRA AIR ONE. WE ARE WHEELS UP AND EN ROUTE TO HYDRA COMMAND SHIP. SHOULD BE ARRIVING IN ABOUT...HANG ON...
NO...
WE'RE JUST EXPERIENCING A LITTLE DRAG HERE. MIGHT BE A WING FLAP MALFUNCTION.
HE'S ON THE PLANE!
TELL CENTRAL COMMAND TO FIRE ON US RIGHT NOW!
SIR, THAT'S NOT POSSIBLE.
SIR... I WON'T DO THAT.
HE'LL KILL US BOTH!
SIR, YOU MUST CALM DOWN.

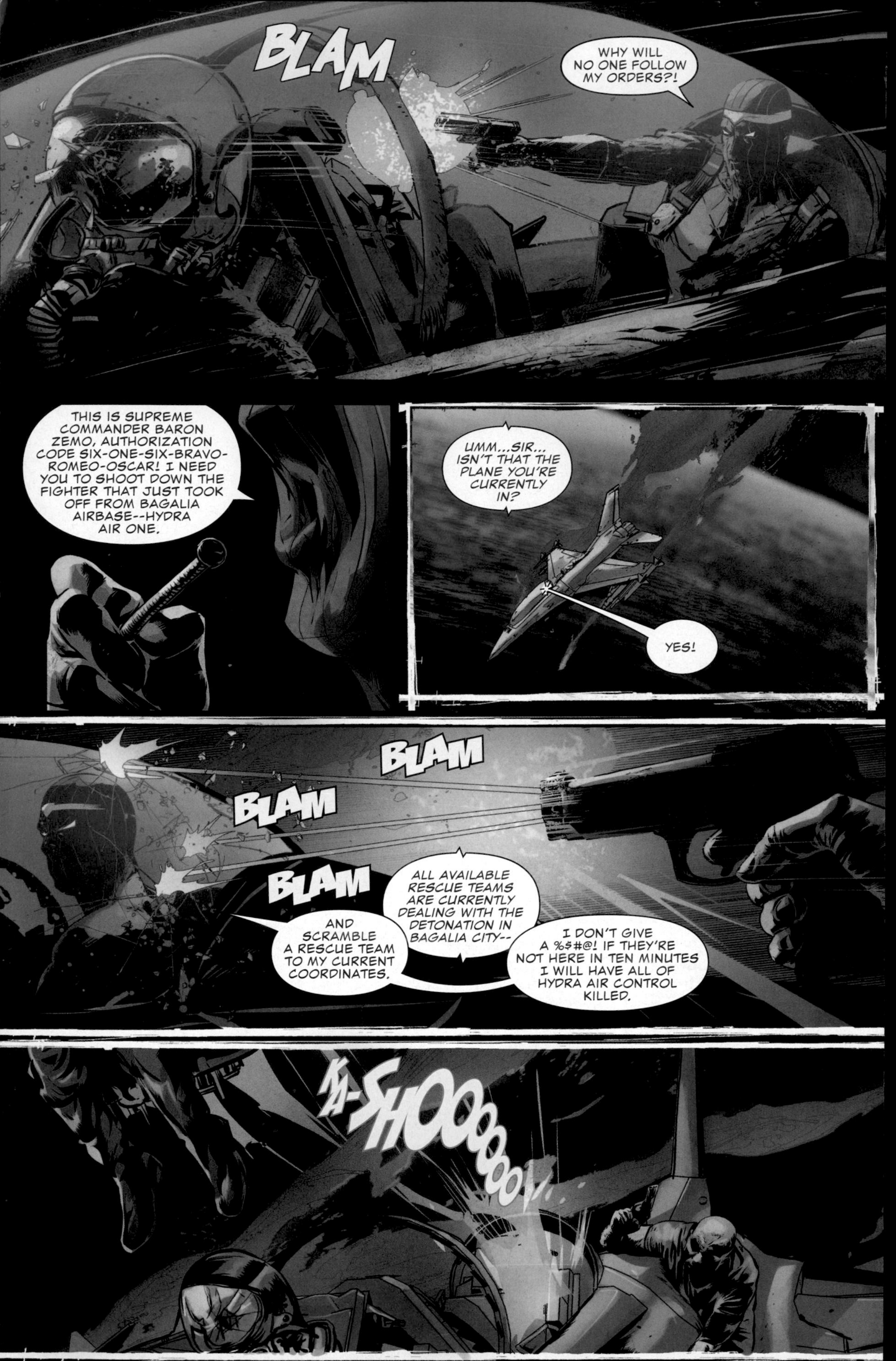
BLAM
WHY WILL NO ONE FOLLOW MY ORDERS?!
THIS IS SUPREME COMMANDER BARON ZEMO, AUTHORIZATION CODE SIX-ONE-SIX-BRAVO-ROMEO-OSCAR! I NEED YOU TO SHOOT DOWN THE FIGHTER THAT JUST TOOK OFF FROM BAGALIA AIRBASE--HYDRA AIR ONE.
UMM...SIR... ISN'T THAT THE PLANE YOU'RE CURRENTLY IN?
YES!
BLAM
BLAM
BLAM
AND SCRAMBLE A RESCUE TEAM TO MY CURRENT COORDINATES.
ALL AVAILABLE RESCUE TEAMS ARE CURRENTLY DEALING WITH THE DETONATION IN BAGALIA CITY--
I DON'T GIVE A %$#@! IF THEY'RE NOT HERE IN TEN MINUTES I WILL HAVE ALL OF HYDRA AIR CONTROL KILLED.
KA-SHOOOOOOM

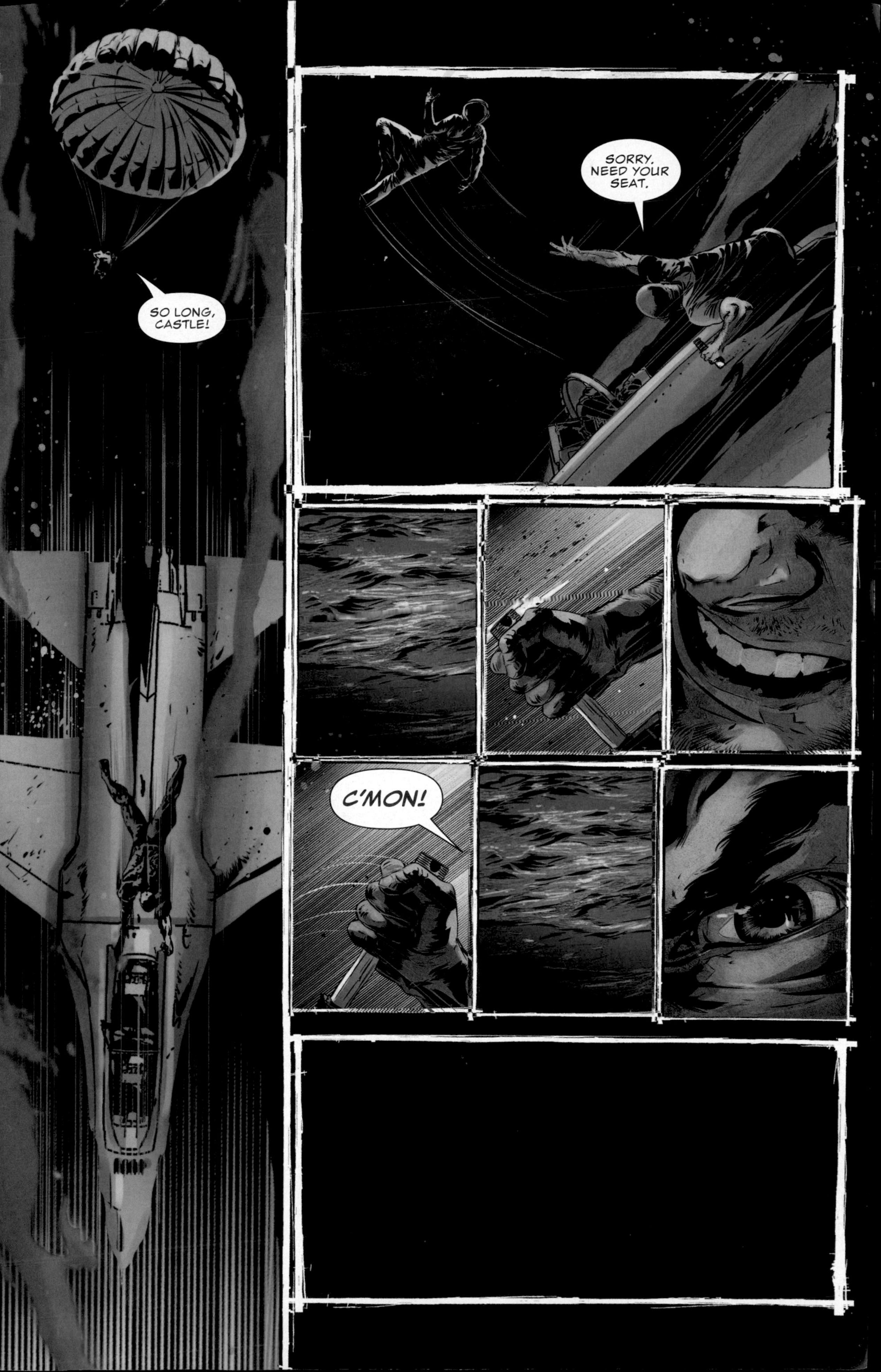
SO LONG, CASTLE!
SORRY. NEED YOUR SEAT.
C'MON!

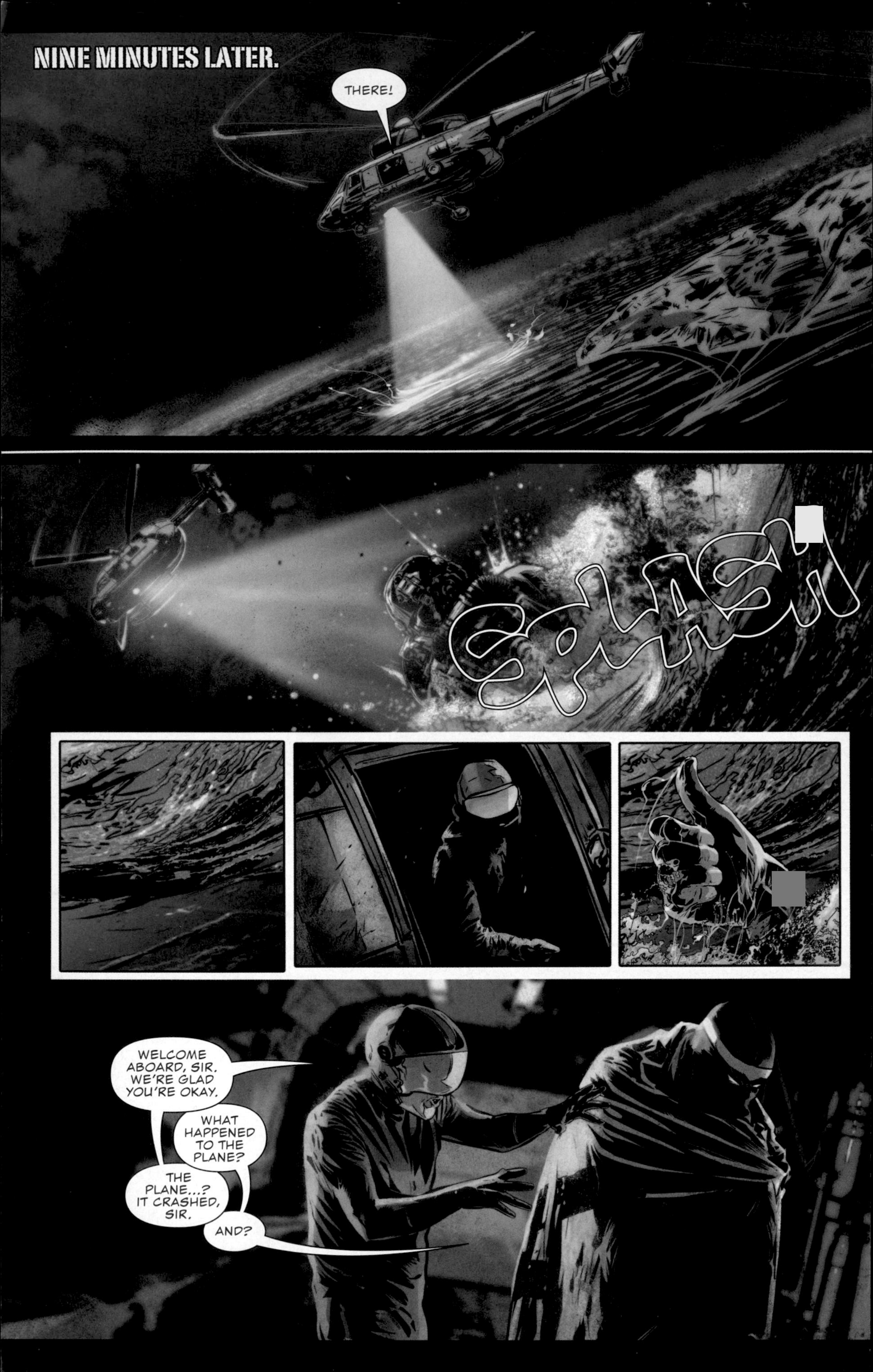
NINE MINUTES LATER.
THERE!
SPLASH!
WELCOME ABOARD, SIR. WE'RE GLAD YOU'RE OKAY.
WHAT HAPPENED TO THE PLANE?
THE PLANE...? IT CRASHED, SIR.
AND?

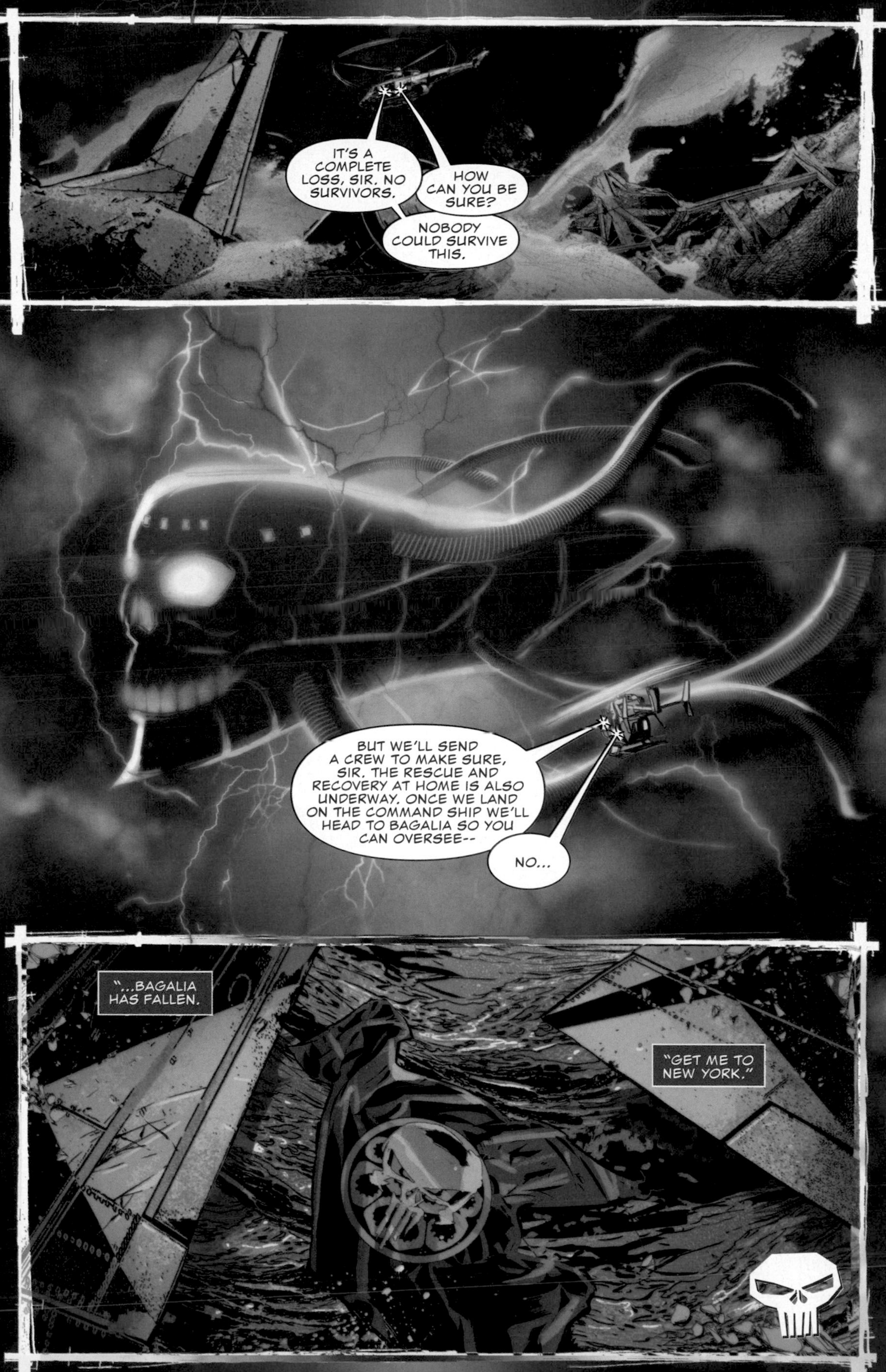
IT'S A COMPLETE LOSS, SIR. NO SURVIVORS.
HOW CAN YOU BE SURE?
NOBODY COULD SURVIVE THIS.
BUT WE'LL SEND A CREW TO MAKE SURE, SIR. THE RESCUE AND RECOVERY AT HOME IS ALSO UNDERWAY. ONCE WE LAND ON THE COMMAND SHIP WE'LL HEAD TO BAGALIA SO YOU CAN OVERSEE--
NO...
"...BAGALIA HAS FALLEN.
"GET ME TO NEW YORK."

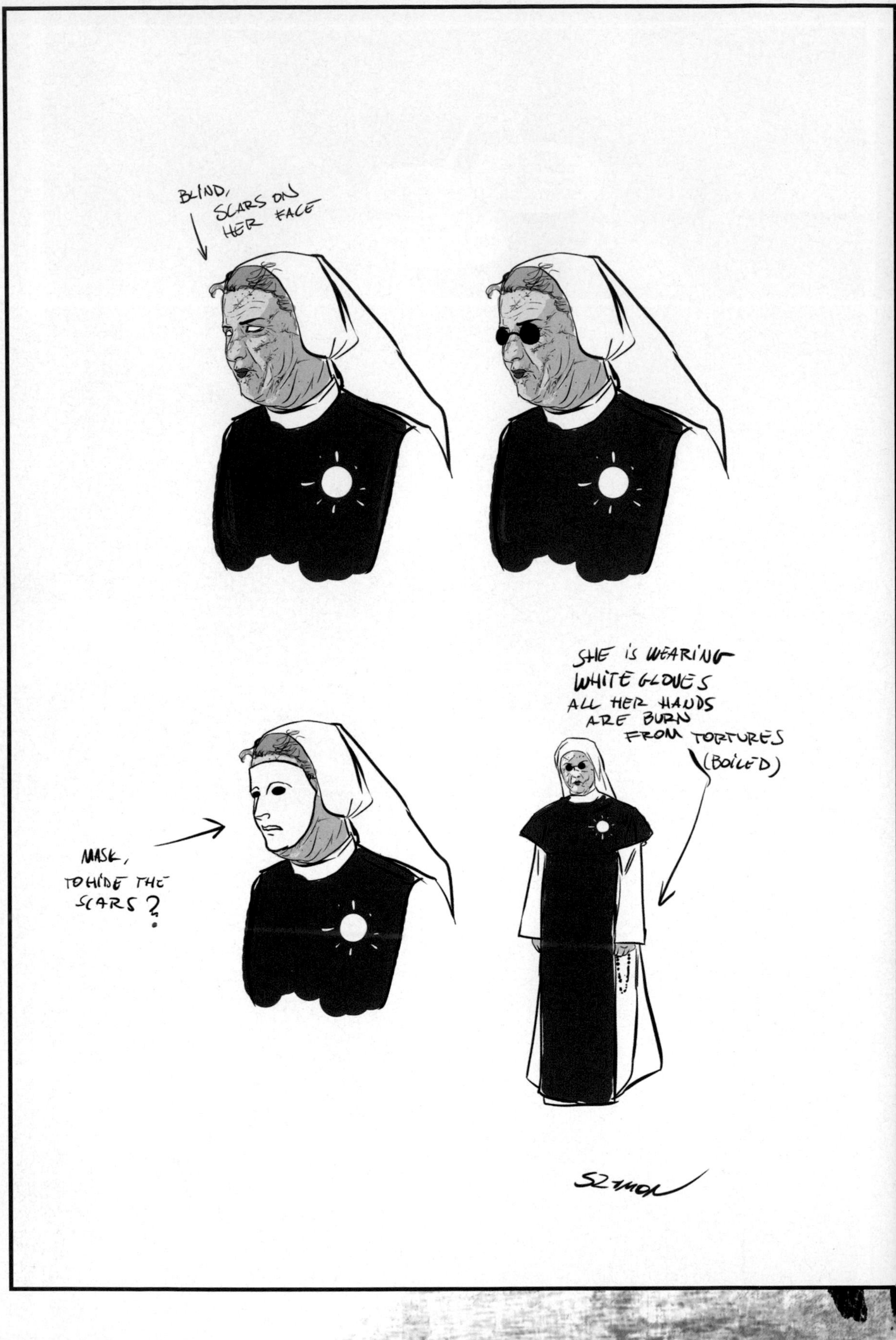
BLIND,
SCARS ON
HER FACE
SHE IS WEARING
WHITE GLOVES
ALL HER HANDS
ARE BURN
FROM TORTURES
(BOILED)
MASK,
TO HIDE THE
SCARS ?
SZYMON

SISTER MERCY CHARACTER DESIGN BY SZYMON KUDRANSKI

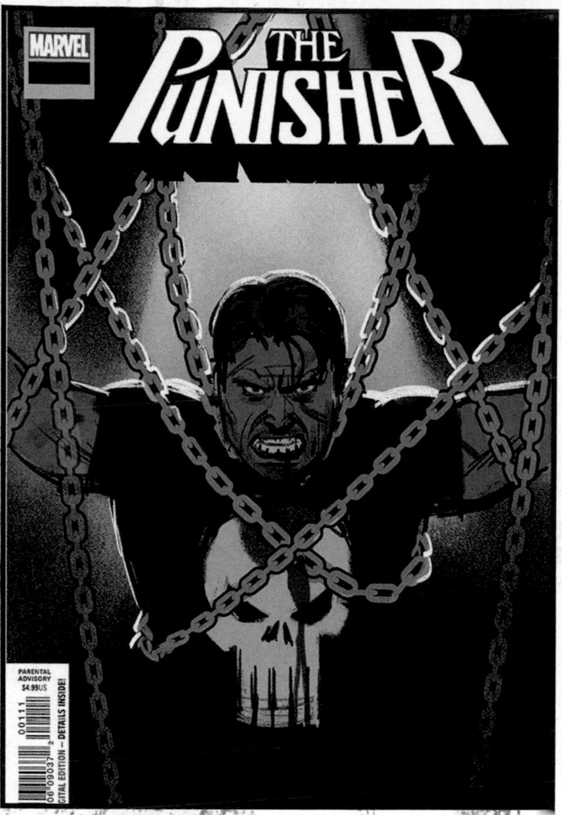
MARVEL
THE PUNISHER
PARENTAL ADVISORY
$4.99US

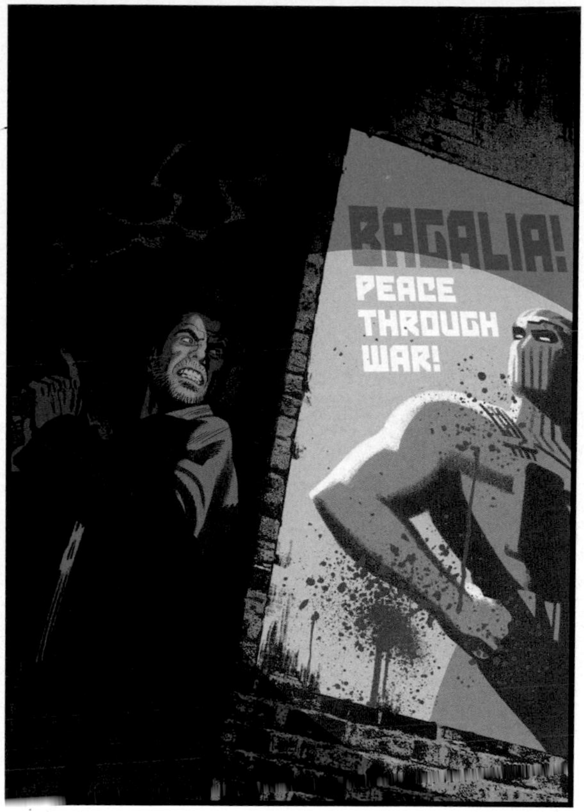
BAGALIA!
PEACE THROUGH WAR!

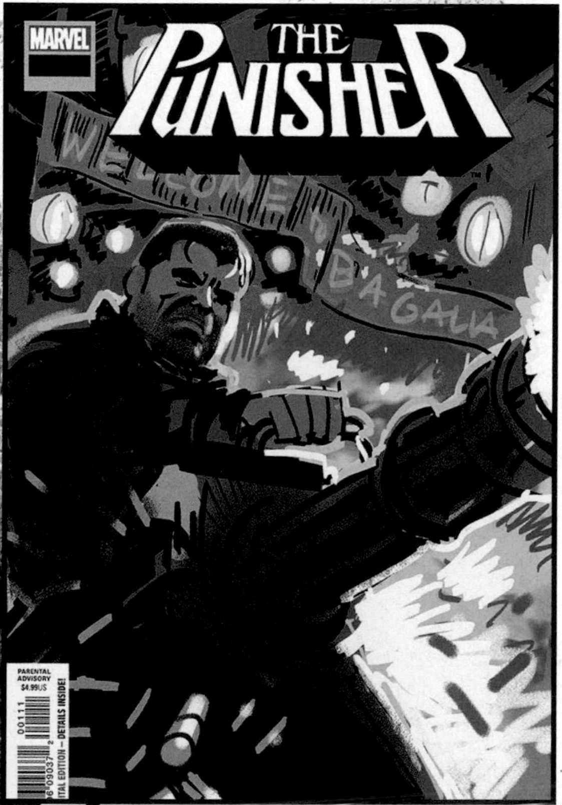
MARVEL
THE PUNISHER
BAGALIA
PARENTAL ADVISORY
$4.99US

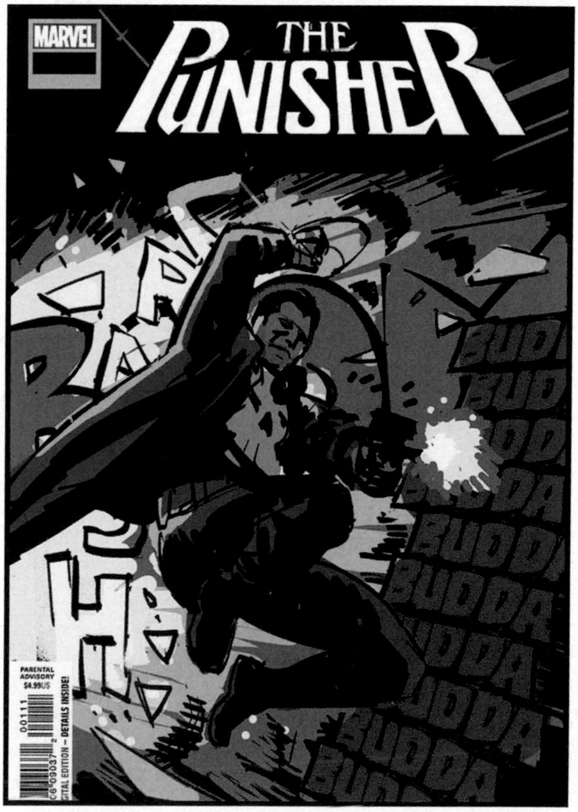
MARVEL
THE PUNISHER
BUDDA
BUDDA
BUDDA
BUDDA
PARENTAL ADVISORY
$4.99US

COVER SKETCHES BY GREG SMALLWOOD

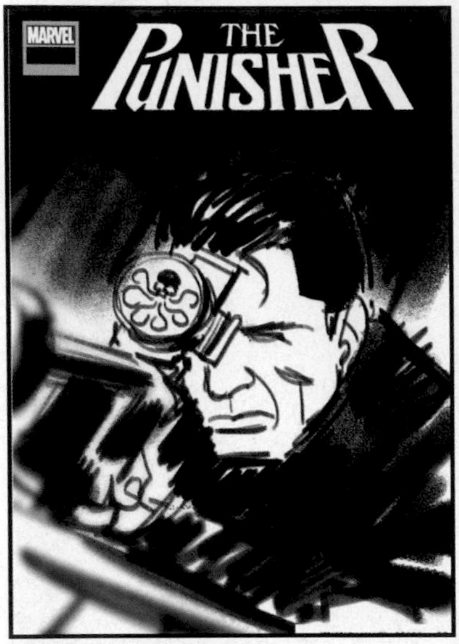
MARVEL
THE PUNISHER
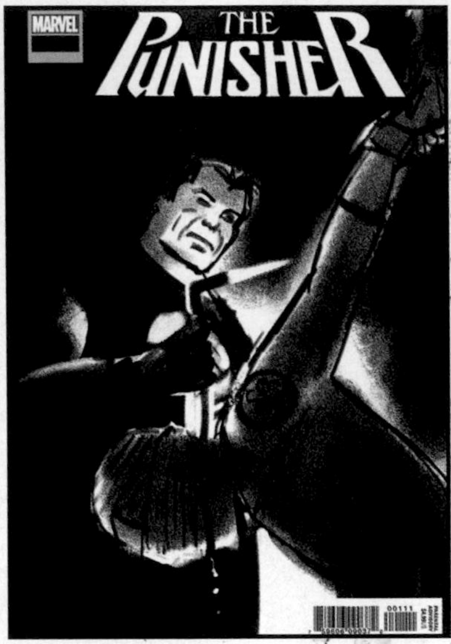
MARVEL
THE PUNISHER
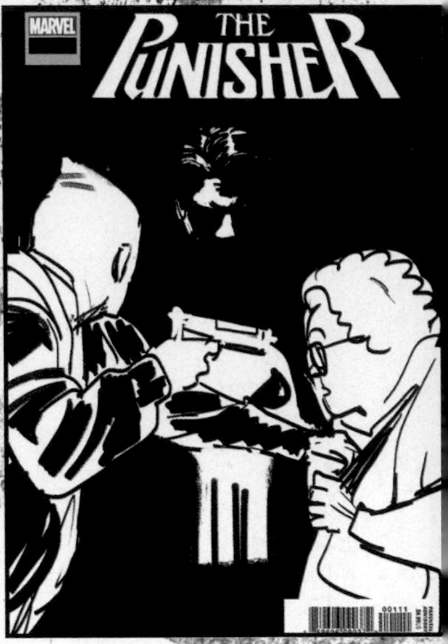
MARVEL
THE PUNISHER
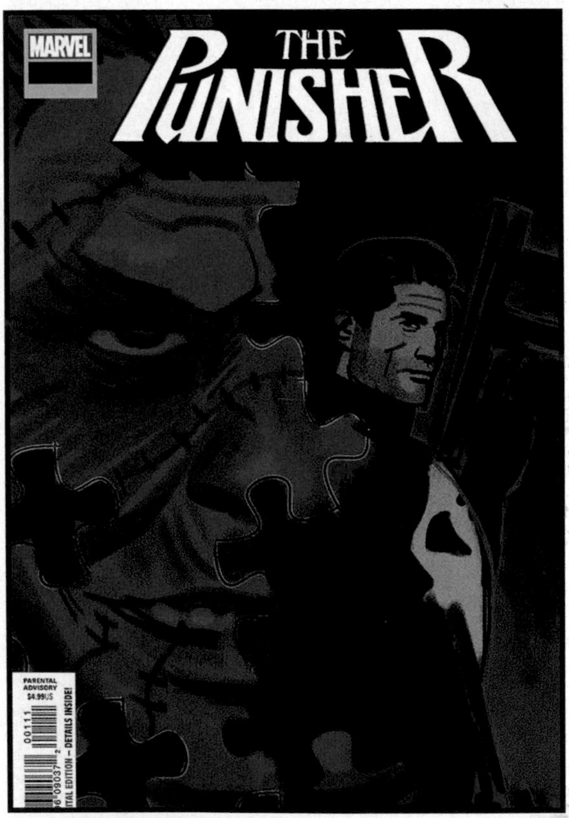
MARVEL
THE PUNISHER
PARENTAL ADVISORY
$4.99US
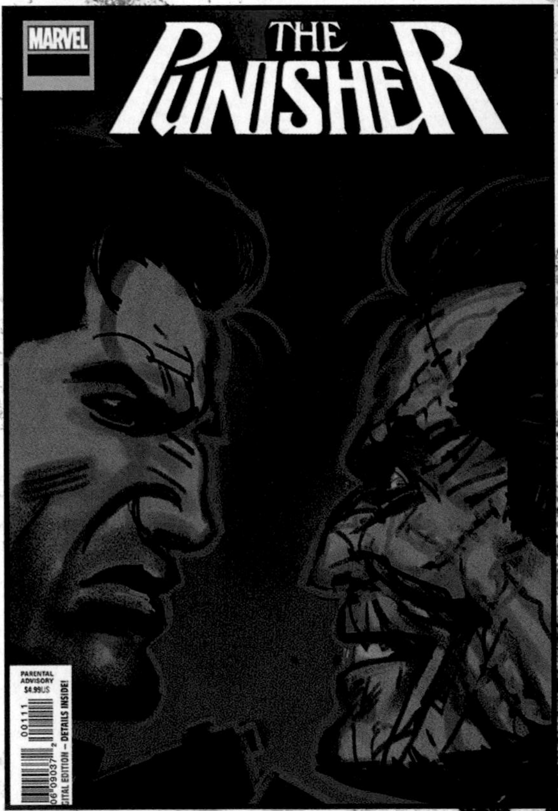
MARVEL
THE PUNISHER
PARENTAL ADVISORY
$4.99US

COVER SKETCHES BY GREG SMALLWOOD

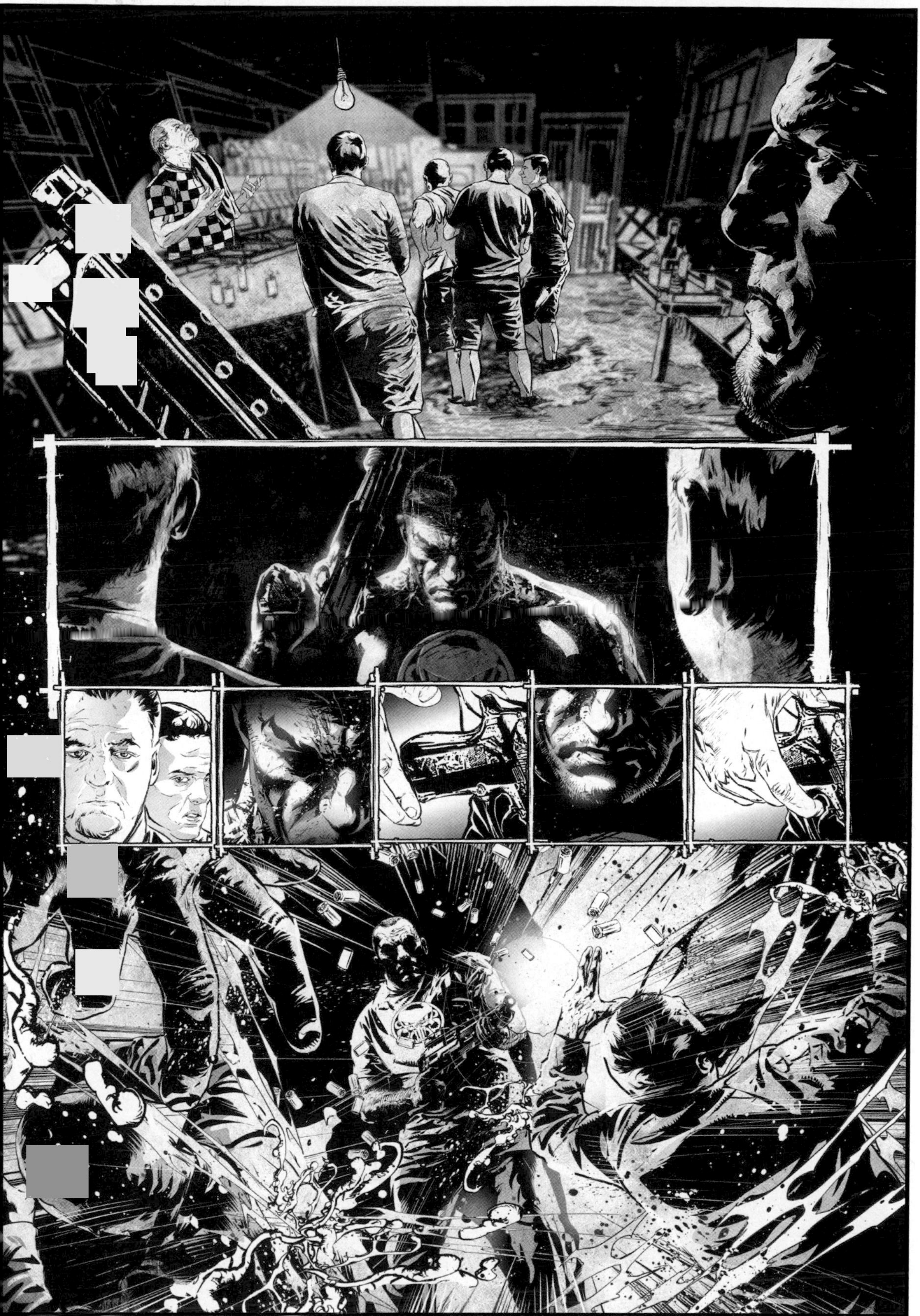

#10, PAGE 12 ART BY SZYMON KUDRANSKI

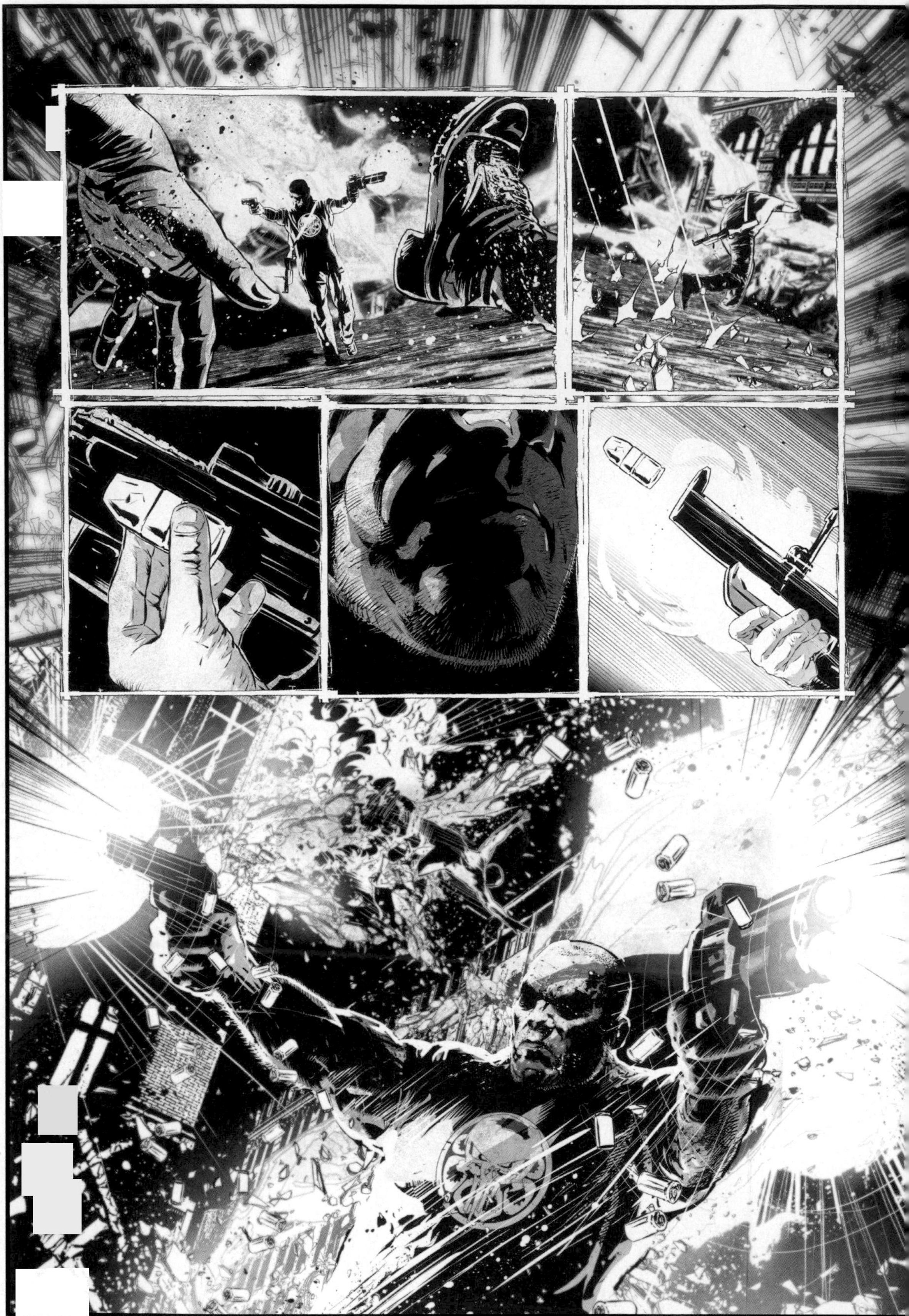

#10, PAGE 14 **ART** BY SZYMON KUDRANSKI